Oedipus in the Stone Age

Oedipus in the Stone Age

A Psychoanalytic Study of Masculinization in Papua New Guinea

Theodore Lidz and Ruth Wilmanns Lidz

With the assistance of
Harriette Dukeley Borsuch

International Universities Press, Inc.
Madison, Connecticut

GN
671
N5
L54
1989

Photographs by the authors

Copyright © 1989 by Theodore Lidz and Ruth Wilmanns Lidz

All rights reserved. No part of this book may be reproduced by any means nor translated into a machine language, without the written permission of the publisher.

Library of Congress Cataloging-in-Publication Data

Lidz, Theodore.
  Oedipus in the Stone Age: a psychoanalytic study of masculinization in Papua New Guinea/Theodore Lidz and Ruth Wilmanns Lidz, with the assistance of Harriette Dukeley Borsuch.
    p. cm.
  Includes bibliographies and index.
  ISBN 0-8236-3727-1
  1. Initiations rites—Papua new Guinea. 2. Ethnopsychology—Papua New Guinea. 3. Oedipus complex. 4. Masculinity (Psychology). 5. Papua New Guinea—Social life and customs. I. Lidz, Ruth Wilmanns. II. Borsuch, Harriette Dukeley. III. Title.
  [DNLM: 1. Anthropology, Cultural—New Guinea. 2. Identification (Psychology). 3. Psychoanalytic Theory. WM 460.5.I4 L715o]
GN671.N5L54 1989
392'.14'09953—dc19
DNLM/DLC
for Library of Congress   88-25796
                                                                    CIP

Manufactured in the United States of America.

To our previous collaborations
Victor, Chuck, and Jer
and their collaborators
Katharine, Lynn, and Melinda

To you . . . we throw
The torch; be yours to hold it high.

J. McCrae

Contents

	Acknowledgments	ix
1.	Apologia	1
2.	The Focus on the Masculinization Rituals	13
3.	The Land, The People, and Their Culture	17
4.	Male Menstruation: Defeminization and Disidentification from the Mother	49
5.	Psychoanalytic Concepts of the Bleeding Rituals	65
6.	Masculinization	81
7.	The Forest Lodge	107
8.	Afek and Yomnok Among the Bimin-Kuskusmin	115
9.	Afek at Telefolip	133
10.	The Papuan Gulf	141
11.	The Myth of Matriarchy	157
12.	Masculinization in Papua New Guinea and Its Impact on Psychoanalytic Theory	173
	References	201
	Name Index	211
	Subject Index	215

Acknowledgments

We wish to express our gratitude to Burton G. Burton-Bradley for his hospitality while we were in Port Moresby in 1971, for inviting us to examine patients with him, and for informing us about the people of that country, then about to become a nation; to Gilbert Herdt, whom we cherish as a friend as well as an advisor, for providing us with his articles prior to their publication, for reading drafts of our papers and spending many hours discussing his studies and answering our questions; to Fitz John Porter Poole, who not only furnished us with his numerous papers and chapters, both published and unpublished, concerning the Bimin-Kuskusmin people, but also spent many hours seeking to improve our understanding of these people; to Robert Brumbaugh for making available his unpublished thesis.

Once again we thank Harriette Dukeley Borsuch who provided invaluable help by tracking down references, checking quotations, reading numerous books about Papua New Guinea, preparing the map, and editing this book as she has most of our previous writings.

We thank the Commonwealth Fund for a grant to help with the preparation of the book. Theodore Lidz was a Career Investigator of the National Institute of Mental Health during the first years of work on this and other studies concerning the peoples of Papua New Guinea.

To study men, we must observe those around us, but to study Man, we must look farther afield; it is first necessary to observe differences in order to discover distinctive attributes.

Jean-Jacques Rousseau

1
Apologia

It may seem presumptuous for two psychoanalysts without formal training in anthropology to venture to write a book about the peoples of Papua New Guinea, particularly as the latter are divided into over 700 discrete language groups and at least as many cultures. Our interest and our effort require explanation. However, we first wish to reassure the anthropologists upon whose field work and writings we depend. The book is not concerned with ethnography, though we do not disclaim the expectation that it will contribute to the understanding of the beliefs and practices of some of the cultures. Our primary interest lies in how the field studies of a number of social anthropologists may clarify, verify, or alter psychoanalytic theory and developmental psychology. To carry out our objectives, we have found it essential to gain an understanding of the basic schemata (Piaget, 1952; Inhelder and Piaget, 1958) or cultural codes (Hutchins, 1980) to which the indigenes[1] assimilate and organize experience, and their concepts of causality, both of which differ profoundly from our own.

[1] The term *native* as applied to the native inhabitants of Papua New Guinea is considered pejorative. *Indigene* is a designation that differentiates the people from the *aborigines* of Australia, the *autochthones* of Irian Jaya, and the *Europeans*, the latter term encompassing all Caucasians even if they come from Australia, New Zealand, or the Americas.

To state the essence of our endeavors briefly: knowledge of the customs and beliefs of the indigenes has led us to change our understanding of the oedipal transition; to reorganize our psychoanalytic concepts of masculinity and femininity, and the reasons for the apparent dominance of males; to review the functions of mourning and the influences of the dead upon the living, and the reasons for the almost universal human need to believe in a life after death; to examine the relationships between sorcery or witchcraft and paranoid delusions, and the ways in which sorcery can serve as an integrative rather than a disruptive force for both the society and the individual; and we learned how the study of cargo cults contributes to our understanding of how divergent basic assumptions and ways of reasoning of peoples play a major role not only in international tensions and conflicts, but more pertinently to our interests, to the genesis of severe psychopathology, including schizophrenic disorders.

This book, however, will be limited to a study of the initiation rituals of various tribal societies scattered within the eastern half of the island of New Guinea—the portion of the island that is part of the nation of Papua New Guinea, and several adjacent societies in the southeastern corner of Irian Jaya. (We should note that the descriptions presented do not apply to the Trobriand Islands, or indeed to many of the other islands that make up the nation of Papua New Guinea, some of which have very different cultures.) Such rituals offer important challenges to some aspects of contemporary psychoanalytic theory. We shall place particular emphasis on the defeminizing and masculinizing rituals of several societies that have been studied intensively by psychologically oriented ethnologists, but we will consider the practices in a few other societies as well.

Tribal practices, including initiation rituals, vary markedly and, as will become apparent, those we describe cannot be generalized to the entire region. However, despite the differences, certain characteristics are present in all of the initiations we shall describe, as well as in still others not described in this work.

How did the authors become interested in the various

1 Apologia

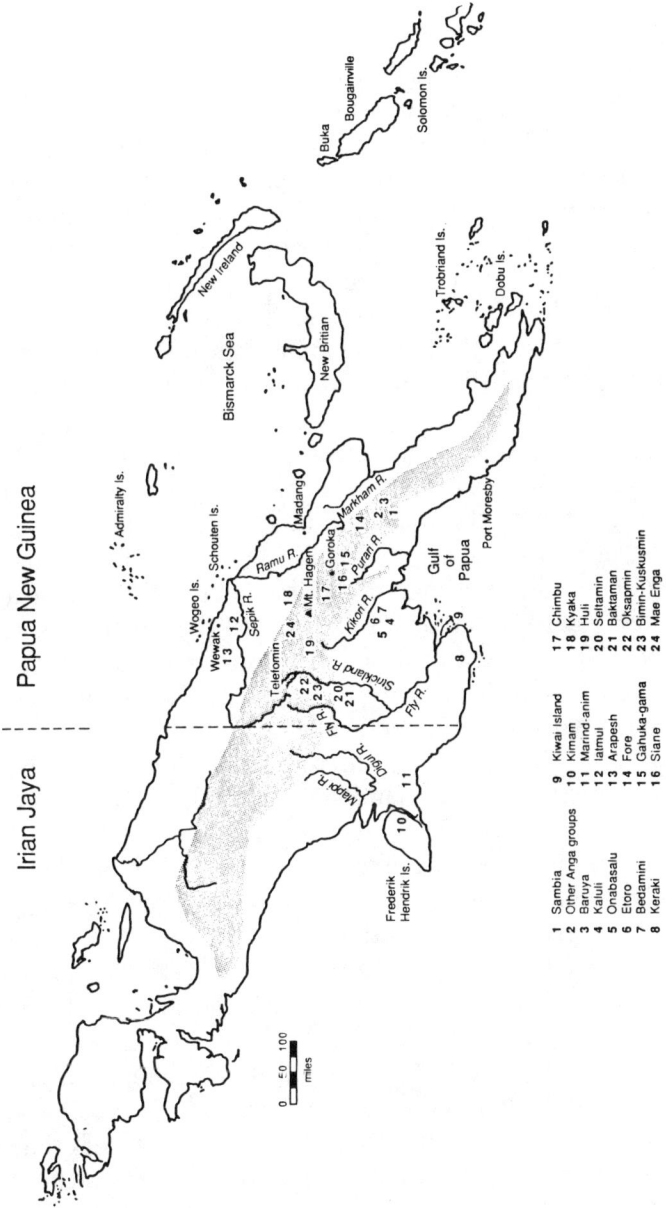

The island of New Guinea showing the location of some of the tribal societies who practice initiation rituals.

cultures of Papua New Guinea, indeed, become preoccupied with reading and thinking about them for 15 years? Both of us had long been interested in ethnology, having lived and studied in many countries, and one (T. L.) had resided in Fiji for two and a half years during World War II, and in proximity to the Naga people of India for almost six months. Then, while conducting a graduate seminar at the University of the South Pacific in Fiji in 1971, learning from our students from ten to 12 different Polynesian and Melanesian societies about how families in each society carried out their basic functions and inculcated their preferred personality traits, we were invited to attend the Melanesian Behavioral Science Conference at the University of Papua New Guinea at Waigani near Port Moresby. In the two weeks of the conference, we learned a good deal about the developing country, the social studies being carried out, and the problems of acculturation of a neolithic people. This experience supplemented the readings of Malinowski (1922), Mead (1928, 1968–1971), Bateson (1958), Fortune (1963), Lawrence, (1964), and Read (1965) we had carried out in preparation for our trip. Before we traveled in the highlands and to the upper reaches of the Sepik River, we remained in Port Moresby to attend the first Niugini Arts Festival. Dr. Burton Burton-Bradley, the only psychiatrist for the more than 2.5 million inhabitants of the then Australian trust territory, invited us to make rounds with him at the Laloki Psychiatric Centre he had established and on the psychiatric unit of the general hospital in Port Moresby.

We are greatly indebted to Dr. Burton-Bradley because some of the patients we interviewed—a few in English and others in Neo-Melanesian (pidgin) with the help of Dr. Burton-Bradley—intrigued and puzzled us. It was not, however, the cultural relativity so much as the nature of their problems that intrigued us and led us to realize that we had a great deal to gain from trying to grasp the nature of the peoples' beliefs that were so antipodal to our own but which had enabled them to function effectively for thousands of years. We were face to face with the critical question of how limiting or how encompassing our psychoanalytically oriented insights into human behavior were.

1 Apologia

Several of the male psychiatric patients we studied together with Dr. Burton-Bradley in the hospital at Port Moresby suffered from severe anxieties about sex, pollution by women, and the effects of witchcraft. One patient, for example, was brought into the psychiatric service of the hospital after a woman complained that he kept standing outside her home, returning repeatedly after being asked to leave, and even after he had been warned by the police. The patient claimed to have been bewitched by the woman who was seeking to seduce him in order to kill him by draining him of his semen and his vitality. He was very agitated and clearly seemed delusional. However, the central "delusion"—the belief that a woman may seek to gain strength at the expense of a man, even of her husband, by depleting him of his semen through engaging in excessive vaginal or oral intercourse—is, we learned, common to various New Guinea societies. A woman who entices a man in order to deplete him rather than to satisfy her needs or to produce a baby may be deemed a witch. Healthy men in many regions have an inordinate fear of female emanations, not just of menstrual blood. This fear seemed to be an important factor in determining the social structure of the villages; and the need to teach boys how to overcome the noxious influence of women and protect themselves from it constitutes a central aspect of male initiation rituals.

Then, when we traveled through the highlands of New Guinea and visited in villages in the middle and upper Sepik River, the vividly painted and tattooed bodies and faces set off by lavish headdresses of bird of paradise feathers, the ritual dances, pig festivals, fertility rites, and a lengthy marriage ceremony provided a vitality and force to what we had read and heard about these various peoples. Our curiosity and psychoanalytically trained passion to understand human behavior and motivation flamed beyond the kindling point. Here there was much to comprehend that lay beyond what we could learn from patients we analyzed but which, we presumed, might clarify aspects of our patients' behavior and fantasies.

Tumbuan, Iatmul people, middle Sepik River.

1 Apologia

Pig festival, western highlands.

In New Zealand, en route to Papua New Guinea, we had made a pilgrimage to Mesopotamia Station, the sheep run established by Samuel Butler. There, some 100 years earlier, Butler, probably inspired by observations of Maori culture, began his account of the fictional land of Erewhon, which he placed across the towering mountains beyond his run (Butler, 1872). The people of Erewhon had long since outlawed machines lest machines, as they subsequently have, enslave humans. Their ways and beliefs, like their country's name, were essen-

Chimbu groom with fifth bride and wedding party.

tially reversals of the conventions of the English whom Butler satirized, and in satirizing held up to the bleak light of reason.

The people of Erewhon believed in the Land of the Unborn where babies awaited and sought parents who would accept them as their children provided the babies signed a pledge exonerating the parents of responsibility for what befell them. Here, criminals were treated by "straighteners," precursors of psychotherapists, whereas persons suffering from communicable diseases were held responsible for their conditions and

1 Apologia

punished severely. The judge at the trial of a consumptive lectured the prisoner:

> "You may say that it is not your fault . . . [however] if you had been born of healthy and well-to-do parents, and been well taken care of when you were a child, you would never have offended against the laws of your country. . . . If you tell me that you had no hand in your parentage and education . . . I answer that whether your being in a consumption is your fault or no, it is a fault in you. . . . You may say that it is your misfortune to be criminal; I answer that it is your crime to be unfortunate" [pp. 134–135].

The inhabitants of Erewhon worshiped conformity, and were shocked at the concept of immortality of the soul, of which Butler's hero tried to convince them. They held the belief highly immoral for it would lead people to cheapen this present life, distract men's minds from perfecting the economy, encourage the poor in improvidence, and allow people to acquiesce to troubles they might well remedy. The visitor to Erewhon had no success in changing their outlandish ideas, but considered that a professional missionary might have a better chance.

Butler was well aware of the influence of culture on personality and how the behavior of parents and not simply their sins could affect their children unto the third and fourth generations, and very pertinent of our studies, that a culture's axiomatic beliefs affected profoundly a people's perceptions, ways of thinking, and interpersonal transactions.

The ways and beliefs of the indigenes are in some ways even more contrary to our own than those of the Erewhonians. They are more difficult for us to understand. The people of Erewhon had different premises, but they thought and reasoned much as did the English, in some respects even more logically in accord with Butler's deterministic philosophy. The peoples of Papua New Guinea not only base their lives on different premises, but divide their world and their experiences into categories that are very different from ours, and their concepts of causality tend strongly to the magical and supernatural. Neither fictional nor satirical, they present ways in which humans can live, survive, and even flourish that are extremely different from ours. Their cultures are very different ways of "carving a space out of chaos in which meaning can exist" (Cowan, 1980) in which people can live together and support one another. These ways form integrated patterns that somehow evolved out of the countless ways in which people can adapt to their environments. However different the ways of adaptation may be, and though humans are very malleable, all cultures must meet peoples' biological structure, physiological limits, and needs, such as the total dependency of infants; the differences between men and women; the need for sexual relations to reproduce, if not to satisfy a basic drive; the child's built-in developmental progression; and many other such matters, including the early awareness of death. The cultural pattern must also take into account the environment in which people live, and which they utilize and seek to modify to their needs.

It had become apparent to us that in order to use our psychoanalytic knowledge to attain some understanding of the indigenes, and to increase our psychoanalytic insights through the study of them, we must first gain a reasonable comprehension of their ways of living and their systems of belief. The task would require time and effort.

Our attempt to understand what we had seen and heard would not involve further journeys into New Guinea but rather into the accounts and cogitations of those who had studied one or more of the cultures intensively. In this country of so many varied cultures, each with a different language, it takes years to gain a reasonable understanding of a single group. When we started our explorations, the careful anthropological studies of Papua New Guinea, and especially the studies of the highland peoples were not extensive. However, the area beckoned many ethnologists, and material has poured forth in abundance during the past dozen years. Societies that had seemed relatively uncomplicated to the casual observer were found to be exceedingly complex and intricate as studies of a new generation of anthropologists such as Poole, Herdt, Tuzin, and others who were psychodynamically oriented appeared. We attempt here to

1 Apologia

convey some of what we have learned to others, but also to raise and hand on questions for others to solve.

After we state in the next chapter why we have limited this book to the study of the rituals that masculinize boys in Papua New Guinea and left other intriguing aspects of these cultures to other publications, we shall provide a brief and therefore a general and only approximate orientation to the peoples of Papua New Guinea for readers who are not New Guineaists, a characterization that encompasses only a few psychoanalysts and a limited number of anthropologists.

2

The Focus on the Masculinization Rituals

From among the various intriguing aspects of Papua New Guinea cultures that are pertinent to the clarification and further development of psychoanalytic theory, we shall in this book focus on the rituals among many peoples of eastern Papua New Guinea that are deemed essential to transform boys into men.

As we have already noted, the way in which children, particularly male children, are raised in many Papua New Guinea societies differs so profoundly from child-rearing practices in Western societies where psychoanalytic theories have developed, that it necessitates a reexamination of some basic psychoanalytically derived theories of child development. A notable modification of concepts of the boy's oedipal transition seems required. As elsewhere, the repression of the erotic component of the boy's attachment to his mother and the potential intense rivalry between father and son are important in Papua New Guinea. However, here the repression or resolution occurs much later in childhood and in conjunction with initiation rituals that place a greater emphasis on overcoming the boy's initial core identification with the mother and fostering, or indeed forcing, the attainment of a firm masculine identity. These are matters that have lately received increased consideration by psychoanalytic theorists. The oedipal transition here transpires as an aspect of the complex process of the boy's separation and individuation from the mother, but the process clearly extends beyond the first several years of life studied by Mahler, Pine, and Bergman (1975) and even far beyond the oedipal period, as Anna Freud (1965) recognized.

The problems involved in the boy overcoming his primary identification with his mother clarify why his development is more complex than that of the girl who properly can retain her primary feminine identification with her mother. The orientation differs from Freud's teaching that the girl encounters greater developmental difficulties because she has to shift her basic choice of a love object from the mother to the father; and because, lacking a penis that in itself makes the male feel superior to the female, she is fated to suffer from penis envy, if not also a pervasive sense of incompletion. The circumstances in Papua New Guinea lead rather to both a recognition of the male's profound envy of women's procreative and nurturant capacities and an anger over the mother's abandonment of him, which combine to contribute to a reactive misogyny and lead to the men's relegation of women to an inferior and even a despised status.

Then, too, the major repression of the boy's libidinal investment of his mother and his identification with her, as well as his concomitant induction into a masculine identity, do not take place at the age of our oedipal transition that is variously placed between the ages of three to six, but later during the so-called latency period. Indeed, in a number of these societies, the latter part of the latency period is strongly erotized through obligatory homosexuality. However, although the evidence is scanty, it seems probable that some decathexis of the attachment to the mother takes place earlier. Moreover, even though the boy is regarded as one of the "people of the women's houses" prior to the first stage of initiation, he is treated differently from young girls, tends to consort with other boys, and knows that as a boy he will have a very different way of life than his sisters.

2 The Focus on the Masculinization Rituals

In considering the initiation rituals, it is necessary to realize that in many and perhaps most of these tribal societies the men believe that a boy cannot mature into a man naturally. The process of turning a boy into a man after he has lived with and been raised by his mother for the first seven to 15 years of his life, with relatively little direct influence from his father, is carried out by the men's cult by means of initiation rituals. These rituals start when the boy is wrenched from his mother, actually or symbolically, and subjected to the first stage of initiation that supposedly enables the boy to become pubertal—always a strange and frightening ordeal and in some places cruel or even extremely sadistic. The rituals, which may continue in stages for ten to 15 years, differ from place to place but, in general, have a basic similarity in that the procedures are intended to defeminize, masculinize, and deerotize the attachment to the mother. These processes are reinforced by the degradation of women, by injunctions of the dire dangers that emanate from women and their sexuality, and in many societies by the isolation of the initiates from all women until they marry. Finally, there is an emphasis on the rewards of ultimately becoming a fully privileged male instead of a despised female.

Thus, although the deerotization of the boy's or youth's attachment to his mother may, among some of these peoples, be furthered by the men's threats of castration or death, the major threat consists of the danger of the emasculating and devitalizing qualities of women and their sexuality, and in some areas their castrating vaginas. The ambivalent longing to return to the protective care of the mother is countered directly by a strong emphasis or exaggeration of the dangers of the mother's libidinal attraction, which is extended to all women.

As the process of masculinization in many areas requires an actual or symbolic insemination of the boys, it becomes necessary to examine how homosexuality need not be, and in Papua New Guinea is not, an effort to deny masculinity or assume femininity but rather an important component in achieving the fierce warrior masculinity necessary for survival in communities engaged in interminable, ruthless warfare with neighboring groups. The scrutiny of the reasons for the homosexuality reveals similarities to the etiology of some types of homosexuality in Western societies, and thereby helps elucidate the psychodynamics of homosexual tendencies and identities.

The rituals, which almost always include a devaluation of women and instill fear of the debilitating and even lethal effects of women's sexuality, not only have a profound influence on the personality development of both males and females, but also upon the social structure. The answer to the question of whether men's fears of women's libido arose from the method of child rearing, or the fears that separate the two sexes led to the method of child rearing lies buried in antiquity. Currently the situation is circular, and we can only conjecture about its origins, seek answers in the indigenes' mythologies, and utilize psychoanalytic insights into human development. Of particular relevance is the omnipresent belief that in primordial times the women invented and controlled the rituals and dominated the men.

We must note that we shall often describe rituals in the present tense, and properly so, as we will be primarily considering rituals as observed and described by anthropologists during the latter half of this century and particularly in the 1970s. Some rituals disappeared following "pacification" by the Australian authorities and perhaps even more so during the rapid acculturation that has been occurring over the past 20 to 25 years. However, writing about them in the present tense indicates our concern with the way of life prior to the impact of missionaries and other Western influences on the indigenes.

3

The Land, The People, and Their Culture

The peoples of New Guinea attract our attention because they, and particularly those of the fertile, high mountain valleys and other parts of the interior, were among the last neolithic peoples to be influenced by outside cultures. Indeed, some of the cultures had been untouched by influences from beyond the island for millennia. The existence of the highland peoples was unknown to Europeans and perhaps even to some of the coastal peoples until 1930, and many places remained unexplored until after World War II. Thus, anthropologists were afforded the opportunity to study numerous neolithic societies free of acculturating influences and were among the first outsiders to intrude into various areas.

The ethnographies provided by anthropologists who lived among various tribes and came to know them intimately have enabled psychologically oriented ethnologists and psychoanalysts to contemplate and study how this particular cultural branch of humankind reached an equilibrium with the environment at a neolithic level. In contrast to the roaming hunting and gathering aborigines of Australia whose cultures formed the basis for numerous conjectures and theories about our primeval ancestors and their religious beliefs, and greatly influencing

A high valley with sweet potato garden.

Durkheim, Freud, and Frazer among others, here were fairly static peoples, some of whom had discovered or at least utilized agriculture just about as long as any peoples on earth. The hundreds of fairly distinct cultures, all without central governments, defined laws, or chieftans but guided by myth, custom, and the need to preserve their own particular way of life, afforded an opportunity to uncover fundamentals of the human condition and very different ways from our own of achieving a workable personality integration.

The vast island of New Guinea extends for 1,500 miles just north of Australia. Though equatorial, its terrain and climate vary widely. There are hot and humid coastal areas with extensive mangrove swamps and mud flats, as well as fine beaches. A spiny cordillera of alpine heights runs the length of the interior containing high valleys that have a temperate climate of between 70° and 80° F throughout the year. Relatively

Central highlands from a mission at 7,000 feet.

free of malaria and with fertile soil, the high valleys contain over 800,000 people or approximately half of the population of the eastern half of the island, the portion with which we are primarily concerned and which is part of the nation of Papua New Guinea. The western half, now called Irian Jaya, belongs to Indonesia.[1]

The regions between the coast and the highlands rise in steplike fashion with an abundance of savannah country and fairly dense tropical rain forest. The island is virtually bisected

---

[1]The eastern half had been under Australian control, but since 1976 it has constituted a major portion of the nation of Papua New Guinea. The division does not reflect ethnic differences but is derived from earlier divisions by colonial powers that we need not trace here. Papua New Guinea encompasses the Bismarck Archipelago with its large islands of New Britain and New Ireland; the two northernmost Solomon Islands, Buka and Bougainville; and numerous small islands, including the Trobriands made famous by Malinowski's writings, and the Admiralties where Margaret Mead studied the Manus; as well as the eastern half of New Guinea.

Chimbu warrior.

just east of the Irian Jaya border by the Fly River that flows south into the Gulf of Papua and the Sepik River that flows northward into the Bismarck Sea. Their many tributaries that drain large segments of the highlands and plateau areas interdigitate. (See Figure 1.)

The tribal peoples of Papua New Guinea are divided into over 700 distinct language groups and at least as many cultures. Despite the similarities that we shall discuss, their ways vary greatly. Although the entire nation had a population of about 2.2 million in 1970, less than that of the state of Connecticut, it has been estimated that it contains a quarter of the languages of the world.

The number and diversity of the cultures derive from the relative isolation of the eastern half of the island from all but adjacent islands;[2] by the separation of its people by high mountain ranges and rain forest, but perhaps even more by the fierce warrior cultures and the interminable warfare between neighboring clans or phratries. Each group of clans, not simply each tribe, ferociously defended its boundaries against intrusion, and sought to preserve its rituals and cultural ways as

[2]The western portion of the island had been visited by Malayan slavers and traders for at least several centuries; they apparently rarely ventured eastward beyond the Fly River in the south and the Sepik in the north. Their influence may have penetrated into the interior of Irian Jaya where the Kapauku people have a complex numerical system probably derived from an old Malayan system (Pospisil, personal communication), in contrast to the extremely simple and primitive counting systems found in Papua New Guinea. The eastern half of the island remained virtually untouched by non-Melanesian influences until the last three decades of the nineteenth century when plantations and trading posts were established along the coasts. The first Westerner to venture onto the eastern half of the island was the adventuresome Russian naturalist, the self-styled "Baron" Miklouho-Maclay. He had himself and two helpers set down on the Rai coast near present-day Madang in 1871. Maclay and one helper managed to survive and make friends with the indigenes in a few hamlets and even travel into the foothills of the mountains. His reports had wide repercussions throughout Europe. His adventures make an incredible saga, but a recent biography (Webster, 1984) is rather disillusioning. Despite Maclay's claims, he actually learned little about the people, and although he wished to be recognized as the representative of the people of the "Maclay Coast," the indigenes would not have considered him to be their spokesman and were scarcely civil to him on his return to the area. However, explorers and plantation owners soon followed. A new account of the experiences of the first Europeans to enter the highlands in 1930 as well as of the indigenes' reactions to them is provided by Connolly and Anderson (1987).

Huli warriors.

handed down from generation to generation. Hamlets were often at war with neighbors to avenge a death, whether a homicide or one blamed on a sorcerer in an adjacent hamlet.

The existence of so many discrete languages, a situation in which the people in some adjacent valleys do not understand one another, indicates that tribes have been separated for many hundreds of years, and some probably for thousands of years. Nevertheless, some societies that are widely separated and have very different cultures may have some very similar, seemingly idiosyncratic beliefs and practices, as we shall note in subsequent chapters.

We can say little about the origins of the early inhabitants of the island. Australia and New Guinea formed a single continent until about 8,000 years ago. According to recent studies, humans or their hominid precursors inhabited the highlands at least 40,000 years ago (White and Allen, 1980; Golson, 1982).

3 The Land, The People, and Their Culture   23

Central highland warriors.

There is evidence that gardens existed in the Mount Hagen area about 9,000 years ago. It is possible that inhabitants of the conjoint continent migrated into the highlands, which probably formed its most salubrious environment. However, many of the present inhabitants came to the island in Melanesian migrations from southeast Asia several thousand years ago and therefore are not descendants, or at least not pure descendants, of the original inhabitants.[3]

---

[3] Although the Torres Strait that separates the northern tip of Australia and the Trans-Fly region of Papua New Guinea is only 100 miles wide and dotted with islands, the influence of the areas on one another has been very slow, as can be noted from the fact that while pigs were present in the highlands some 8,000 years ago, there were no pigs in Australia until modern times; and although dogs existed in Australia 4,000 years ago, they did not cross the Torres Strait for 2,000 years and it took another 1,000 years for them to reach the highlands. It seems likely though that the cultures of the Marind-anim of southeastern Irian Jaya and some Trans-Fly peoples have some similarities to those of peoples in northern Australia. However, several very useful importations

Even after plantations and towns were established along the coasts, exploration and settlement of the interior remained very sparse aside from journeys up the Sepik and Fly rivers. The peoples of the highlands remained unknown to the Europeans, and apparently to most of the coastal peoples, as well, until 1930 when two gold prospectors, Michael Leary and Michael Dwyer, inadvertently entered the fertile and thickly populated highland valleys from the north and crossed the mountain ranges to reach the south coast.[4] As the highlands were explored, the Australian administration set up a series of base camps at five or six places prior to 1935 and patrols sought to pacify the warring peoples. Missionaries as eager for souls as the prospectors were for gold established two missions. However, in the years 1934 to 1935 a prospector and two missionaries were killed and a patrol was attacked, and in the ensuing battle several patrol officers were wounded and 19 indigenes killed. The administration closed the highlands to all except those already there and the area remained virtually barred to outsiders until after World War II.

The highland peoples in turn had little if any knowledge of the outside world prior to 1930, and even though they greatly prized gold-lipped kina shells, which they obtained via a long

---

reached the interior from the coast rather quickly. The sweet potato reached New Guinea in the middle of the seventeenth century and soon started to modify the way of life in the highlands because it can grow at higher altitudes and in less fertile soil than taro and yams, which in turn led to a greater accumulation of pigs for ceremonials and trade. The steel axe reached the highlands decades before the Europeans and changed the way men lived, for it greatly reduced the time and energy needed to clear and fence gardens every few years as required in swidden agriculture.

[4] Leary and Dwyer, experienced bush travelers, set out to find the camp of a successful gold prospector in the upper Ramu Valley, but followed the wrong river and found themselves in the previously unknown highlands. Unable to find their way northward, they followed valleys cut by the Prurari River to reach the Gulf of Papua. Because of their fitness and skill, but also because the inhabitants took the white men for ancestor spirits and were awed by their equipment, they survived the arduous and very dangerous trip through country filled with cannibals hostile to outsiders. When Leary and Dwyer reached the Wahgi River, they saw numerous bodies and skeletons that had been carried down the river and laid on the banks and knew that even more densely populated areas lay to the west. They returned to explore the Asaro Valley, and later still other areas. A succinct account of their early explorations and the settlement of the highlands can be found in J. Sinclair's *The Highlanders* (1971).

Very old man describing ambush of first Australian patrol in his area.

series of trade partners who passed articles from one to the other, they knew nothing of the ocean,[5] and as far as we have been able to ascertain, their myths contain nothing about the sea.

Although Vicedom and Tischner made important anthropological observations in the Wahgi Valley and vicinity prior to World War II, the collection of any appreciable knowledge about

---

[5] According to Meggitt (1965) the Mae Enga of the western highlands believe the kina shells grow on trees in a distant land and are harvested by the natives.

the people of the highlands started only after the war (Vicedom and Tischner, 1943–1948). The Australian ban on warfare, homicide, and cannibalism was accepted by most tribes, even by some who did not have direct contact with patrol officers but had simply heard of the new laws. The Australian patrol officers as superordinate authorities with guns that they used only in dire emergencies managed to bring a peace that was broken only occasionally to a region where intratribal warfare had been an essential part of the way of life.[6]

Schools, missions, coffee plantations, cattle ranches, roads, a few towns, and the end to warfare, cannibalism, and head-hunting (but the introduction of alcohol and capitalism) have brought profound changes to the highlands, though peripheral areas of the highlands and the rain forest have been less affected. Although our interest lies in the beliefs and ways of the people prior to the advent of Europeans, it is essential to remember that most reports of even remote areas have been affected to some extent by the presence of Europeans, even when they had not yet actually entered the area. Poole (1983a) could witness Bimin-Kuskusmin cannibalism in the form of ritualized necrophagia of relatives, but had to reconstruct from narratives how they used ritual cannibalism to counter witchcraft and how they had eaten enemies killed in battle. Rappaport (1984) did not actually witness the ritual preparation for war he described; or Schieffelin (1976, 1982) the *Bau A* ceremonial practice of the peoples of the Great Papuan Plateau, which he reconstructed from accounts of participants. Still, Read (1952) was wrong in his surmise that he might be the first and last white man to witness the Nama cult initiation, for Newman (1965) also witnessed it, and Herdt (1981) not only saw but participated in the closely related but more complex Sambia initiation rituals. Poole (1982a) managed to observe and study the extremely involved initiation rituals of the Bimin-Kuskusmin as well as obtain the participants' understanding of, and reaction to, them as late as 1970.

[6] However, two patrol officers were killed and eaten near Telefomin in the mid-1960s; and there have been new outbreaks of warfare in the interior since the Australians withdrew their patrols in 1976.

Social Structure

The peoples of New Guinea are divided into a host of tribal societies that do not have chiefs or any central government and are simply a conglomeration of clans or larger phratries living proximately that have a common language, beliefs, and customs.[7] Most peoples live in hamlets consisting of groups of huts and one or more men's cult huts. In the western and southern highlands, they may live in groups of scattered homesteads united into "parishes" that are usually patrilineal and virilocal. On the sparsely populated Great Papuan Plateau, they live in long houses that supposedly contain two intermarrying patrifilial moieties.[8] The hamlets and parishes are, in general, united into subclans and clans, and the clans into phratries who claim a common primal ancestor or ancestors, have common customs, unite for ceremonials and initiations, and often intermarry, even though some of the subgroups will be at war with others in which they are supported by fairly permanent or shifting alliances with other subclans or clans. Along the great rivers a few villages contain a thousand or more inhabitants.

The hamlets or parishes that in most areas form the basic

---

[7] Just what constitutes a tribe is not always apparent. Thus Read (1965) originally wrote about the Gahuka-Gama as if they were a tribe, but he later designated them as a phratry (Read, 1984). The very large Enga tribe of the western highlands consists of subtribes speaking different dialects or related languages and with somewhat different customs. In contrast, the Baktaman and Seltamin, small groups who live near one another in the bush, have been considered separate tribes though they speak closely related languages and participate in each other's initiation ceremonies (Barth, 1975).

[8] We are obviously excluding the Trobriand Islands, the site of Malinowski's studies, as the inhabitants have chiefs, are matrilineal, permit considerable premarital sexual freedom, and have artifacts that seem clearly related to the Indonesian in design, and differ in still other ways from the cultures of the main island.

Even the groups that are formally patrilineal and virilocal make exceptions as outsiders—men who decide to live in their wives' hamlets, refugees from defeated and demolished hamlets, and adherents to a Big Man—may be accepted into the patrilineages. The constituents of the long houses on the Great Papuan Plateau are, in actuality, from diverse patrilineages (Schieffelin, 1976).

Village on a Sepik River tributary.

unit beyond the family have, as we said earlier, neither chiefs, laws, nor formal means of adjudicating disputes but are governed by tradition, following a way of life the people believe was given the clan or phratry by its primal ancestor or pair of ancestors in mythic times. Conduct is controlled by the fear of sorcery and ghosts and by fear of antagonizing the ancestor spirits who mediate between the living and nature, control the fertility of the women, pigs, and soil, and protect from epidemics. In most areas, each hamlet or parish has a men's cult house in which the sacred objects are stored, and where the men gather to debate custom and a proper course of action when necessary. In many, and perhaps most, regions, a hamlet has one or more Big Men[9] who has emerged as a leader because of the

---

[9] Big Men do not exist everywhere. The Baruya, for example, who live on the periphery of the eastern highlands (Godelier, 1982), have something of a hierarchy of "great" warriors, shamans, cassowary hunters, salt makers with varying degrees of

3 The Land, The People, and Their Culture

A cult house, middle Sepik River.

power of his personality, often though not necessarily, because of his prowess in war, or the force of his oratory, or his ability to settle disputes amicably. He can lead, persuade, or dominate by the force of his fierce personality but he cannot command, for these are egalitarian societies—as far as the men are concerned.

The family forms the basic societal unit; but, as we shall consider in some detail, the unit of husband, wife, and children does not properly meet the requirements of a true nuclear family. In many and perhaps most of the tribal societies the husband does not live in the hut with his wife and children but sleeps in the men's hut because of fear of contamination from his wife's sexual secretions and emanations, which also contaminate her children. In those localities where he sleeps in the family hut he remains in an area in which his wife is not permitted to enter. In many societies the father has little direct influence upon his small children. Commonly, when a man has more than one wife, each wife lives with her children in a separate hut. Nevertheless, the family forms a social and economic unit with tasks shared between husband and wife. The man's primary loyalty, particularly in the highlands, is not, or is not supposed to be, to his wife and children but to the men's cult into which he is initiated before he reaches puberty.

Although some villages may be divided into moieties that can intermarry, the rules of exogamy usually require that many of the wives come from other hamlets. As the range of interchange is limited and some proximate hamlets are enemies, men may marry women from enemy communities and in some areas the majority of men do so. The Mae Enga, for example, say, "We marry the people we fight" (Meggitt, 1970, p. 139) which increases husbands' distrust and even fear of their wives

---

prestige, and honored agriculturists. Whereas a great warrior was an essential and powerful protector prior to pacification, he was not a civil leader, and if he overstepped his use of power by seducing wives of covillagers or preempting pigs, he was likely to die quickly—presumably by accident or through information given the enemy. The various societies of the Great Papuan Plateau apparently do not have Big Men and the initiative for various ventures, including raids, rests upon almost any individual (Schieffelin, 1976).

and affects many other aspects of societal life. For example, when the Baktaman were unable to even the number of killings with their neighbors the Seltamin, they killed and ate a Seltamin woman who had married a Baktaman and had two Baktaman children (Barth, 1975). The Bimin-Kuskusmin tend to fear that wives taken from their enemy the Oksapmin may be witches (Poole, 1983a). Other peoples such as the Kuma (Reay, 1959) specifically avoid such potentially dangerous marital ties.

The dichotomy between men and women is among the most striking aspect of New Guinea societies, particularly in the highlands. The women are derogated and despised. They are forbidden to enter the cult houses on pain of death; and may, to the outsider, seem to be treated as little more than beasts of burden. The men, particularly in most of the highlands but also in other regions, fear the polluting and even lethal qualities of female sexual fluids and emanations, which leads to a separation of the sexes more or less in proportion to the severity of the fears of the noxious qualities of the female libido. Women share the belief that their vaginal secretions and odor and particularly menstrual blood are antipathetic and even potentially lethal to men's virility and health. Men, particularly young men, are weakened and their health undermined not only by frequent intercourse but even by frequent contact with women. In most regions, though not all, boys cannot mature into men if they continue to live with their mothers. The dangers of the female libido and women's emanations and exudations thus have a profound influence on the social structure, interpersonal relations, and child rearing.

Despite the contumely, female babies are usually welcomed. In some places they will later be given in exchange for a bride for a son, or to gain bride-wealth for her father or brothers. A man may say of his sister, or rather of his sister's vagina, that it is "the road along which pigs come."

The dichotomy between the sexes has led some anthropologists to speak of an antagonism between the sexes, and even of a dual cultural system with different subcultures for the men and women. Although there are reasons for both theories, neither is

Bride-wealth, central highlands.

really warranted, for the men and women fill complementary functions, and contrary to appearances women can, at least in many places, be very influential in making important decisions (Brown and Buchbinder, 1976; Herdt and Poole, 1982). Moreover, women fill important functions in establishing and maintaining relations between hamlets and clans, and even in maintaining a network of hamlets. Women are likely to keep in contact with their agnates. If a woman cannot visit with her mother who lives in an enemy hamlet, she may be able to meet with her in the mother's native hamlet. A woman's father and brothers will keep track of her, and if her husband mistreats her, they will threaten vengeance; her death or the death of one of her children may require compensation or provoke vengeance through murder or sorcery. Among the Bosari a man's affines are often his closest associates (Schieffelin, 1976).

Optimally marriages are arranged between cross-cousins. Among the Sambia and some other peoples a man is married to his father's sister's daughter when feasible, but among many tribes to his mother's brother's daughter. In many localities an adult male's closest and safest relationship with a woman is likely to be with a sister, though among some tribal societies the relationship is antagonistic. A sister's emanations are usually considered less dangerous than a wife's. A man may feel secure in eating his sister's food, whereas in various societies if he eats food prepared by his wife, it is with trepidation. Among the necrophagic Fore of the eastern highlands, a man eats his dead sister's vagina but eating his wife's would endanger his health (Lindenbaum, 1976). The closeness probably derives from brothers and sisters having lived together under their mother's affectionate protection before the boy was separated from the mother.

Various Mae Enga myths (Meggitt, 1976) reflect an ideal of a brother and sister living together without a dominating father or the dangers of sexual relationships; but there are also myths or tales of their unknowingly marrying or committing incest.

In many of the tribal societies a mother's brother often serves as a sponsor who seeks to protect and solace her son during the ordeals of the boy's initiation; and among the Kimam (Serpenti, 1984), Marind-anim (van Baal, 1966), and some Trans-Fly peoples, a very complex relationship exists between a boy and his mother's brother in which the uncle assumes many paternal functions and also transmits the semen that transforms a boy into a man (see chapter 10). A man recognizes his matrilineal and affinal ties even during battle and he will not engage in direct combat with his mother's brothers or his wife's father or brothers.

The men's central tasks are to protect their women, children, and land from the almost constant danger of attack; to avenge their kin and covillagers; and to maintain the traditional ways handed down to them. They carry out rituals to maintain harmonious relations with the ancestor spirits and conduct the complex initiations that transform boys not just into men but into stalwart warriors. They maintain relations with a trade partner, clear the garden plots of trees and fence them to keep the pigs out (time-consuming tasks prior to the acquisition of steel axes), and hunt marsupials and gather fruit in the forest. They arrange for their daughters' and often their sisters' marriages, and participate in running the affairs of the community. In many societies a man will not marry until his midtwenties, and as the average life span formerly was less than 40 years, the portion of his life spent as a husband was relatively brief. In the societies in which homosexuality was obligatory in boyhood and youth, the homosexual period could be longer than the time that remained for marital heterosexuality.

The maintenance of a reasonable equivalence between men is a major determinant of behavior, even though the men differ in fighting ability, wealth, prestige, sacred knowledge, and the power of their magic. It is a means of minimizing envy and domination, essential to the unity and harmony of a group whose men tend to be extremely phallic in their masculinity and aggressivity, but who must cooperate in the defense of their communities and in carrying out rituals and ceremonials. Their aggressivity is difficult to judge from their behavior since pacification. Read (1954) who lived among the Gahuka-Gama shortly after World War II wrote:

> They are jealous of their reputations, and an undercurrent of tension, even latent animosity, accompanies many interpersonal relationships. Dominance and submission, rivalry and coercion are constantly recurring themes and there is an unmistakably aggressive tone to life. The majority of awards go to the physically strong and self-assertive, to the proud and flamboyant, to the extroverted ex-warrior and orator who demands, and usually obtains, the submission of his fellows [p. 866].

Indeed, the men can be cruel to initiates (Tuzin, 1982) supposedly because they believe pain and suffering hardens the boys. Then, many of these tribal peoples, though far from all, were anthropophagic, and might tauntingly cut up and eat enemies they killed in full view of the dead man's kinsmen; though more customarily only after the proper ritual was held. Not all cannibalism indicated bloodthirstiness. Among some peoples, such as the Fore and Bimin-Kuskusmin, it was obligatory to eat dead relatives, or at least portions of them to preserve their essential spirit.

The "equivalence," together with the nonaccumulation of wealth by individuals in most of the societies, requires explanation for it holds only as an approximation. A man, particularly in the highlands where the culture of pigs flourishes, gains prestige by possession of a large number of pigs, usually possible only if he has several wives to raise food for the pigs and to care for them. However, the pigs are not primarily for his and his family's consumption. Pigs, in general, are accumulated to be killed at various ceremonials at which the roasted pig meat is distributed with considerable care so as not to offend kin, covillagers, and allies. In most highland societies, roasting a rather large number of pigs is the sine qua non for holding a ceremonial at which the dead as well as the living must receive a share. If pig culture is meager, large supplies of marsupials, fish, grubs, vegetables, pandanus nuts, and so on, are collected and distributed. Pigs are also used to indemnify for such grievances as adultery or even homicide, and thus avert vengeance through sorcery or a war. A man may be wealthy in the sense that his contributions will eventually be repaid by the recipients or their descendants. However, great care is taken not to incite the envy of others, particularly concerning the possession of magic that induces women to yield to a man. Such capacities leave a man open to attack by sorcery that endangers his life. Still, a man may be held in awe because his ability to accumulate wives, pigs, and taro, and to seduce women without becoming ill, indicates the power of his magic, which enables him to withstand the sorcery directed at him.

The woman's role has been essentially domestic. She is usually married to a man considerably older than herself and goes to live with him shortly before or after her menarche, though among some tribes she is transferred to the care of her husband's parents much earlier. She bears and raises children: a woman often has a toddler by her side, a baby at her breast, and an abdomen protruding over another waiting in her womb. She grows vegetables, gathers certain foods, rears the pigs that may be almost a part of her family, and carries burdens of foodstuffs and wood and sometimes an infant or pig in a net bag suspended from her forehead onto her back.

Though marriages have often been arranged during the girl's childhood, among some groups a girl and man may have considerable say concerning whom they marry, or at least must acquiesce to the selection. In general a woman will not remain with a man who mistreats her too severely or for whom she has an aversion. However, her agnates regard such desertions or "divorces" with disfavor, as they will be obligated to repay the bride-wealth they had received. Then, as we have commented, women often exert a quiet but strong influence in important matters, and an industrious, faithful wife attains esteem and even prestige, and older, post-menopausal women may no longer be considered dangerous to men.

The hamlets or subclans tend to be almost economically self-sufficient. Each hamlet or parish possesses land around which the people can move their gardens and around which their sows wander, and forests where men gather fruits and hunt small marsupials. Some exchange of food, such as fish for sago, may take place between neighboring villages, and pig meat given to kin and allies at ceremonials will be reciprocated at some later date. Articles that are needed but are not available locally are attained through exchange for an object of equivalent value from a trade partner in a nearby community, often an affine who may have obtained it via a chain of such trade partners.

Though highly traditional, change does come about, though usually very slowly. It comes in some areas through expansion

3 The Land, The People, and Their Culture 37

Mother and children, central highlands. Mt. Elimbari in the background.

due to population pressure, or through the "borrowing" or actual purchase of rituals from neighbors, through the transmission of cultural ways at "trade fairs," particularly in the populous and prosperous western highlands, and along the coasts and rivers by the greater mobility of traders and raiders.

Some Basic Concepts

Understanding the people of any culture requires knowledge of the basic beliefs they accept as axiomatic; the shared cultural code (Hutchins, 1980) that enables them to understand one another and live together. Even without laws, the people adhere to customs that provide a consistency of behavior and expectations without which societal existence would be chaotic if not impossible. People make many inferences and assumptions from innumerable references and signals derived from the assimilation of a common cultural heritage.

The basic beliefs of a culture largely determine which experiences persons assimilate and how they think about and utilize them. A child, indeed any person, can assimilate only to preexistent cognitive structures that become altered through accommodation to the new experience (Piaget, 1952). Cognitive structures (or schemata) do not develop simply from a child's perceptions and experiences but are greatly directed by, and assimilated from, those who rear the child, and, in the process, knowingly or unknowingly convey the culture to the child. A great deal of a culture's codes are simply taken for granted, and many must be challenged by contact with other cultures before they reach conscious awareness.

We have already considered some critical basic beliefs that are common to most New Guinea cultures; the belief that the culture was given by the group's primal ancestors, the importance of the ancestor spirits, the division of the societies into male and female, the need to initiate boys to enable them to mature, and the limitations on individual power and wealth. Here we wish to clarify some of these concepts and add a few other pertinent basic beliefs.

The behavior of these various peoples can scarcely be understood without reference to the dead. The primal ancestors who gave the people their culture departed, and in many places, perhaps particularly in the highlands, are totally removed and can no longer be influenced. However, as we have noted, the collectivity of ancestor spirits guard the integrity of the culture and the territory and are not only propitiated at all ceremonials by sharing the food with them, but their beneficence is maintained by adherence to the cultural traditions. One might venture to say that they form a cultural superego. However, they are kept satisfied when their descendants follow tradition correctly rather than by their good or evil behavior. That is, judgment regarding the morality of a particular behavior does not come into question. However, except for certain higher religions and for persons capable of very abstract conceptual ways of thinking, the difference between right or wrong and good or evil may be a matter of cultural mores. The ghosts of the recent dead remain among their living kin for varying lengths of time. They are more powerful and all-knowing than when alive, and are ready to take vengeance on those who neglected them before or after they died.

There are no accidents. The indigenes are strong determinists and everything has a cause. No one, aside from very young infants or occasionally a very old person, dies from "natural causes." All illnesses, accidents, or deaths are either caused by a ghost or by sorcery or witchcraft. The sorcerer, the person instigating the sorcery, or the witch must be appeased when a person becomes ill and following a death becomes the object of vengeance. Sorcery is usually attributed to a person in a nearby hamlet who is avenging some offense by the victim. Thus, warfare or attempts to "payback" by sorcery are perpetuated until the score is even, a state that is rarely attained.

Although a people will believe that their culture was given them virtually in its current form by the primal ancestor or pair of ancestors at the very beginning of their existence, they may at the same time believe, as do the Gururumba (Newman, 1965) and the Karavar (Errington, 1974), that before they received their culture, they were unregenerate savages who ate their infants, committed incest with their mothers, and constantly fought and killed one another over women. In brief, like Freud, they believe that humans are fundamentally impelled by aggressive and lustful impulses but the need to live in societies delimits and constrains. Outlets for aggression, rape, and cannibalism exist in warfare with enemy groups and in raids on other tribes, which, at least, alleviate the discomfort and discontent that Freud believed arose from the repressions imposed by cultures (Freud, 1913).

The depths of the past are shallow, not much beyond the time when people lived whom the elderly can still remember or had heard about from their parents or grandparents, beyond which there was a mythic time, perhaps not very different from the dreaming or dream time of the Australian aborigines. It was then that the primal ancestors or culture heroes of the group emerged and gave rise to their descendants and established their way of life. The indigenes do not know their ages or mark the years. Though festivals are generally scheduled to start at a full moon, they do not clearly count the days in the lunar cycle. Events are likely to be timed in terms of how long it takes for taro roots to mature, or to acquire the necessary number of pigs to hold a ceremonial, or when certain trees blossom, and so forth. Their numerical systems are limited to counting by designating parts of the body and thus do not extend beyond counting to the teens.[10] They tend to live in a time that is cyclic rather then sequential. The emphasis has been on continuity of a way of life, reinforced by fear of the wrath of their ancestors.

The continuity of the clan or phratry must be preserved and children created despite the men's ambivalence concerning marital sexual relations. Babies are formed of womb blood and the semen from numerous inseminations. Womb blood forms the "female parts"—the blood and certain organs—of both men and women, whereas the semen forms the "hard parts," which

---

[10] The Kutulus are notable in having a system that extends to 37 parts of the upper extremities and neck and head (Bjerre, 1964).

include the bones and heart. The precise division of organs into male and female varies from culture to culture. Whereas girls mature into women naturally with the aid of little, if any, ritual, boys must be transformed into men ritually, which often includes a symbolic rebirth from men with the ritual help of ancestor spirits. Some peoples explicitly, and others implicitly, believe that ancestors are reborn or enter into a boy when he is initiated (Herdt, 1981). There is a definite belief among some groups that the essential spirit of men is transferred from generation to generation via semen.

Payback is a major tenet. This Neo-Melanesian or "pidgin" term covers both retribution for death in war or through sorcery, and also the expected and required repayment for favors, including presentations of food at festivals. It not only helps control the power of individuals but is also a major source of security because the killing of a covillager or kinsman will be avenged, very much as in feudal Europe. Since deaths are often attributed to sorcery, it does not require an actual killing or rape to reinstitute warfare between enemy groups, which therefore may be virtually perpetual. Nevertheless, long periods of uneasy truce exist because of adherence to traditions concerning ritual obligations; and despite murderous animosities, men from enemy groups may play essential roles in various initiation procedures, as we shall examine in subsequent chapters.

Cognition

If Comte were correct, the beliefs we have cited that are common to most cultures in eastern New Guinea might suffice to enable the reader to grasp the fundamentals of how the indigenes relate to their world and to follow the practices we shall present. He wrote: "The laws of logic which ultimately govern the world of the mind are, by their nature, essentially invariable; they are common not only to all periods and places but to all subjects of whatever kind, without any distinction even between those that we call the real and the chimerical;

they are to be seen even in dreams" (quoted in Lévi-Strauss, 1962, epigraph). However, the premise cannot be accepted. One of Freud's major contributions was to distinguish between primary and secondary process thinking—between conscious reflective thought as against the logic or illogic of dreams and unconscious processes. Moreover, studies of the development of cognition and language (Piaget, 1926; Inholder and Piaget, 1958; Vygotsky, 1962; Werner, 1964) have demonstrated the changes in cognitive capacities and ways of thinking that take place over the developmental years.

It is probably correct to state that the indigenes tend to divide experiences dichotomously, or into opposites as structuralist theory holds. Among the basic dichotomies are the polarities we have noted between life and death, male and female, war and peace, and also between the affinal and agnatic, the cultural and the wild, and probably between the sacred and profane. Nevertheless, we note that most of these contrasts are "bridged" or vitiated because even though people tend to think in contrasts or opposites, neither the environment nor people's behavior exists in such dichotomous ways. For example, among virtually all peoples, the dead are believed to continue to exist and influence the living; both men and women are composed of both masculine and feminine parts, and, as we shall examine, men seek to preempt female capacities, such as giving birth and menstruating. The division between war and peace is often far from clear-cut because very long periods of truce often prevail; affinal and agnatic lines will cross and intermingle if cross-cousin marriages continue over several generations; men preserve the culture whereas women are "wild," that is, licentious, but it is the men who hunt in the wild and women who remain largely in the hamlet and tend the cultivated crops. The sacred and profane intermingle, for the indigene does not distinguish clearly between the technical work that makes a drum or a canoe and the ritual that is essential to make such artifacts into functioning objects. However, the thinking of the indigenes has not developed in the same directions as the cognition of peoples in Western cultures. The indigenes have a different logic, concepts of causality, and ways of dividing experiences into the categories with which they think.

Our efforts to clarify the fundamentals of the indigenes' ways of thinking, including their ways of reasoning, conceptualizing, and finding causes can only be halting and tentative for the matter is very complex and the guidelines available (Freud, 1913; Levy-Bruhl, 1923, 1926; Sapir, 1949; Boelaars, 1950; Whorf, 1956; Bateson, 1958; Lévi-Strauss, 1962; Geertz, 1973) do not seem sufficiently comprehensive or consistent with one another. In discussing the limitations of the indigenes' cognition, we wish, at the outset, to make it clear that we are not considering their potential intellectual capacities. It is obvious that indigenes with university educations have become as competent as university graduates elsewhere. It is a matter of the nature of the cognitive tools and the education provided the nonacculturated indigene.

Cognition develops in the child to some extent through maturation of the brain, but clearly through experience, the assimilation of the culture's system of meaning and logic, and through formal education by adults.

It seems apparent that the indigene's use of magic and sorcery as well as his belief that he can control nature by means of ritual via omnipotent ancestors are residues of preoperational modes of thinking that continue into their adult lives to a far greater degree than is the case with people living in industrialized societies.[11] The indigenes do not remain completely fixated at such levels for they form categories, but the categorizations are largely concrete. We might follow Lévi-Strauss (1966) and consider that by a "science of the concrete" they slowly discovered various basic techniques such as making stone axes and weapons, plaiting, pottery, agriculture and animal husbandry, roasting and boiling, and so forth to satisfy human

[11] Of course, animistic and other types of preoperational thinking were not only extensive in Europe during the Middle Ages but continue in the belief systems of most Western religions, particularly fundamentalist religions, though they do not pervade everyday matters to the extent they do in Papua New Guinea and most other nonliterate societies.

needs, but they had not become capable of more "abstract" types of thought. However, it is difficult to judge just what is concrete and what abstract thought. Surely there is something "abstract" about the concept that the living and dead rotate through a cycle, in part as tangible people in the community and in part as spirits in the place where dead ancestors dwell (Poole, 1982b), and in the metaphor of the Gisaro songs of the Kaluli in which place names evoke misfortunes associated with them (Schieffelin, 1976). It seems more correct to say that the indigenes' "formal operational" thought is limited and continues to contain many preoperational influences. The people of Papua New Guinea can certainly develop theories and reason from them, one of Piaget's criteria for "formal operations." The theories may not be scientifically valid but the indigene has theories about why a person becomes ill, why girls mature more rapidly than boys, how to make crops grow, and so forth. The theories contain animistic and magical types of thinking but the thinking is not childish. Pospisil (1978), for example, tells that an old man traveled a long distance to have the anthropologist clarify a problem for him before he died. He was puzzled how Europeans could be so ingenious in designing guns, medicines, and airplanes and still be so illogical in their religion. How could they think a person can sin and have a free will, and at the same time believe God is omnipotent and determined all that would happen in the world He created? "If He determined all that happens, and also the bad deeds, how can a man be held responsible?" The old Kapauku puzzled over what has puzzled many learned theologians.

The child in our industrial societies does not abandon childhood "egocentric" ideas of causality simply because they are not found to be instrumentally useful, but also because adults cease accepting them and teach different concepts. They are taught that it was not their wishes or actions that caused it to rain, but God; or more scientific ideas of why things happen. In contrast, indigene children are not only taught to continue their ways of thinking about causes, but are instructed in animistic and mythic, ritualistic ways of understanding their experiences. Indeed, the fear of alienating the ancestor spirits, the reverence of tradition, and the paucity of outside influences are powerful forces against innovative ideas.

The problem of understanding the ways of the peoples of Papua New Guinea transcends questions of the preoperational and concrete character of their thinking. Sapir (1949) and Whorf (1956) established one of the cornerstones of contemporary anthropology when they emphasized the circular problem confronting both anthropologists and linguists: that to understand a language, it is necessary to understand the culture; and that one cannot understand a culture without understanding the language. They did not mean the ability to translate words, but rather that every culture divides up the continuity of experience into different sets of categories which are, by and large, designated by the vocabulary of the language. Every culture divides experiences into somewhat different categories, and often the words used to translate them do not cover the same concept. The Mexican *mañana* is not the same as the English word *tomorrow* nor are *love* and *amour* synonymous. German has no word equivalent to the English *mind*, and most Americans have difficulty in discussing a person in terms of "body, spirit and soul" (*Leib, Geist und Seele*). Very disparate cultures are likely to categorize very differently and the cultures of Papua New Guinea are in many ways antipodal to our own. As might be anticipated, the people's ways of categorizing are so different from ours that it impedes our understanding of their communications, customs, and general behavior and, as has been illustrated in our paper on cargo cults (Lidz, Lidz, and Burton-Bradley, 1973), led to tragic misunderstandings between the indigenes and most missionaries.

Some different categorizations are readily grasped. The Bimin-Kuskusmin have a word to designate the mother and infant as an entity—and we realize that it would be useful if we had a smiliar categorization. On the other hand, without knowledge of the culture, it is difficult to grasp why an ancient stone axe head, a python, and the sounds of a pair of flutes should be categorized together; or what a sister's vagina and pigs have in common. Perhaps the problem can be illustrated most readily by following Buchbinder and Rappaport (1976) who explicate a critical dichotomy of the way indigenes categorize male and female. Among the Maring, as elsewhere in Papua New Guinea, the terms do not apply just to humans and animals or to vegetal life, but divide much of the world. They point out that the concept of male includes "high-hard-hot-dry-strong-spiritual-immortal" versus "low-soft-cold-wet-fecund-mundane-mortal" that are female. We can amplify. Females are polluting and "wild" with the connotation of lasciviousness, in contrast to men (Lindenbaum, 1976). Parts of the body, of both men and women, are either male or female. In most places taro is male and strengthens men, whereas sweet potatoes are female. As will become apparent, the categories of male and female have even more sweeping significance in the lives of the people, not simply in terms of their behavior but their perception of their universe.

There are other conceptual problems that are difficult, at least for us, to understand or explain. For example, taro, at least among the Dobu, can be talked to and influenced by incantation to migrate underground from one garden to another. Then, too, animals, vegetables, and humans can descend from one another. As Poole (1988) has clearly designated, the part-human androgynous ancestors of the Bimin-Kuskusmin people were the offspring of a lizard, and had both human and marsupial offspring. They believe the sweet potato to be the descendant of the cassowary and echidna and so forth. Thus, the boundaries of such concepts as animal and vegetal are extremely loose, and even the category of "human" has a nebulous quality to it.

We must further emphasize an aspect of indigene concepts that will become apparent in subsequent chapters. Many ideas are held and many things are done simply because they are part of the group's mythology. Among the Bimin-Kuskusmin (Poole, 1988) many details of the initiation rituals are simply part of the lengthy and complex "Afek myth cycle"—the myths about one of the two primal ancestors. Presumably a ritual elder will eventually learn the entire myth, but if a unified Afek myth actually exists, it is so sacred and secret it cannot be disclosed. The primal ancestors, or some ancestor spirit, may be supposed to have the vision and ability to understand life and various rituals in their entirety, but the reality or the truth is dangerous, particularly to the uninitiated, and must be revealed gradually in symbols that convey an impression and a feeling state rather than definite knowledge.

Reasons that arise from myths will share many of the characteristics of dreams. In dreams, for example, various experiences are condensed into one image; seeming opposites, rather than being contradictory, indicate similarities between matters that apparently are divergent. They are timeless in that the symbols join events and feelings from different occasions; they permit disguised expression of unacceptable impulses, and so forth. Myths, in contrast to most dreams, are likely to have gained a degree of permanence because they express shared unconscious and partly conscious desires, impulses, and thoughts of the persons of a given culture, or of persons everywhere.

We have not been able to define or properly describe the indigenes' ways of reasoning, their ways of forming categories, or their ideas of causality. We have sought simply to prepare the reader to understand them symbolically, and to appreciate that in the absence of more scientifically valid concepts, such beliefs about nature and ways of influencing events beyond the people's control are useful in diminishing a sense of helplessness and provide them with a means of attempting to control their fate.

4
Male Menstruation: Defeminization and Disidentification from the Mother

We shall start our scrutiny of the rituals that transform prepubertal "feminine" boys into men by a consideration of the forced vomiting and particularly the bleeding which in various places is termed *male menstruation*—practices that are central to the first phase of initiation in many Papua New Guinea societies, and a critical, though seemingly incidental event in many others. Male menstruation in different forms is a practice among Australian aborigines and Mohave Indians as well as the indigenes, and we focus on the practices in Papua New Guinea because we believe they provide important insights into the young boy's initial identification with his mother, his problems in achieving a masculine identity, and also into the obscure subject of men's overt and latent envy of women.

These topics have aroused considerable attention in recent years both because of the psychoanalytically oriented studies of transsexuals by Stoller (1966), Greenson (1968), Socarides (1973), and others, and because of various challenges to the psychoanalytic emphasis on women's penis envy without a counterbalancing interest in men's envy of women's generative capacities (Greenson, 1966; Bettelheim, 1971; Lidz and Lidz, 1977; Stoller and Herdt, 1982). It is evident from Jaffe's (1968) review of the psychoanalytic literature pertaining to masculine envy of women, as well as Tyson's (1982) review of the literature on gender identity, that these topics require clarification. The examination of a way of life that differs profoundly from our own enables us to set aside our cultural preconceptions and take a fresh look at some cardinal problems of human development.

Before we consider the implications of male menstruation to psychoanalytic developmental theory, we shall examine the actual practices. We shall first turn to Kenneth Read's (1952) description of the Gahuka-Gama ritual, which started a new era in the study of initiation rituals. We shall then focus attention on the initiation rituals of the Sambia who dwell on the fringe of the eastern highlands and those of the Bimin-Kuskusmin who inhabit an area near the headwaters of the Fly River near Telefomin, though we shall refer as well to the practices of various other peoples. We do so because Gilbert Herdt who has lived among the Sambia and Fitz John Porter Poole who studied the Bimin-Kuskusmin intensively are both psychologically oriented ethnologists who gained the confidence of the people among whom they lived. They were not only permitted to witness and participate in various stages of the initiation rituals but also to discuss the pertinent myths and traditions with the cult leaders and study the meanings of the rituals and the reactions to the rituals of both the novitiates and initiators. Few, if any other anthropologists have been able to provide such intimate, firsthand knowledge of initiation rituals in Papua New Guinea. Further, since writing a first draft of this book several years ago, our task has been lightened considerably for it is no longer necessary for us to describe a variety of initiation rituals or document the widespread practice of ritual homosexuality in Papua New Guinea. Two books edited by Gilbert Herdt, *Rituals of Manhood* (1982) and *Ritualized Homosexuality in Melanesia* (1984), have carried out these tasks more amply and authoritatively than our attempts.

Although the rituals in these localities are very different,

4 Male Menstruation: Defeminization and Disidentification from the Mother

we believe that underlying similarities and the purposes they serve will become apparent. Kenneth Read (1965), who, we believe, was the first trained anthropologist to enter the highlands after World War II, has provided us with a vivid and dramatic account of the male initiation ritual of the Gahuka-Gama people in the Asaro valley, a high plateau country divided by 13,000-foot mountain ranges. The Gahuka-Gama were still an almost pure neolithic people when Read studied them in 1950. Philip Newman (1965) has described the similar practices of the Gururumba in the same valley, and Herdt (1981) the related rituals of the Sambia people. Male menstruation forms a central part of the initiation into what Read named the nama cult, common to various cultures of the eastern highlands.

Among the Gahuka-Gama the boys live with their mothers until some time between the ages of ten and 15, and during that period are raised primarily by their mothers. Their fathers sleep in a men's cult hut because of their fear of contamination by menstrual blood and other female exudations and emanations. The boys are subjected to a mild, preliminary ritual experience some time between the ages of five and seven when they are taken to the river to the accompaniment of the shrill sounds of hidden "nama," the sacred flutes, which they and their mothers believe are the voices of ancestors in the form of mystical birds. At the river, the boys find themselves surrounded by a throng of armed and decorated warriors whose continuous chanting is accompanied by hidden flutes. The experience is probably quite terrifying for the children but they are then returned to their mothers.

The critical prepubertal rites are carried out only once every five or six years because they must be accompanied by an elaborate ceremonial pig killing and food distribution that drain the community's resources. Thus, the initiates vary in age but with rare exceptions are still prepubertal.

After many weeks during which the sacred flutes resound through the hills every night and preparations for the pig festival are made, one morning the boys are assembled together with all the men who are in full warrior regalia. The mothers are in mourning dress, their bodies smeared with clay in recognition of their separation from their sons who are "formally crossing over to the male division" of the society (Read, 1965, p. 158). Then the men, with the novices bunched in their center, rush down the mountainsides, crashing through the bush, shouting and chanting, the sounds of the flutes beating in their ears, until they reach the river toward which warriors with novitiates from other hamlets are descending in a symbolic show of strength.

The boys, placed in the front ranks of the vast crowd, see a score of naked men standing in the river exhibiting their erect penises and masturbating. Then, several of the men stride into the river where one takes two rolls of razor-sharp leaves and pushes them up and down his nostrils until blood gushes into the water, an act rewarded by shouts of approval from the multitude. When the bleeding stops, he staggers to the river bank, his knees buckling from the pain. After a half-dozen men simultaneously follow his example, each initiate, with his mind "numb with the apprehension of pain, the urge to struggle and escape constrained only by the greater fear of shame" (Read, 1965, p. 167), is held firmly by his sponsor, while another man thrusts the leaves back and forth in his nostrils until the boy bleeds profusely into the river. After all of the initiates have been bled, the men who had bled themselves reenter the river where each doubles a length of cane and thrusts it down his esophagus like a sword swallower and draws it back and forth until he vomits into the water. The dangerous procedure is then carried out on the initiates who are now weakened and slack from the bleeding.[1]

When, after some hours, all the boys have been bled and forced to vomit, some of the stronger men take the initiates on their shoulders and make their way uphill to the hamlets. As they approach their hamlet, the men are suddenly attacked by the massed women of the village who hurl rocks and clubs at them and even threaten them with bows and arrows. Although the attack is, in a sense, symbolic, it is clearly a release of pent-

---

[1] The blood, vomitus, and semen are extruded into flowing water, like the bleeding into the fire in the Wogeo ritual we shall describe, to prevent their falling into the possession of a sorcerer.

up hostility by the women who are enraged at having had their sons taken from them and forced to undergo a ritual they know is painful and dangerous. Some men may be rather seriously hurt and they finally abandon their disdainful reserve and counterattack, scattering the women.

The initiates are carried to the men's hut where the secret of the sacred flutes is disclosed to them; namely, that the sounds are made by flutes rather than by ancestor spirits in the form of mystical birds. The secret must be kept from the women and children on pain of death. During the ensuing six weeks the boys remain secluded in the hut where they are taught to play the flutes, after which they are paraded around the village in their new ceremonial outfits to be greeted by their women kinfolk who pretend to have difficulty in recognizing them now that they have become men. The youths return to the men's cult hut and remain there for five to ten years, permitted only minimal contact with women.[2] When the youths are between the ages of 15 and 19, but probably older,[3] and have been betrothed, they go through the ceremony again. After a period of stringent dietary restriction and intense practice playing the flutes, and when their duties and rights as men have been fully explained, they emerge at the start of a pig festival with full male status.

To comprehend the importance of the bleeding and vomiting rituals and why they are deemed essential to enable the boy to become pubertal, we must not only recall various aspects of male-female relationships in the highlands, but also consider the

---

[2] Read (1984) is fairly certain that the boys and youths isolated from women do not have homosexual relations as Freud (1913) postulated they might, and as is now known is required in a number of other Papua New Guinea societies. Still, it should be recognized that at the time Read lived among the Gahuka-Gama he had no reason to believe ritual homosexuality might be important; and that his stay was cut short by a serious illness (Read, 1965).

[3] Sexual maturity comes very late in these highland societies. Brown (1978) and Herdt (1981) judge that menarche occurs between the ages of 16 and 18 or even later—and thus boys would not be expected to reach puberty before the age of 18. It seems likely that Read underestimated the ages at which the youths attain full male status.

people's concepts of how babies are made, and why girls can mature naturally but boys must be turned into men by ritual.

Among the Gahuka-Gama and Gururumba, as among most highland peoples, the men sleep in a men's hut in which they also keep and conceal their ritual objects, while a man's wife, or each of his wives, lives in a separate hut with her children. Because of the permanent warfare with some neighboring hamlets, it had been imperative that each hamlet or village rear the boys to become strong warriors who can defend the community's territory and protect its women and children from murder, cannibalism, and rape. The practice of exogamy usually requires most men to marry women from other villages, and in some localities almost 70 percent of the wives come from enemy villages, so that a man's mother and wife may both be from enemy villages. In these patrilocal villages, the mothers of the boys may have been raised in a tradition that differs to some extent from the one that must be handed on to their sons. The separation of the sexes is heightened by the men's marked fear of menstrual blood and women's sexual emanations, which keeps men from sleeping with or near their wives. Contact with a menstruating woman will make a man seriously ill. The danger from menstrual blood, however, provides a source of protection to women living among alien men. A husband who mistreats his wife does so at the risk of his life, for she can kill him by putting menstrual blood in his food.

The danger from women, however, extends beyond contamination by her menses, for there is something about the vital essence of women that is antipathetic to men's vitality, and young men in particular will be weakened and their health undermined by prolonged proximity to a woman. Loss of semen in heterosexual intercourse is also considered weakening, and young men are stringently warned against overindulgence as they are not yet strong enough to withstand the powers of women and the loss of semen. A man runs the additional danger that his wife might give his semen to a sorcerer—a certain way of procuring his death. We believe it is apparent, even without further elaboration, that any pleasure derived from sex is greatly diminished if not offset by the multiplicity of dangers it entails and that many barriers exist to comfortable relationships between men and women.

The dangers of female contamination extend beyond direct contact. Men may be very cautious about being near their young infants or in handling their children because they carry contamination from their mothers. Among some peoples, the men and women walk on separate paths so that men can avoid the women's contamination that has brushed off onto the bushes and vines. Herdt (personal communication), who has lived among the Sambia for several years, has never seen a husband and wife purposely touch one another in public.

The men's secret cult forms the core structure of the society and the secret of the sacred flutes or, in some places, the secret of the bullroarers is kept from the women and children. Both instruments are considered to be the voices of the ancestors, or the means of summoning them, and are central to most rituals. (Bullroarers are fish-shaped pieces of wood that make a whirring or thunderous sound when whirled on a string, and are recognized to be phallic symbols.) Initiates are warned on pain of death not to reveal the secret that the sounds are made by men. Indeed, the punishment extends beyond death, for their bodies would be thrown in the river rather than disposed of with proper ritual so that their ghosts would never find rest but forever haunt the forest as malignant spirits. Women are said to have been put to death because they have inadvertently seen men playing the flutes or witnessed some other secret ritual. However, it seems clear enough that many if not all women know that the sounds are made by flutes, as well as many other secrets of the initiation rituals. We have been told that women take the attitude that as they have everything of importance—the babies, the pigs, the gardens—they let the men have their flutes and their ceremonies if it makes them feel satisfied and if they are willing to accept these crucial responsibilities. Nevertheless, the women firmly believe that the well-being of the group and the fertility of its women, pigs, and crops depend on the rituals the men conduct to influence the ancestor spirits.

They also believe that males will be harmed by undue exposure to women's genital odor, and are trained to avoid stepping over a husband's possessions.

It is of interest and of theoretical importance that virtually everywhere in Papua New Guinea, myths teach that originally the flutes, bullroarers, and the rituals themselves belonged to the women but were taken from them by force or guile.

Now, although it is essential for the villages to raise powerful warriors, the boys are raised primarily by their mothers for the first seven or even 12 to 15 years of their lives. The boy's bonding to his mother and his identification with her is fostered by the way of life. The children are breast-fed for several years, and in many places sleep alongside their mothers for many years while the father tends to keep his distance. As sexual intercourse is believed to weaken the mother's breast milk, there is a strict postpartum sexual taboo that keeps the parents from having sexual relations for at least a year, and commonly for two or three years, thus enhancing the mother's erogenous investment of her child. As the relationships between the newly married parents are rarely intimate or even satisfactory to the wife, a woman's major gratification is apt to come from her children. The mother is the principal authority and refuge for a boy until he is separated from her very late in childhood. However, in some, if not most, localities, the father takes an interest in his sons after they have been weaned, plays with them and teaches them, though the mother's brother may relate more actively than the father. Even though the bonding to the mother may be intense, the boy knows that he is a male and is treated as a boy from a very early age. The boys also become aware when very young that men dominate their wives and treat women with contempt.

In Papua New Guinea, babies are not conceived by sperm fertilizing an ovum, but rather a fetus is comprised of womb blood and an abundance of semen produced by multiple acts of intercourse.[4] In some societies a young man must summon up

---

[4] When the authors were in Papua New Guinea in 1971, a magistrate dismissed paternity charges against a man because the woman agreed that she had intercourse with him only once.

his courage and the various protective techniques he has been taught, be willing to weaken himself by expending his store of semen, and repeatedly expose himself to his wife's dangerous vaginal emanations in order to have a child.[5] However, a man has little status in the community, and in some places is unable to complete his initiation into manhood, until he has had at least one child (Herdt, 1981).

With this somewhat sketchy background, let us consider what the initiation ritual and, in particular, the nose bleeding, vomiting, and the sacred flutes are all about. What do the indigenes consider the purpose of the rituals and what has seemed fairly obvious to the ethnologists who have observed and studied them? It is apparent to all that the initiation serves to separate the boys from their mothers and replace their attachments to their mothers with a new solidary relationship to the men's group, makes them obedient to older men, and take them as models for identification. In addition, it establishes an intimate relationship with their male agemates with whom they spend many years as novitiates and who will be their companions in warfare. They are symbolically reborn as males. They are no longer "persons of the women's houses" but are in the process of becoming men of the cult house who are not only independent of women but markedly superior to them.[6]

---

[5] Among some peoples of southeastern Irian Jaya, a woman is inseminated by serial intercourse with her husband's patrikin, not only at the time of the marriage but also when she has finished nursing a child and is in condition to become pregnant again (van Baal, 1966; Serpenti, 1984; chapter 12).

[6] Jane Harrison (1912, p. 26), the great scholar of pre-Olympian Greek religions, on the basis of her knowledge of Greek mystery rites and her readings about the Australian aborigines wrote, "The initiators dress up as the ancestral ghosts of the tribe, sometimes even wearing the actual skulls of their ancestors, and in this disguise dance round the catechumens and terrify them half out of their senses. It is only when fully initiated that the boys learn that these terrific figures are not spirits at all but just their living uncles and cousins. The secret is never imparted to women and children. To do so would be death . . . (p. 26).

"The birth from the male womb is to rid the child from the infection of his mother—to turn him from a woman-thing into a man-thing. Woman to primitive man is a thing at once weak and magical, to be oppressed, yet feared. She is charged with powers of childbearing denied to man, powers only half understood, forces of attraction, but also of danger and repulsion, forces that all over the world seem to fill him with dim

The vomiting is said to rid the boy of any of the mother's womb blood swallowed in utero and of any dangerous menstrual blood he had inadvertently ingested with the food his mother prepared for him, as well as residues of "female foods" permitted women and children but deemed weakening to men. Further, according to Newman (1965), the use of the vomiting cane performs a function analogous to the artificial breaking of the hymen in a girl at the time of her menarche that enables her to menstruate and thereby mature. The cane is believed to break a membrane inside the body that permits the boy to develop secondary sexual characteristics and become a man.

The nose bleeding, which, at least in some places is clearly referred to as male menstruation,[7] is essential for the boy's physical maturation because it rids the boy's body, at least symbolically, of his mother's womb blood that entered into his composition, and thus makes it possible for him to move on to be reborn as a man. Beyond symbolically ridding the boy of his mother's womb blood, it is a means of purifying him from menstrual and other female contamination, particularly from

---

terror. . . . Man cannot escape being born of woman, but he can, and, if he is wise, will, as soon as he comes to manhood, perform ceremonies of riddance and purgation. . . (p. 36). The child . . . might remain with its mother for a time. She will practise on it her mother-rites . . . but sooner or later, the day of separation is at hand. The Kouretes of the tribe will come and take him away, will hide him for weeks or months in the bush, will clothe him in strange clothes, teach him strange dances and strange lore, and bring him back all changed, with a new soul, the soul of his tribe, his mother's child no more, trained it may be henceforth to scorn or spit at her. He belongs from henceforth to his father and to the Man's House" (p. 37).

Here, as elsewhere, Harrison's insights based on meager evidence were profound.

[7] It may seem strange that bleeding from the nose is equated with bleeding from the genitals as in menstruation. However, in Papua New Guinea the nose is clearly equated with the penis, as can be noted in many of their artifacts, particularly in the Mwai masks of the Iatmul. When the Awa people cut wedges in each side of the glans penis, they say that it is like bleeding the two sides of the nose. When an older Sambia warrior was telling Herdt about raids in which he had participated prior to the pacification of the area, he narrated that a young woman he had captured begged him not to kill her and said, " 'I will help you clean out your nose' "—clearly meaning that she would have sexual relations with him (Herdt, 1981, p. 61).

Although Herdt does not believe that the Sambia people equate the nose bleeding with menstruation, they go into the forest and bleed their noses each time their wives menstruate, and as we shall note, the men on Wogeo have a similar practice.

the dangerous vital essence of women. Men envy women's natural means of self-purification by menstruation that preserves their health, and men who are properly concerned with their health, strength, and attractiveness will periodically purify themselves both by vomiting and nose bleeding.

Male menstruation is also considered to be an essential precursor of learning to play the sacred flutes. As the flutes represent the ancestor spirits[8] who control the fertility of the people, pigs, and soil, the possession of the flutes and the rituals that influence the ancestor spirits bestows upon men the control of fertility, balancing the natural creativity of women. Because of the flutes, the women became spiritually dependent on the men who have control over the ritual contacts with the ancestor spirits without whom the people cannot survive.

Initiation rituals are also held among some peoples for girls at the time of their menarche, though the rituals are not as serious, prolonged, or painful as the initiation rituals for boys. Whereas female initiation celebrates the fact of growth and the onset of reproductive power and teaches the adolescent girls to control this power lest it have a deleterious effect on others, the male initiation has the purpose of inducing sexual maturation, growth, and reproductive power rather than celebrating its existence. It is apparent that in Papua New Guinea the first stage of the initiation rituals is not a puberty rite, but rather enables boys to mature into men. In the process, the rituals serve other purposes that we shall discuss more fully in later chapters. They remove the boy from his mother and rid him of the womb blood that went into his makeup and the inhibiting influences of contamination from female emanations, but they also provide some of the characteristics of women that men envy. The disparity between women and men is overcome. The youth begins through initiation to assume a ritual control over vital powers that the female acquires naturally: the flutes

---

[8] The flutes are always blown in pairs, a musical necessity as they have no vents and a single flute can be played to render seven notes over several octaves. It is only by combining flutes pitched differently that tunes can be played. Perhaps flutes, like people, require the combination of a male and a female to function properly. A large horn used to summon the flutes is called "the mother of the flutes."

control fertility akin to women's reproductive capacities; nose bleeding enables men to purify themselves from sexual contamination much as menstruation rids the woman of contamination by males; breaking the imagined membrane during the first vomiting ritual is similar to breaking the hymen that enables sexual maturation (Newman, 1965). Newman points out the rather apparent identification of the vital essence with sexual energy; or, as we might wish to say, with libido.

Although we may seem to have presented a multiplicity of purposes for the male initiation ritual, including the artificial menstruation, they all relate to a single theme: freeing the boy from his initial feminine identification with his mother while at the same time providing substitutes for the female characteristics he must renounce. We have, however, been dealing only with the first stage, or part of the first stage of a series of initiation rituals. When we examine the subsequent phases of the rituals that accentuate the masculinization process, we will also elaborate on the means of fostering renunciation of the mother. But first let us consider briefly how some of the other Papua New Guinea cultures carry out the defeminization of their boys.

Hogbin (1970) described ritual menstruation practices he witnessed in 1934 on the island of Wogeo in the Schouten group not far from the mouth of the Sepik River. Although separated from the Asaro valley by only 400 or 500 miles, the cultures have clearly been separated for many hundreds and perhaps thousands of years, and though the actual rituals differ markedly, they serve the same functions. On Wogeo, the culture differs significantly from those of the highlands; but notable similarities are also apparent. The hamlets on the island are not at war with one another and there is less of a pressing need to raise fierce warriors. Men have much less fear of contamination by women. The sexual mores are freer and premarital intercourse is the rule. However, "the social separateness of the men and women . . . is constantly underlined, and generally when working or at leisure they remain apart" (Hogbin, 1970, p. 86). The sexes are in more or less balanced opposition. Men blame women for undermining male solidarity; and at a girl's puberty rites women make fun of men's assumed self-importance. Here, rather than only women being dangerous to men, each sex is dangerous to the other. "The established doctrine is that the members of each sex group would be safe and invulnerable, healthy and prosperous, if only they were to keep to themselves and refrain from mixing with members of the other sex group" (Hogbin, 1970, p. 87). However, small children would die without mothers, couples are dependent upon one another economically, and sexual drives force them together, with the result that everyone is "perpetually weakened, liable to disease and misadventure" (p. 88). The females are considered more fortunate than males because menstruation regularly frees them from contamination whereas the men must take positive measures to purify themselves.

Despite the differences from the Asaro valley and its nama cult, the secret of the sacred flutes and the belief that boys must be bled before they can mature are central aspects of the rituals. Here, too, there is a simple preinitiation ritual for boys between the ages of three and five when the flutes summon the mythical Nibek monsters, representative of ancestor spirits, from the sea. During the ceremony the little boys are blindfolded and have their ears pierced. They are frightened by being told that "the Nibek monsters have bitten you; they have made their first mark and will come back later and eat you up." Like preliminary ceremonies elsewhere, it seems to mark the boy's first major movement following weaning toward separation from his mother.

When the boys are about ten, they are taken to the men's hut, terrified because they are now to be eaten by the Nibek monsters. Here, too, mothers weep and sing mournful songs. The boys, however, are soon reassured that if they remain quiet, they will not be hurt when eaten. Then after some scrubbing to remove traces of the Nibek's excrement,[9] and being dragged from the sea by a spear blade twisted in the hair to make them

---

[9] Similar procedures in some other Papua New Guinea societies are performed to cleanse the boys of their mothers' contamination.

grow, the flutes are played and the secret revealed that the flutes are the Nibek monsters.

Back in the men's hut, the novitiates are told that the ceremony was invented by the culture heroes "to separate them from their mothers, to make them grow, and to prepare them for handling the instruments" (Hogbin, 1970, p. 110). They are warned not to reveal the secrets to the women or children and after a further series of rituals they return to the men's hut. The following day pairs of boys from opposite moieties drink from a brook together and become blood brothers, and are considered closer than siblings. Here, too, the boys will live in the men's hut for some years with minimal contact with women.

On Wogeo, the initial bleeding ceremony does not take place until the boys begin to develop pubic hair and have greater self-control, for should a single drop of blood fall upon the boy he would surely sicken and die. A boy cannot grow into a man unless he learns to play the flutes after being purified by eliminating the various polluting elements absorbed from women during childhood. The tongue is chosen as the site of the initial bleeding because the boy has absorbed the pollution through nursing and the inadvertent ingestion of menstrual blood, but also because abrading the tongue makes it more pliable for playing the flutes. In an extremely elaborate and difficult ceremony, each initiate sits with his head protruding over a small fire with his tongue thrust out while a specialist carefully scrapes the boy's tongue with an abrasive leaf until blood drops steadily into the fire. The boy is repeatedly warned not to swallow or let a drop of blood fall upon him rather than into the fire. The men who carry out the procedure become severely polluted and must undergo stringent cleansing following it, and are subject to extreme taboos for some weeks.

The boys are now told of the grave risk of indulging in sexual relationships before they learn how to purify themselves by inducing menstruation by cutting the glans penis, a procedure that the youth is taught when about 18 or 19 years old. He wades into the ocean and cuts the head of his penis with a sharp crab claw deeply enough to produce a gush of blood. Men are not required to menstruate each month but ought to do so regularly. In actuality, however, most men wait until they become ill, which they blame on female pollution. The benefits of the procedure are immediate—the man's muscles harden, his hair and skin become more lustrous, and he feels stronger and more self-confident. Therefore, men will be certain to menstruate before setting out on a raid or trading expedition.

As in the Asaro valley, the youth does not attain the status of manhood until he goes through one more rite. Here, the ritual has to do with growing his hair long enough to wear through a wicker cone in the traditional manner.[10] He is then considered capable of marrying and having children.

In other localities, still different means of bleeding the initiates are used. Among the Ilahita Arapesh (Tuzin, 1982) and the Awa (Newman and Boyd, 1982), the glans penis is cut, and at a later stage the Awa cut wedges out of each side of the glans, and drive the instruments used for nose bleeding into the nostrils with a stone.[11] The Bimin-Kuskusmin incise near the

[10]This strange practice has its analogues elsewhere, and its symbolic meaning is obscure. We conjecture that it may relate to the practice among some groups, even one as far away as the Kimam-Papuans (Serpenti, 1984) of shaving the initiate's head as a means of separating him from the mother, but leaving for a time, a single topknot tuft—the first part of the infant to emerge from the mother—as a tie to her that must not be broken too abruptly. The topknot is cut at a later date. Perhaps it is for this reason that when the youth has grown long hair that is not symbolically related to his mother he is considered ready to marry. We are also led to wonder if pulling the boy out of the ocean by his hair may not be symbolic of rebirth from the sea or from the Nibek ancestor spirits who inhabit the ocean.

[11]Despite the stringent preparations, the Awa consider that intercourse with a virgin bride is still too dangerous for her inexperienced husband. Here, along with still other precautions taken before the marriage is consummated, the bride is taken to a place at the edge of the forest by several of the husband's older patrikin and their wives. The bride must then submit to as many of those future male affines who wish to copulate with her as often as they desire. The purpose of this prolonged, serial copulation is not only to prepare the bride for procreation by opening her vagina but also to force out any bloody fluids that would harm her young husband and thereby impair successful reproduction. The older men who have already fathered several children are less susceptible to the dangers of contact with such potent female substances and are thus protecting the well-being of their young relative and promoting procreation. The pain the bride suffers is thought to invigorate the life force in her body and strengthen her reproductive organs. Perhaps, the European noblemen who exercised *le droit du seigneur* had similar altruistic motives.

navel, the major source of maternal influence (Poole, 1982a); in some places slivers of bamboo or small wads of sharp leaves are inserted into the penile urethra to scarify it (Berndt, 1965; Salisbury, 1965). Among the Chambri, bleeding is an important aspect of the scarification of the initiate's back (Gewertz, 1982); and the Kimam-Papuans (Serpenti, 1984) bleed the initiates by forcefully perforating the nasal septum to permit insertion of boar tusks.

Although the ritual procedures among the Gahuka-Gama and the peoples of Wogeo upon which we have been focusing are painful and frightening, the procedures we have considered thus far are not so much threats of damage, such as castration threats to keep the initiate in his place and bring about repression of oedipal longings, but primarily rituals of riddance; that is, to rid the person of the mother's influence that impedes maturation and the lengthy process of becoming a man.

It is of interest that serial copulation with the male patrikin is used for very different reasons in at least three other localities: among the Kimam-Papuans to collect semen to smear on the groom to make him grow and to see if the bride is ready for marriage (Serpenti, 1984); among the Marind-anim to provide the collective semen necessary to form the fetus (van Baal, 1966); and among the Fore (Lindenbaum, 1976) and elsewhere to subdue a bride who refuses to have intercourse with her husband.

5
Psychoanalytic Concepts of the Bleeding Rituals

We now turn to examine from a psychoanalytic perspective why it is essential that the prepubertal boys are subjected to rituals that include vomiting and bleeding, taught the secrets of the sacred flutes, and are symbolically reborn as men from men or male ancestor spirits. As part of our inquiry, we shall consider why menstrual blood and women's sexual emanations are so dangerous to men, and why the men need to degrade women to an extent that creates a profound divisiveness between men and women.

A study of the purposes of the ritual bleeding, termed *male menstruation* in some localities, requires consideration of two topics that have each received considerable attention from both psychoanalysts and ethnologists: the fear of menstrual blood and the male adolescent initiation rituals.

The common psychoanalytic explanation of men's dread of menstruating women and menstrual blood—a fear that is found all over the world—is based on the belief in the universality of the castration complex and of the childhood belief that women have been castrated: the sight of menstrual blood reawakens a man's childhood fears of castration either as punishment for his oedipal wishes to possess his mother, or because of his masturbation with unconscious fantasies about his mother. Two Papua New Guinea myths we know seem to relate menstruation to childhood concepts that women have been castrated. Williams (1936) tells that the Kwavaru believe that their primal ancestor Tiv'r had a wife, Engu, who suffered from some malformation so that she did not become pregnant with a human child but with a bullroarer. When Engu moved, the bullroarer emitted its characteristic sound which puzzled Tiv'r. Engu refused to tell Tiv'r what caused the sound, but he eventually commissioned his birds to steal the bullroarer from his wife. After various birds failed, one succeeded. When Engu had her legs spread while sweeping, the bullroarer protruded from her vagina and the bird swooped down and snatched it. Engu was left lying on her back screaming, with blood flowing from her vagina—the origin of menstrual bleeding. The bird gave the bullroarer to his master who hugged it to his chest and declared that from then on it would belong to man alone. In a related Keraki account (Williams, 1936), Yumar, the wife of Kambel, the primal ancestor of the people, had the bullroarer in her genitals which Kambel managed to snatch from her when she was sweeping.

These myths, and others we shall consider in subsequent chapters, indicate that the primal ancestress possessed a penis as well as a vagina, and the primal male ancestor gained superiority by taking it from her.

Although such theories help explain men's fears of menstruation and menstrual blood, they do not explain why menstrual blood is considered lethal, and perhaps, even more important, why vaginal secretions and odors are deemed so damaging to males in Papua New Guinea. While we cannot explain the fear of menstrual blood, which is so widespread that it must reflect something rather fundamental about human behavior, we wish to make several observations that we believe help elucidate the fear of both menstrual blood and women's sexual secretions and vaginal emanations.[1]

---

[1] Gillian Gillison's unpublished study "The Moon Is Our First Husband" requires particular consideration because the author, in contrast to most male anthropologists in Papua New Guinea, was able to study the women's myths and beliefs about menstrua-

If we pay attention to the sentiments expressed by people in New Guinea, we must seriously consider that menstrual blood, and thereby the menstruating woman, are dangerous because menstrual blood is the essence of antilife. As babies are formed out of womb blood and semen, womb blood is the very core of the woman's procreative power. Menstrual blood is dead womb blood, the negation of life and creativity. It has the capacity to kill a man in Papua New Guinea, but even in Western societies many persons believe that if a menstruating woman touches or waters a plant, it will wither. Further, in Papua New Guinea, if not elsewhere, the woman's essence, vital spirit, or libido is considered oppositional to that of the man and deleterious to his well-being, and menstrual blood is considered an excretion that is a filtrate of all that is polluting in a woman. It clearly has to do with danger from her sexuality. Menstrual blood, then, may be so dangerous because it is both the antithesis of life and at the same time the filtrate of woman's libido that is so threatening and dangerous to men.

A psychoanalytic explanation of the fear of menstrual blood that differs from the castration theory was offered by Daly

---

tion while living among the Gimi people of the eastern highlands. Gillison found that Gimi belief that the danger of vaginal intercourse and vaginal secretions derives from fear of residues of menstrual blood; a belief which would not hold for the Sambia who fear the genital odor. Gillison cogently challenges the general acceptance by anthropologists that menstruation is a natural function of women because, as she states, in Papua New Guinea nothing happens naturally but is always caused. She considers that menstrual blood is transformed from the father's semen that the woman absorbed in utero, a sort of intrauterine incest. The concept is somewhat akin to the Bimin-Kuskusmin belief (see chapter 10) that the woman's vital fluids that enter into the formation of the fetus come from her father's semen. However, Gillison finds evidence that the Gimi fears of menstrual blood relate to both incest and castration—evidence based on interpretations of myths that we find somewhat confusing. The moon, as the primal father, let down his long penis (as a little girl imagines her father's penis); with each menstrual period another piece of the penis that remains in her vagina is lost. However, she also deems the menstrual blood to be a dead, or "failed," child that resulted from the intrauterine incest with the father.

We may not have conveyed Gillison's concepts altogether correctly and certainly have not presented her evidence. If her concepts adequately explain the Gimi fear of menstrual blood, they cannot hold for peoples in other parts of the world, unless Gillison is suggesting that everywhere the fear of menstrual blood relates to the taboo on father-daughter incest.

(1928) many years ago. Daly took off from his studies of the Hindu goddess Kali. He marshaled evidence that a taboo of the menstruating woman became essential to the continuity of the family and society as well as for the maintenance of the incest taboo because the menstrual odor made the woman irresistibly sexually attractive to the male. The repression of the desire aroused by the odor has been so intense that most persons now find the odor to be very disagreeable rather than attractive. The argument almost eliminates refutation, but studies seem to indicate that women's secretions of pheromones that are sexually attractive are highest around the time of ovulation, not during menstruation.

We wish to offer an hypothesis that is the opposite of Daly's that may shed light on the male indigene's fear of women's sexual secretions and odors as well as menstrual blood and relates to the men's denigration and avoidance of women. We consider that the mother's odor and particularly her genital odor is important in fostering a child's attachment behavior (Lidz, 1976) or bonding to the mother. Further, a woman's genital odor and that from her apocrine glands when sexually excited are important factors in arousing men sexually. To the child, the mother's odor provides a sense of security and attachment. The menstrual odor displaces the customary odor and disrupts the sense of comfort and security, perhaps to a frightening degree. The dysphoria produced by the menstrual odor may well persevere into adulthood in the male, and be reinforced by a shift from the woman's usual odor that attracts sexually to one many men find repulsive. However, it is the attraction of women's genital odor that tempts Papua New Guinea men to a regressive dependence upon and attachment to a mother figure that they counter by strong reaction formation for reasons that will become apparent in later chapters. The importance of the mother's genital odor to the boy's attachment to her may be the reason why in many places the boy's ritual bleeding is from the nose.

A basic psychoanalytic theory concerning male puberty rites has been presented by Reik (1946b). It also focuses on the oedipal conflict and castration anxiety. Fathers, remembering their death (or castration) wishes toward their own fathers, seek to force the repression of such wishes in their sons—or to forestall their sons from acting on such wishes—by subjecting them to a rite of death and rebirth; frequently, as with the people of Wogeo, through being devoured by a monster and then anally reborn from him, much as a child may conceive of birth through the digestive tract. The ritual of death and rebirth is a symbolic warning and substitute for actual sacrifice and is, Reik seemed to believe, usually followed by circumcision as a substitute for castration. It reflects the father's ambivalence toward his son, his fear and hostility as against his desire for a son and his love of him. The effects of this cycle of fathers' fear of sons and sons' fear of fathers on the integration of the self, the family, and society has been examined by Lidz (1975) in his study of Hamlet.

Although Reik's and other closely related theories are attractive and mesh with other psychoanalytic concepts, they do not properly explain the first-stage initiations in Papua New Guinea. As we have emphasized, they are not puberty rites but rites to enable the boys to become pubertal and grow into powerful warriors—just what fathers would seek to prevent according to Reik's theory.[2]

Another reservation to Reik's theory concerns the equating of all ceremonials of blood-letting in males with castration. Subincision as practiced by the Australian aborigines makes the male genitalia resemble the female and therefore can be considered castrating; but, as Bettelheim (1971) has argued convincingly, it does not seem to be carried out as a threat or

---

[2] There is also the theory promulgated by Whiting, Klukhohn, and Anthony in 1958, which sought to explain why puberty rites take place in some societies and not in others. They believe they uncovered statistical evidence that pubertal initiations take place in societies with lengthy postpartum bans on sexual relations, and in which the small child sleeps with the mother for several years. Norbeck, Walker, and Cohen (1962) could not replicate their ratings for various societies. Statistically significant findings can only indicate that a hypothesis may be on a useful track; exceptions must be explained before a rule can be established. Moreover, the length of the postpartum sexual taboo is only one aspect of a situation that fosters a child's strong libidinal attachment to the mother, as well as an identification with her.

punishment, but because of male envy of women's creative capacities and as a means of partially assuaging men's bisexual desires. The reasons for the widespread practice of circumcision remain obscure, and it may be prudent to avoid reaching premature and possibly erroneous closure about the origins and meaning of circumcision by considering it a modified form of castration. Indeed, there is ethnological evidence that circumcision accentuates maleness and makes the penis more attractive and acceptable to women, who wish their men to be circumcised. In any case, it seems clear that the procedures that induce bleeding from the penis, nose, or tongue in Papua New Guinea are a means of purifying the boy of his mother's womb blood and menstrual contaminations and mimic women's self-purification via menstruation and do not form substitutes for castration. Indeed, as we have noted, the men in the eastern highlands demonstrate the procedures on themselves, as if to indicate the masculine power achieved through the ritual; and both Sambia and Wogeo men periodically purify themselves and believe they improve their health and strength by such bleedings.

We believe that Burton and Whiting (1961), even though they also emphasized the importance of circumcision as a substitute for castration, helped formulate a more coherent theory concerning the purposes of male initiation rites. They considered that the initiation rituals are a means of counteracting a conflict in sexual identity that arises from the boy's early identification with his mother, particularly when the mother is the primary influence and controlling agent during the boy's early years.

Allen (1967) pointed out:

> The most highly developed sex division is found in those societies in which all or most of the men . . . are members of a single exogamous patrilineal descent group . . . [and] constitute an enduring and corporate body . . . whereas the women . . . depart on marriage. . . . When spouses are taken from remote, strange and, above all, hostile groups, the sex division is likely to take an extreme form [pp. 12–13].

The same may apply when the society is matrilocal and the men come from a variety of other localities and need to find and express their common interest in the performance of the ritual from which women and children are excluded in order to achieve the necessary solidarity in the face of the underlying strength and unity of the women. The more any given society conforms to one or other of the above models the greater is the probability that the sex dichotomy will manifest itself in residential separation, an ideological polarity of all things male and female, and the performance of exclusive rites, including the initiation of boys into male "associations in which membership is compulsory for all adult and adolescent males of a particular community" (Allen, 1967, p. 8).

We are now in a position to examine more directly the meaning and purposes of the first stage of male initiations that include bleeding and vomiting as well as the separation of boys from the women of the community that Freud postulated in *Totem and Taboo* (1913). We shall consider the importance of the practices to both the boy's development and to the society in which it takes place. In so doing we shall develop some ways of regarding masculine development which, while not new to psychoanalytic theory, diverge from the more customary views.

In line with Mahler's (1971) emphasis of the importance of the child's separation-individuation from the mother, we shall consider how the boy's initial symbiosis with his mother, his ensuing primary identification with her, and his object love for her can impede his integration and his achievement of a male identity (Greenson, 1966). We shall at the same time emphasize the importance of men's envy of women that derives not only from the boy's early identification with his mother, but also from men's envy of women's natural creative and nurturant capacities (Bettelheim, 1971). Further, we shall discuss the boy's fear of, and wish for, reengulfment by the mother as a critical developmental problem for the boy (Loewald, 1951) and the likelihood that fears of castration by either the father or mother can reflect an ambivalent wish for a female identity and not simply a projected fear of the father.

Bettelheim was drawn to studies of the Australian aborigines' practice of ritual subincision, which produces artificial hypospadias in the man, by his observation that some of the disturbed boys in his institution envied the girl's genitalia and feminine attributes just as girls showed penis envy. He broke away from the theory that ascribed various types of ritual operations on the penis to the fathers' desires to control their sons' oedipal rivalries by provoking or augmenting their castration anxieties, and instead emphasized men's envy of women's physical makeup and particularly their inherent capacity for creativity and nurturance. He concluded that to understand rites such as subincision which make the male genital resemble the female more closely, it is essential to consider the child's early preoedipal experiences "including the close attachment of the infant, boy or girl, to his mother . . . and the ambivalence of boys and girls, originating in pregenital fixations, about accepting their prescribed adult sex roles" (Bettelheim, 1971, p. 19).

Bettelheim believed that the subincision ritual was a means of dealing with the ambivalence about one's gender when such ambivalence was no longer compatible with adult status in the society. He also suggested that subincision was a means of allowing the man to realize, in part, his ambivalent desire to possess female sexual organs, and that penile blood-letting from the subincision area reflected an envy of menstruation, and that the ritual of rebirth expressed an envy of women's abilities to give birth to children. He specifically countered the idea that the ritual mutilation and the accompanying practices were imposed by adults to increase castration anxiety; rather, they filled adolescent needs to resolve conflicts about sexual identification and went a long way toward overcoming castration anxiety (Bettelheim, 1971). The subincision rituals are efforts to master the conflicts that arise "from man's instinctual polyvalent desires; also the conflict between such desires and the role society expects him to play" (Bettelheim, 1971, p. 148).

Although in general agreement with Bettelheim's deductions, we believe that the problem is more complex, as the remainder of this book will demonstrate. Here, we wish to pursue further some theoretical implications that emphasize different aspects of men's envy of women's physique and capacities to menstruate; and also examine why, because of the nature of the social system in which these people live, the male menstruation ritual is important to foster the boy's differentiation from his mother and his achievement of a firm masculine identity.

Although the boy's fear of castration by his father and the girl's belief that she had been deprived of a penis by her mother are often important to our understanding of both male and female development as well as of psychopathology, we do not believe that they are basic, universal phenomena. From studies of schizophrenic patients and various disturbances in sexual identity such as transsexuality, and then perhaps even more clearly from attention to the rituals we have described, we have come to consider that the oedipal transition as initiated and impelled by castration anxiety is only one alternative means of *reinforcing* a more fundamental series of transitions that are essential to the development of children everywhere. Parin (1972) reached a similar conclusion from his studies of the resolution of the oedipal conflicts in two dissimilar African cultures.

All children must differentiate or individuate from their symbiotic union with the mother and establish firm boundaries between the self and the mother; and then as the child's symbiosis shifts to become both a somewhat amorphous identification with the mother and also an object love for her, the boy must overcome his primary identification with his mother and eventually gain a clear gender identity as a male.[3] The mother is a source of security and comfort to the infant and small child, and the loss of the sense of being one with her, of being protected by her omnipotence, and of being essential to her becomes an unavoidable source of some discomfort and anxiety. It is essential that the mother rescind something of her

---

[3] Freud paid little attention to the child's initial symbiosis with the mother and rather focused on an autoerotic phase and primary narcissism. In his paper on Leonardo da Vinci, Freud (1910) considers the identification with the mother made by male homosexuals to follow upon repression of the child's love for his mother: "he puts himself in her place, identifies himself with her, and takes his own person as a model in whose likeness he chooses the new objects of his love. . . . What he has in fact done is to slip back to auto-erotism" (p.100). While, as shall be seen, we agree with his general concept of the origins of some types of homosexual tendencies, we believe he had, in a sense, reversed a sequence of development.

erotically toned gratification of the child to foster the separation. As Parsons (1954) emphasized, the incest taboo is universal not only because it is essential for the preservation of the family and society but also for the harmonious development of the individual, a thesis that Lidz (1976) amplified in his presentation of the preoedipal and oedipal phases of development. However, the individuation from the mother, and for the boy, the disidentification from her, are equally, and perhaps more, important. Still, as the boy individuates, he internalizes something of his mother and thus acquires a basic feminine component that remains at the very core of his self. Horney's (1932) concept that men's fear of women and dread of the vulva derive from the boy's fear of loss of self-esteem because his penis is not large enough to satisfy his mother and his subsequent fear when a man of being sucked in or engulfed during intercourse should not be taken too literally, but rather in terms of the pull of the wish/fear for reunion with the mother and reengulfment by her.

Loewald (1951) considered the ambiguities of the young child's identification with his mother and his object love for her and called attention to the importance of the "paternal veto against the libidinal relationship with the mother" (p.15), to support the boy against the threat of the engulfing, overpowering womb; and that "Against this threat of the maternal engulfment, the paternal position is not another threat or danger, but a support of powerful force" (p. 15). Although Loewald emphasized the role of the father's castration threat rather than the more clearly positive supporting paternal influences, his recognition of the boy's need to identify with a paternal figure in order to counter the regressive feminizing pull toward reunification with the mother that could also demolish the developing ego formed a significant landmark in psychoanalytic theory. Stoller (1974) in his studies of transsexualism has depicted a type of mother who, because of her own background and needs, is unable to help her son break his identification with her and move to identify with his father. Socarides (1973) through his work with homosexuals and transsexuals reached a very similar orientation. Greenson (1968) also emphasized the fear of losing one's gender identity which he believes is stronger in men than in women "because the boy must attempt to renounce the pleasure and security-giving closeness that identification with the mothering figure affords, and he must form an identification with the less accessible father" (pp. 372–373).

In considering the problems that arise in overcoming the symbiotic tie to the mother, most investigators emphasize that the child's individuation depends primarily upon how the mother relates to the child, particularly in the first years of his life. However, it is apparent that the task is usually neither accomplished by the mother alone nor is the differentiation completed in early childhood. It depends on the development and maintenance of a proper dynamic family structure to *reinforce* the shift away from the mother and to support the boy's move to identify with the father and the girl's to form an object relationship with him—a process in which the father properly plays a very major role. Stoller (1968) appreciated the role played by a weak, disinterested, and absent father in the genesis of transsexuality, and Greenson (1968) more specifically emphasized not only the need for the mother to allow the boy to identify with his father, but also the vital moment of the motives offered by the father for identifying with him in the boy's switch from identification with his mother to identification with his father.

Freud's original conceptualization of the oedipal transition and its vicissitudes paid little attention to the mother-child symbiosis and the child's early identification with his mother, and emphasized the boy's renunciation or repression of his libidinal attachment to his mother because of his projected jealousy of his father and his ensuing fears of castration by his father. The conceptualization can, we believe, be reformulated to include the transition as it frequently occurs with more nurturant fathers and which does not lead to internalization of a sadistic father image: as the child moves beyond his early childhood egocentricity and begins to recognize his father's prerogatives with his mother, he then identifies with his father who could obtain a wife like his mother, particularly when the mother, through her admiration and love of her husband, fosters the boy's identification with his father. Lidz (1963) elaborated further upon how the parental relationships and the family structure promote proper gender identity formation in children, and also upon how membership in peer groups of the same sex strengthens gender identity (Lidz, 1976). Stoller (1974) appreciated the need for such continuing influences beyond the first few years of life to assure proper gender identity when he wrote, "masculinity . . . in boys and men, does not exist without the component of continuous push away from mother, both literally in the first years of life and psychologically in the development of character structure that forces the inner mother down and out of awareness" (p. 169).

Unless the individuation from the mother and the renunciation of the primary identification with her is adequately reinforced, when the boy grows up he may fear intimacy with girls, and particularly sexual intimacy, for the sexual act can rekindle fears of loss of the self, of engulfment by the mother, and of fusion with her. These fears are born of the latent wish for total nurturance, for surcease from responsibility, and for total safety by reincorporation within the powerful mother figure. As Ferenczi (1924) noted long ago, sexual intimacy for the man is at one level a symbiotic return to the womb, a symbolic merging with the mother. Loewald (1951) considers that the fear of loss of the ego through regression to the primary narcissistic identity with the mother is the source of men's deepest dread. Stoller (1974) properly wonders if "some of the uneasiness men feel about women . . . reflects the need to raise this barrier against the desire to merge with mother" (pp. 170–171).

We have been examining primarily the boy's oedipal transition rather than the girl's. The fundamental task that must be carried out in all societies is the differentiation of the child from the initial symbiosis with the mother and establishing adequate boundaries between the child and mother; and then in guiding the boy to rescind his initial identification with his mother and gain a firm identity as a male. Whereas the girl must establish boundaries, she does not rescind the initial identification with her mother as a female.[4] Herein lies one of the reasons why Freud's early efforts to describe the girl's oedipal transition as a mirror image of the boy's failed. It also seems to be one reason why in Papua New Guinea it is believed that the girl matures naturally and female puberty ceremonies celebrate the girl's maturation whereas the first stage of the boy's initiation is required to induce maturation. The boy does not grow into a man spontaneously because he was born from a woman and initially identified with a woman. He must be rid of his female identification and be reborn as a man. Although the girl has to reverse her choice of love object from the mother to a man, the boy's developmental task of reversing his basic identification is more difficult and thus requires more reinforcement than does the girl's achievement of a firm gender identity.

In the Papua New Guinea societies we have been examining, the family differs profoundly from a family in which both parents live together with their children and are major influences upon the child through much of childhood. The crucial transition takes place and is reinforced very differently than in Western society where the oedipal situation plays a major role.[5] In Papua New Guinea, the boy's emotional separation from his mother, his identification as a male, and his internalization of a superego in the form of the male mores and ethos does not come about because of the oedipal threat projected onto his father; or through his father's presence and his mother's affection for or admiration of his father. Here, the boy's separation and differentiation from the mother is largely the task of the men's cult.

Although in the eastern highlands as well as in other

---

[4] She may, of course, later seek to disidentify with a mother who is unsatisfactory to her father or even hated by him, and attempt to become one who will be more satisfactory to the father—sometimes to become boyish, and sometimes through identification with the father.

[5] We are aware that in places like Wogeo couples live together amicably and perhaps affectionately even if guardedly and uneasily and that Newman tells of a Gururumba couple in which the man remained monogamous and because of his affection for his wife refused to divorce her and remarry even though they were childless; but in general the separation of the sexes is profound and closeness between married couples uncommon, at least during the early years of marriage.

localities the collectivity of men will threaten the boys, particularly at puberty, with castration or death if they have extramarital intercourse with any woman in the community, a much greater emphasis is placed on the dangers of women's sexuality. The young boy is warned that continued proximity to the mother will endanger his health and sexual maturation; that, in a sense, the mother's very presence is emasculating. Later, they warn that closeness to women can cause death through ingestion of, or even contact with her menstrual blood; and then, that sexual intercourse and even women's libido can sap a youth's strength and cause him to fall ill.[6]

The boy's identification with his mother and his ties to her are symbolically broken by the bleeding ritual that at least in some places is thought to rid him of his mother's womb blood that went into his composition. The Siane people's comment on the ritual, "his mother's blood 'is being washed away'" (Salisbury, 1965, p. 62), suggests that the procedure can be considered a tangible symbolic means of doing away with his mother's investment in him and her influence upon him. The ritual vomiting similarly helps rid him of menstrual contamination from his mother and may also serve to counter his oral desires for continued nurturance from his mother. The initiate is symbolically reborn from men as a man and is impressed with the collective power of the men's cult into which he is being initiated. His desires to remain identified with his mother or to remain feminine to avoid the hazardous life of a man who will be engaged in perpetual warfare are countered by the men's persistent degradation of women as polluted and polluting; and by providing equivalents of what in a woman a man might envy—the ability to purify the self through menstruation, and her natural creativity that the man attains by playing the sacred

---

[6] Among the Kimam-Papuans (Serpenti, 1984) and Marind-anim (van Baal, 1966) myths of the primal ancestors contain many tales of castration (but by women, not by men), particularly of the need to cut off a male ancestor's penis after a couple became locked together while having intercourse; and the Kimam men have a great fear of a witch with a castrating vagina who seeks to seduce men. We suppose that such tales of being locked to a woman and losing one's penis reflect unconscious wishes to be reunited with the mother and to lose one's male identity (see chapter 10).

flutes which form a bond to the ancestor spirits who control fertility, as well as other substitutes we shall present below.

After inculcating such deep fears of women and their sexuality, it becomes essential to undo these fears sufficiently to permit procreation and to provide the youth with a sense of strength and power in relationship to women. Among various groups the boys are taught to purify themselves by "menstruation," and in others by magical procedures, but, as we shall see, among some people the means of protection from the dangerous female sexuality are much more complicated. Despite the precautions, among some tribes such as the Mae Enga, men copulate infrequently and primarily for procreative purposes— at least so it is said (Meggitt, 1970). Among the Marind-anim the birth rate is so low that the population is maintained by child purchase or capture (van Baal, 1966).

We have in this chapter been concerned primarily with the boy's identification with and dependence upon his mother that results from living with her for the first seven to 15 years of his life, during which the father plays a very secondary, or at least a "behind-the-scenes" role in the boy's life; and the primary measures taken by the men to overcome the identification and attachment, and then forcefully and forcibly initiate him into the men's cult and inculcate a strong masculinity. The rituals we have described may be the only means, or at least the primary means of carrying out the transition among the Gahuka-Gama, Gururumba and the people of Wogeo but among many other peoples who have been studied more intensively, the measures we have considered constitute only the first of a series of rituals that extend over many years to assure the essential transformation to manhood.

6
Masculinization

The Sambia

Thus far, our primary focus in the transformation of boys who are considered feminine persons of the women's houses into fierce warriors has been on the rituals that promote their defeminization and their disidentification with their mothers. We now turn to the processes that actively foster their masculinization, including their sexual maturation.

The process of masculinization in Papua New Guinea varies from culture to culture. In most places the boys are reborn as men from men, the boys and adolescents are isolated from women, and taught that women's sexuality is dangerous and emasculating; in many places the men believe that boys must be provided with semen in order to mature. They also counter envy of women's generative and nurturant capacities that derives from the boy's initial core identification with his mother by further arrogations of such capacities as well as through the disparagement of women and the aggrandizement of men.

In promoting the boys' sexual maturation and development into young men, the men of the preceding generation find themselves in a "bind." They require new warriors, but in creating them they are also producing potential sexual rivals for their women. The danger is not simply a residue or projection of their own oedipal desires. Their wives, who are often much younger than their husbands and left sexually unfulfilled because of their husbands' fears of female sexuality, can be desirous of the attractive youths.

The men, however, are not simply concerned about oedipal conflict. They had been thoroughly indoctrinated with the belief that women and their sexuality are dangerous to men and particularly to youths who would be weakened by women's emanations and might even die from the debilitating effects of heterosexual intercourse. If the men wish to have strong successors to protect the community from enemies, they must imbue the initiates with the same fears. They can go further and, as Freud (1913) postulated in *Totem and Taboo*, isolate the youths from the women. The isolation not only prevents the youths from having incestuous activities but from seducing, or being seduced by, married women, which would disrupt a community surrounded by enemies; and it also teaches the boys that they can manage without their mothers or, indeed, without any women.

The boys require semen in order to mature, and the bachelors—adolescents beset by strong sexual urges—require outlets. In some cultures, indeed, in many Papua New Guinea cultures, enforced ritual homosexuality serves both purposes. The homosexuality, however, is not an effeminate or feminizing practice, but rather the road to a fierce warrior masculinity. Still, as we shall discuss, it is also a means of coping with the separation and disidentification from the mother.

We shall examine how the various means of fostering the boy's masculinization interrelate and contribute to the psychoanalytic understanding of male development everywhere. We shall find ourselves confronted by a conflict between the expressed purpose of inseminating to masculinize, and the unexpressed, or at least hidden, purpose of providing a sexual outlet for youths that keeps them from heterosexuality prior to marriage. Some Papua New Guinea tribal societies do not have obligatory initiation into the men's cult, and many do not practice ritual insemination. However, among those peoples in the western and southern highlands where initiation into the men's cult is voluntary, the men's fears of sexual relations are particularly marked and may be limited to the purposes of procreation (Meggitt, 1970); but, as we shall present, in some cultures the men have little fear of women's sexual emanations.

Now, confronted by a wealth of material concerning the different ways in which societies in Papua New Guinea utilize rituals to guide the boy's development into a proper masculine member of the specific society, we turn first to the Sambia[1] in our efforts to clarify and understand the various functions of the rituals. We do so not only because Herdt has described them so fully and thoughtfully but also because Herdt's penetration of the men's most deeply concealed myths reveals the importance of oedipal conflict in their ways of raising their sons. Further, his discussion of the rituals with both initiates and initiators has contributed greatly to our understanding of initiation rituals and these peoples' concepts of masculinity (Herdt, 1977, 1980, 1981, 1982, 1984, 1987, personal communications).

The Sambia are a tribe of about 2000 people who live in the rain forest on the fringe of the eastern highlands. They are an Anga (Kukukuku) people (Herdt, 1981) and their tradition tells that they had been forced to migrate to their present locality 200 or more years ago after defeat in a war.[2] The Sambia social organization resembles that of other eastern highland peoples in many ways, but prior to pacification they, as other Anga peoples, had been a particularly fierce warrior group with considerable conflict between hamlets and phratries, which, nevertheless, could join together for initiatory ceremonies and other rituals. The hamlets generally consist of two patrilineal moieties that permit considerable intrahamlet marriage between moi-

---

[1] Herdt has designated these people by a false name to conceal just who the people are who practice ritual fellatio and who among them revealed their secrets.

[2] According to Godelier (1982), the Baruya, neighbors of the Sambia, are also an Anga people who migrated to the area, and two of the subclans fused with the original inhabitants they conquered. Herdt (personal communication) does not believe that the Sambia fused with or assimilated earlier inhabitants.

eties, but exogamous marriages, including marriages between persons from enemy hamlets and phratries, predominate.

Among the Sambia the dichotomy between men and women is particularly marked. During the later stages of initiation, men are taught to be hostile to their wives (Herdt and Poole, 1982). The men greatly fear pollution from menstrual blood, vaginal fluids, and emanations. The women believe that they would impair a son's growth and health should he inhale their vaginal odor if they inadvertently open their legs when he is near. The men and women walk on separate paths, lest the woman's polluting contact with a bush or vine rub off on a man. Men fear to touch nursing children and tend to remain aloof from young children because of their close contact with the mothers. However, in contrast to the usual highland practice, husbands usually sleep in the same hut as their wives, though in a separate area that the wife never enters. Sexual relations never take place in the family hut and heterosexual intercourse in a garden will, in contrast to homosexual intercourse, impair its fertility.

The Sambia initiatory cycle starts when the boy is between the ages of six and ten, and proceeds through six stages until he becomes the father of one, or preferably two children, some ten to 15 or 20 years later. Although the first stage resembles the rites of the Gahuka-Gama in that nose bleeding and the revelation that the mystical sounds are made by flutes, the Sambia rituals differ markedly. We do not know if Read witnessed and was made privy to only one portion of the Gahuka-Gama ritual, or if the Sambia first-stage initiation is actually far more complicated.

What follows is an effort to present in summary form, Herdt's several accounts of the initiation ceremonies. The 1975 rituals which Herdt has described were rather unusual because the Sambia hamlet in which he lived and their closely affiliated hamlets journeyed to hold the ceremonies together with a phratry with which they had long been mortal enemies. The three stages of initiation were incorporated in elaborate ceremonies that lasted for some weeks.

First-Stage Initiation

The first stage marks the removal of the small boys from their mothers and their induction into the men's cult. As new second- and third-stage initiates are needed for the transformation of the novitiates, the third-stage and then the second-stage initiations precede the critical and most complex first stage. However, our primary interest lies in the elaborate rituals and ceremonies that transfer the boys to the men's half of the society and we shall describe them first.

The ceremonies last for seven days, and Herdt has divided them into 18 rituals, or perhaps we should say ordeals, to which these young boys are subjected, children who had previously been carefully sheltered and even pampered by their mothers. They are being hardened, tested, and united into a group of agemates as well as being started on their way to becoming fierce warriors soon after they reach puberty.

On the first day the novitiates were taken from their grieving mothers. Several, knowing that their greatly feared initiation was about to take place, fled into the forest and had to be captured and restrained. The boys accompanied by their sponsors walked for several hours to the dance ground of the last friendly hamlet. There they emerged from the men's house on the backs of their sponsors. The sponsors among most of the tribal societies are preferably the mother's real or classificatory brothers, but among the Sambia are commonly a good friend of the boy's father, perhaps a man from a different hamlet who had been initiated together with the father. The women and children watch. The mothers weep both because they are now being separated from their sons for many years and also because they know that the boys are about to undergo arduous and painful rituals.

The boys are carried by their sponsors toward the forest where they are suddenly beset by two lines of men and are thrashed severely with sticks as their sponsors carry them through the gauntlet. Many of the terrified boys cry and a few defecate involuntarily.

Next, the procession arrives at a platform where a purificatory ritual is held. The boys are rubbed with the top leaves of a black palm tree, and the leaves are twisted into their hair. They are thus symbolically united with a fast-growing and sturdy tree, and like the tree have the sun's power and vitality enter into them by the act. Such symbolic unification of the initiates with strong trees occurs among various tribes in New Guinea. Then, the boy's nose ornaments, worn through the hole that had earlier been made in the nasal septum, are removed and placed in a branch of the tree, an act that supposedly strengthens the boys for the coming ordeals. The boys are then secluded in the men's hut of the hamlet and carefully guarded. A ceremonial nose-piercing ritual soon follows that is mainly symbolic as all except a few boys already have pierced septums, but the ritual together with several other symbolic acts and a feast of pieces of taro—the first food the boys have had all day—are believed to strengthen the boys.

The initiation party accompanied by women and children then proceeds to the hamlet where a great cult house had been constructed some weeks previously for a third-stage initiation. A large crowd gathers in the hamlet where a festive atmosphere pervades. A great bonfire illuminates the dance ground where the men perform various public rituals. Groups of men dance and older warriors sing war songs and carry out several rituals. The women, in turn, hold a "firewood ritual," an unusual participation of women in an initiation ceremony. The women carry smoke-blackened sticks of firewood, symbols of their domestic role (Herdt, 1987, p. 134) and hit the initiates with the sticks and castigate them harshly while admonishing them that when they are older and go into the forest they must bring firewood for their women. The boys are gravely shaken by this attack by their habitual protectors. When the boys are removed, the antagonism between the men and women flares and passes beyond verbal abuse to some scuffling.

Following the firewood ceremony the weary initiates again sing and dance until the "frog feeding ceremony" takes place toward dawn. The ritual will enable a last reunion between the mothers and initiates. The women struggle with the men to extract their sons from the continuing circle of the dance. Finally, the boys are collected and the dancing stops. The women feed the boys smoked frogs, urging them to eat all they can, as frogs will be tabooed food until they have their own children. Finally, the mothers weep and tell their sons that they must now go to the men's house. The first day, the first very long day, of initiation has come to an end.

Herdt (1987, p. 136) reports that the second day "repeats many events of the first day." It is on the third day that the crucial rituals are carried out and the initiates' lives change profoundly.

Soon after dawn the novitiates are taken to the dance ground where they receive another thrashing. This time the thrashing is public, witnessed by the women and children. The initiates are tied to their sponsors' backs and again led through a gauntlet of men who take delight in swatting the boys on their backs and buttocks. Now, however, the mothers follow their sons and try to protect them from the blows by holding cordyline leaves over their backs, and in the process are beaten themselves. Here, as on other occasions, a boy who resists going through the ordeal is beaten more severely than the others. Further ceremonies continue throughout the morning, but the key nose bleeding and flute rituals take place later in the day.

The nose bleeding ritual is similar to that of the Gahuka-Gama we have described and is carried out for the same purpose. However, the use of the vomiting cane had been discontinued about 20 years previously as being too dangerous (Herdt, 1981). The initiates are by now worn and weary from lack of sleep, constant activity, minimal food and water, as well as apprehension. The mothers, who will not be permitted to witness the ceremony, are told that their sons are about to be killed, and then reborn as men.[3] As the mysterious hidden flutes

[3] The threat of being killed and eaten is not akin to the threat of a "Boogey Man" in the United States. There is no definite evidence that the Sambia had been cannibals, but many Anga peoples had been cannibals and anthropophagic peoples were not very distant.

resound, the boys are warned that something ominous is about to befall them.

In midmorning the boys are taken to the ritual site deep in the forest where they face a massive wall composed of green saplings that have been tied together, and with pieces of shaman's red head bands amidst the foliage. The foliage is shaken by a group of bachelors hidden behind it. From the distance it appears as if "blood were dripping from the branches" (Herdt, 1987, p. 141). The initiates are again tied to the backs of their sponsors and carried through a small opening in the fence into a muddy inner chamber. They are then carried through a very narrow, 20-foot-long passage while being beaten on their backs and legs with ginger stalks by numerous warriors. Ginger grows rapidly and the pounding supposedly fosters the boys' growth. The boys are terrified and some cry for their mothers. The passageway leads to a clearing beside a small brook. Herdt (1982) has suggested that the procedure resembles a passage through a womb and birth canal.

A crowd of men hem the boys in beside a pool in the brook. Here, as among the Gahuka-Gama, a war leader enters the pool and plunges sharp cane grasses up and down his nostrils until his nose bleeds profusely into the stream, an act greeted by loud war cries. Then each initiate in turn is held firmly while the initiator shoves sharp cane up the boy's nose until blood flows profusely. The men repeat the war chant for each boy. Here, again, an initiate who struggled and sought to escape was treated more harshly and bled more severely. Herdt, as an observer, felt stunned and almost overwhelmed by the brutality of the scene.

Following the bleeding, the initiates are told that they are being punished for their previous disrespect for their elders, but also because their mothers' "bad talk has entered into their noses," and their mothers' influence has kept them from growing. Prior to pacification, the initiates had been told that the bleeding ceremony would make them into strong warriors and they would be less afraid of losing blood on the battlefield; and rather than becoming distraught when their comrades were wounded, the sight of their blood would spur them to vengeance.

Several hours after the nose bleedings the novitiates are taken to a deeper part of the forest where their bodies, including face and genitals, are rubbed with stinging nettles. The process is extremely painful and the boys scream and struggle. Its purpose is to flake away the childhood skin to enable it to be replaced by new masculine skin. The brutal action leaves the boys even more frightened of what follows immediately—the culminating flute ceremony.

The reader will recall that following the nose bleeding, the Gahuka-Gama initiates were returned to the cult hut where the critical secret was revealed to them; namely, that the mysterious musical sounds they had previously been told were made by mystical birds, the voices of the ancestors, were simply sounds of flutes played by men. Then, after being displayed to the women in their new outfits, the initiates were secluded in the cult house for many years with minimal contact with women. This may be all that transpires among the Gahuka-Gama and the Gururumba, but the fate of the Sambia initiates is very different.

Here, near the cult house but hidden from the women and children, the initiates are dressed in new outfits by their sponsors amidst a great deal of lewd joking and horseplay, for unknown to the boys the new clothes indicate that they are no longer neuter children but have been transformed into sexual objects for the bachelors.

The sacred flutes are heard approaching and then two groups of four bachelors playing the flutes slowly circle the initiates. It is the first time the boys have seen the flutes whose sounds they had been led to believe were the voices of female hamlet spirits in the form of birds (Herdt, 1984) (see chapter 12). The players and their flutes are paired: the longer, wider flute is considered both a penis and a vagina, and the smaller flute which is placed inside the larger one has a tip called both the "nose of the penis," that is, a glans penis, and also a "breast nipple." The dual name is meaningful for the initiates have the tip of the flute placed in their mouths and are urged to suck it. The flutes are thus literally being used to teach the boys the mechanics of fellatio. Those who comply with the instructions are praised, whereas those who refuse to suck the flute may be beaten with a long flute (Herdt, 1981, 1987).

Older men now tell the boys that the bachelors are going to copulate with them orally in order to make them grow. Several elders testify that boys are unable to mature into men unless they ingest semen and that all men have "eaten the penis." Semen is the same as breast milk and the boys will come to enjoy it. The initiates are admonished to ingest as much semen as possible to store for future use, as men cannot make semen themselves. They are told that many men from different hamlets are present and the boys should use the opportunity to ingest their semen. The same kinship taboos hold for homosexual as for heterosexual intercourse. They, like the Gahuka-Gama initiates, are warned that if they ever reveal this secret to the women or children they will be killed and their bodies thrown in the river so that their ghosts will never come to rest among the ancestors. They are also warned against ever committing adultery with married women for if they do the woman's husband will kill them or the elders will cut off their penises and then kill them. The threat is reinforced when an elder takes a machete and slices the boyhood pubic aprons the initiates are still wearing, cutting them midway between the abdomen and the genitals.

After the boys receive this information, which shocks them, they are paraded in their new outfits of novice warriors before the women and children. This is the last time the women will see their sons and brothers for many years to come. Until they begin to live with their wives some ten to 20 years later, they must not look at women or allow women to look at them, but go around with their heads and faces hidden by bark capes. Isolating youths and preventing them from seeing women and being seen by them, the converse of the Hindu and Islamic purdah, is widespread in Papua New Guinea. The novitiates are then led into the men's cult house where they will sleep for the

6 Masculinization

first time instead of in the shed in which they had been sleeping whenever the ceremonies permitted.

As soon as the boys are out of sight, the men verbally attack the women for being bad mothers and delaying their sons' growth. A warrior holds up a bunch of leaves soaked by the blood from the boys' noses, and again tells the women that they had to kill the boys to turn them into men. Then, two men seize one of the mothers and a warrior forces the bloody leaves down her throat while cursing her, perhaps the epitome of the men's degradation of women. The woman looks humiliated and her women friends become furious, but their show of force is cut off when the men threaten them with sticks and chase them away.

Within the men's house, the boys' new clothing is removed and they are hit and stung with cassowary quill bones. Then after the boys are fed, the elders depart and leave the bachelors in charge. Again two groups of flute players enter, but now in old bark capes disguised as women. They represent the female hamlet spirits. The boys are told that the hamlet spirit "has come to cry for you. . . . You must help straighten her out" (a metaphor for sucking a penis to ejaculation) (Herdt, 1987, p. 154), which means that the boys should serve as fellators and relax the bachelors' erect and tight penises. The request to help the female hamlet spirit by relaxing her penis is puzzling if not incomprehensible unless it is understood that the hamlet spirit is androgynous (see chapter 10) or that the penis is being equated with a breast filled with milk.

After the formal ceremonies end, the bachelors make erotic advances to the boys and homosexual activity takes place outside on the darkened dance ground (Herdt, 1981, pp. 233–234). Not all initiates will participate but by the end of the initiation some five days later, all but a few will have practiced fellatio at least several times.

The early morning hours of the fourth day are spent in a song fest and another tree ceremony is held at dawn. Later, the initiates, exhausted from lack of sleep, the beatings, and nose bleedings, are shut in a "birth house." As they approach, they hear the cries of a newborn infant, sounds actually made by flutes. They spend the night lying still, but awake. In the morning they are moved to the cult house where they ingest hallucinogens and the shamans divine or predict which boys acquired spirit familiars—spirits who will turn them into great warriors, shamans, or hunters; but also which boys will die at an early age (Herdt, 1981, pp. 231–232; 1987, p. 185). They are also taught the numerous and onerous food taboos they must observe to enhance their maturation as well as various men's secrets. According to Herdt's first description of the ritual (1981), an initiate who has acquired a spirit familiar is praised for his good luck. He has, in a sense, been reborn and acquired an identity in the birth house. The concept of a cycle of life, in which a period after death spent as an ancestor spirit is followed by rebirth as an infant, occurs in various forms in Papua New Guinea. Among the Sambia it is part of gaining a specific identity as a man.

On the afternoon of the fourth day the women reassemble on the dance ground bearing gifts of sugar cane and bananas for the name changing ceremony. The mother has a say in the choice of the name and now is the first person to say her son's new adult name. Adults will refer to the boys by their new names but the boys do not refer to themselves or their agemates by either the childhood or adult names, but soon devise nicknames that they will use until after the third-stage initiation.

The rituals continue for another three days. Ceremonies on the fifth day celebrate and teach the economic responsibilities of initiates. In the afternoon they are taught fire making and hunting rites. The last rituals teach the secret of the bullroarer, an instrument that plays a major role along with, or instead of, the flutes in other cultures.

At the end of the rituals, the initiates are taken to a "forest lodge," here called the "rat house." They are removed from all contact with women and hunt rats and possum. They remain isolated with bachelors for some weeks, hazed and forced to follow the bachelors' orders, but essentially to ingest as much semen as possible from the bachelors. Although this sojourn in the "rat house" does not seem central to the Sambia initiation, we wish to call particular attention to it, because it is of major importance in the transformation of boys into men in some other Papua New Guinea societies, as we shall present in subsequent chapters.

Whereas the Sambia believe that the boys must undergo nose bleeding to rid them of their mothers' womb blood and female contaminations in order to mature, they also believe, as do other peoples in Papua New Guinea (Herdt, 1984), that boys cannot become men unless they are inseminated repeatedly. They believe that a girl possesses a blood-forming organ, a "tingu," that causes her to mature sexually and supplies her with womb blood that goes into the formation of the fetus. The boy's "tingu" is inactive, and although males have a semen organ, a "keraku-keraku," it is simply a receptacle. Boys and men cannot make their own semen, but after their mothers' blood and its inhibiting influence have been eliminated, they must ingest semen in order to mature and provide themselves with a store of semen that forms their vital essence and gives them strength as well as the ability to make babies. Their supply of semen for life depends primarily on how much they ingest between this first initiation and puberty, and they are repeatedly admonished to do so regularly and frequently. Although when they become adolescent, the bachelors will expend a good deal of semen by inseminating boys, this is not deemed to be as depleting as vaginal intercourse. Losing too much semen through heterosexual intercourse weakens a man and makes him vulnerable in battle as well as to illness and, if carried to excess, leads to premature death. However, semen expended in heterosexual intercourse can be replenished by sucking the milk sap from the aerial roots of certain trees, a practice sexually active men carry out regularly. The milk sap becomes semen and enters into the store of semen of the patrilineage that is transmitted across the generations (Herdt, 1984).

The belief that boys cannot turn into men unless inseminated repeatedly is more widespread in Papua New Guinea than the practice of ritual homosexuality,[4] for in many places the insemination is indirect. Although in some areas along the Gulf of Papua, girls are fed or anointed with semen to make them grow, the Sambia (and others) believe girls mature naturally because they have an active "tingu," and acquire strength from their husbands' semen, sometimes even before reaching puberty (and later are regularly purified by menstruating).

Aside from the initiate's sponsor, who serves as something of a mother substitute during the initiations, another man plays a very significant role in the boy's life—the boy's primary inseminator.

A boy will be inseminated by many bachelors, including enemies, but the boy's father usually selects a primary inseminator. As in ancient Greece, the boy is believed to assimilate characteristics of the bachelor along with his semen, but also runs the danger that his inseminator may be a witch and turn him into a witch. The preferred primary inseminator is the boy's sister's betrothed or husband who has not yet had a child.[5] The question arises whether the practice exists to provide the girl's husband with a sexual outlet until his wife reaches puberty; or to counter the initiate's envy of women, particularly of his sister, by allowing him also to be her husband's sexual partner and form an erotized relationship with him. The practice would seem to foster an identification with his sister that

---

[4] Herdt (1984, pp. 1–82) has reviewed the numerous societies in which ritualized homosexuality is known to have been practiced, but he does not include peoples who feed the boys food mixed with semen or fertilized by semen; or who anoint with semen or substitutes believed to be akin to semen. The widespread practice of sodomy in the Trans-Fly area was reported in the last century (Beardmore, 1890); and Williams (1936), the government anthropologist, learned that the Keraki believed it essential for the maturation of boys into men. When he asked the men if they had been subjected to anal intercourse, they replied, "Of course, how else would we have grown into men?" However, it was Herdt's report of the actual rituals that drew attention to their significance.

[5] We note that among tribes of the Trans-Fly and southeastern Irian Jaya, the mother's brother who here is the protective sponsor, is also the primary inseminator (see chapter 10). Here we note only in passing that whereas the semen of the father's patrilineage enters into the formation of the fetus, the rules of exogamy properly have semen from the mother's patrilineage turn the boy into a man.

6 Masculinization

replaces the earlier identification with the mother. It may also enable a displacement of incestuous feelings between a brother and sister, much as psychoanalytic experience has shown that the sharing of a sexual partner often indicates an unconscious homosexual attraction between the sharers. Commonly, the most trusted relationship among the Sambia and many other Papua New Guinea peoples is between brothers and sisters and not between husbands and wives.[6] It is of interest that in some Papuan Gulf societies, the maternal uncle is both the boy's sponsor and inseminator (see chapter 10).

The ritualized homosexual insemination is critical to transforming boys who had grown up permeated by feminine influences into men. The men know that they cannot make babies, but they have convinced themselves that women cannot make men. Along with the assumption of other feminine attributes, they have arrogated from women the capacity to give birth to men rather than simply boys. Moreover, in the process, the bachelors compensate, we assume unconsciously, for women's abilities to nurse babies by enabling the boys to grow into men by sucking their penises—a carry-over from their frustrated identification with their mothers. The initiates who have become regressed by their separation from their mothers and the multiple traumata they have suffered are now given the penis as a substitute for the breast to suck. Although we know from Herdt's (1981) talks with initiates that at first they are shocked to learn that their elders had practiced fellatio and some were reluctant to comply, it soon becomes enjoyable to most of the boys and strongly erotized.

---

[6] Brother-sister relations can remain close into adulthood even when the siblings live in different hamlets. A man, at least in many Papua New Guinea cultures, trusts his sister more than his wife. He will, for example, eat food prepared by his sister but not by his wife. Women depend on their brothers to protect them from cruel husbands and mistreatment in their husband's community. There is considerable evidence that a girl's primary libidinal attachment is to a brother, and that men displace their attachment to their mothers with affection for sisters with whom they lived prior to being taken away by the men's cult. There are stringent taboos against brother-sister incest, but folk tales tell of unwitting (Meggitt, 1976) and conscious (Malinowski, 1929) breaches of the taboo.

Indeed, at the initiation ceremonies that Herdt (1987) attended in 1975, he was amazed at the open homosexual wooing and stimulating of bachelors by first- and second-stage initiates that took place prior to the third-stage initiation. He was surprised to see the young men and boys who usually behave in a very prudish manner engage in open homosexual play in the cult house. The period of initiatory rituals seemed to be "a time with the license to act out normally forbidden impulses" (Herdt, 1987, p. 118), very different from normal life. After dark the dance ground became a scene of rampant homosexual contacts, but couples withdrew from the dance ground into the darkness to carry out fellatio. Boys sought out their favorite bachelors and sought their favor by openly stimulating their genitalia. Several boys pursued the same young man in very openly provocative ways. The atmosphere was carefree. One little boy, for example, impatiently asked a favorite to "shoot him," that is, to orally inseminate him. There can be no doubt that the first- and second-grade initiates, or at least some of them, have highly erotized homosexual relationships with their inseminators. Herdt (1987, p. 123) was taken aback to witness such open homosexual behavior on the part of friends he thought he knew well. It revealed further something he had long since learned, how difficult it can be for an anthropologist to know just what transpires in a culture he studies.

Second-Stage Initiation

The second stage of initiation does not change the boy's status greatly, but it continues over several days with various purificatory rites, and notably strong admonitions to continue to ingest as much semen as possible to enable them to become strong warriors and hunters. Many food taboos had been imposed during the first-stage initiation and now the feast at the end of the ceremonial brings an end to many of these taboos. The rites are usually held just prior to the more significant first-stage initiation to enable these boys to help in those ceremonies.

Third-Stage Initiation

The third stage, in contrast, brings about a very important change in the youth's status and activities. It is a puberty rite that marks adolescence. The boys become bachelors and shift from being inseminated to becoming inseminators, and prior to pacification they were prepared to fight as warriors and warned to be prepared for an enemy attack at any time. The rites are violent: the adolescents are severely beaten and forcibly nose bled, and repeatedly warned against any sexual contact with women and particularly against being seduced by lustful women. They must obey strict taboos during the period when the rituals are carried out: they are forbidden to drink water, eat, or talk. They are again purified at certain very strong trees to remove any traces of female contamination that may remain. After a wearing day, they must dance until a very late hour when they are fed cold taro, a masculine food.

After another forest purification on the second day, they are thrashed with cassowary quill bones. Then they are unexpectedly and violently subjected to another nose bleeding. That night they are permitted to sleep for the first time in several days. On the third day a ritual identifies each of the new "bachelors" with a masculine black palm tree. At the very end, warrior arm bands are placed on their forearms, the mark that they are postpubertal and they receive new nose ornaments that also identify their status. Now that the adolescent becomes an inseminator, he can no longer be inseminated and he has his strong adolescent sexual drives satisfied by the first- and second-stage initiates. Before pacification the new bachelors were taken on a war raid against another tribe, a practice similar to the headhunting and cannibal raids conducted for initiates by the Marind-anim (van Baal, 1984) and Kimam Papuans (see chapter 10). A daring bachelor might try to capture a woman to take back to his hamlet as a wife, apparently an uncommon feat. Should he manage to kill an enemy warrior, he was taught not to give the coup de grâce to his helpless foe until he ingested his semen. The semen, the essence of the masculine spirit, would transfer to the new bachelor warrior the power and strength of the dying enemy. The act of slaying an enemy was the ultimate rite of passage that confirmed the youth as a warrior. Apparently only a few managed to accomplish the deed, but those who did were on their way to becoming war leaders.

The Fourth and Fifth Stages

The subsequent three stages of initiation are essentially marital rites and are not determined by the initiate's maturation but by his wife's. The fourth stage occurs when he is married, usually to a child bride obtained for him by his father or older brothers. A youth will not start living with his bride until shortly before or after her menarche. However, he is now told how to protect himself from women's genital odor while having intercourse and warned that when he has intercourse, he must not penetrate too deeply lest her secretions enter his urethra and make him ill.[7] A ceremony again links the youth's growth, strength, and longevity to that of a specific tree.

The fifth stage of initiation takes place at the time of the wife's menarche. His nose is again bled, now preferably by himself. He is told how to protect himself from women's pollution in greater detail. Among other precautions, he must stuff mint leaves in his nostrils and chew a certain bark while having intercourse in order to absorb his wife's genital odor and spit out the bark as soon as he leaves her. He should rub the lower parts of his body with nettles and bathe them in mud. Then, he must bleed his nose each time his wife menstruates. He is taught to be hostile to his wife and dominate her because

---

[7]The belief would seem to be related to the fear that exists among several other tribal societies that if vaginal fluids enter the man's urethra he can become pregnant, and without a vaginal opening he will die (Kelly, 1976). Williams (1936) was told by the Keraki that they had killed a pregnant man lest the women learn of their secret practice of sodomy.

he has to go through the ordeal of nose bleeding because she pollutes him and endangers his life.

The initiate is now a man who has been isolated from women for a dozen or more years, practiced homosexual fellatio actively and passively, and had the dangers of vaginal intercourse and even of contact with women pounded into him. He is not likely to make the shift to vaginal intercourse readily. His young wife has been taught to practice fellatio on him for some months before they attempt vaginal intercourse. The ingestion of semen is essential to strengthen her bones, fill out her breasts, and provide her with the breast milk she needs when she gives birth to a child. Indeed, breast milk is only transformed semen so that men even believe that it is their semen that indirectly nourishes the baby.

The Sixth Stage

The sixth and last stage of initiation bestows the full rights of manhood and takes place after the man has proven that he has achieved masculinity by having a child, and preferably two. The requirement may be a necessary incentive for the men to risk intercourse repeatedly. The ritual includes nose bleeding but also feasting. The man is instructed to refrain from intercourse with the new mother and keep away from the child until it is weaned, a matter of several years. He need not bleed his nose during this period unless he has another wife. The new father is also told the most secretly held sacred myth of the male cult—a myth that changes our, and we assume the initiate's, understanding of the five previous stages. Until this juncture the dominant emphasis of the proceedings has been the promotion of the boy's maturation and the protection of the initiates from the noxious and even lethal secretions and emanations of women and then to make it possible for him to have heterosexual intercourse and become a father despite the dangers. Of course, there had been warnings and threats against premarital and extramarital intercourse, but now the myth follows Freud's belief that the youths are isolated and their homosexuality fostered to prevent oedipal conflicts. Freud did not intuit obligatory homosexuality, but suggested that homosexuality might take place during the youths' isolation from women and serve to unite them.

The essentials of the myth that Herdt (1981, pp. 256–260) has recorded in detail are as follows:

The primal ancestors or culture heroes of the Sambia were Numboolyu and Chenchi who emerged from a tree. Both are said to have been male, though their anatomy seems to have been rather ambiguous, and *chenchi* is the men's slang word for "dog's vaginal bleeding." Numboolyu eventually started having erections which were uncomfortable. He masturbated and saw that the ejaculate looked like the juice of the pandanus nut and might be good to eat and, therefore, he copulated orally with Chenchi. Chenchi did not like the practice until she slit Numboolyu's foreskin, after which Numboolyu's penis grew bigger and nicer and Chenchi began to enjoy sucking it.[8] Numboolyu's breasts receded whereas Chenchi's filled out. After a time Chenchi's abdomen enlarged and then she started to have severe pains. To relieve the pain, Numboolyu finally slit Chenchi's pubic region and created a vagina through which a baby came out. It was only because Numboolyu made Chenchi's vagina that women came into existence and were able to bear children. Now that Chenchi had a vagina, Numboolyu, just as men do today, sometimes copulated with her orally and sometimes vaginally. Time passed and eventually Numboolyu's oldest son came to him and asked what he should do about his erections. Numboolyu thought to himself, "Should I send him to my wife Chenchi? No, she is my sexual outlet and my son and I would fight over her." He told his oldest boy to go and copulate orally with his younger brother but he did not tell Chenchi about

---

[8] Slitting the foreskin or the practice of supraincision is not uncommon, though it is not mentioned in the numerous articles and books we have read about Papua New Guinea. According to the Sambia myth, it certainly is not a substitute for castration but is carried out by the woman to make the erect penis more pleasing to her.

it. If the boy became pregnant, he would tell Chenchi; but as he did not, the Sambia continue to keep the practice of homosexual fellatio secret from women. Herdt's informants insisted that had Numboolyu sent his son to his wife Chenchi, Sambia men would now turn their wives over to their pubertal sons. They also agreed that had it not been forbidden by Numboolyu's example, wives would gladly copulate with their sons. Thus, we learn that a fundamental reason, and perhaps the original reason, for making the practice of fellatio obligatory is to provide adolescent sons with a sexual outlet in order to keep them from having intercouse with their mothers; or perhaps, it would be more correct to say, to keep mothers from having intercourse with their sons.

Herdt considered that the Sambia men kept the myth of Numboolyu and Chenchi a closely guarded secret because of their shame over the hermaphroditic origins of men. It seems clear enough that Sambia men as well as those of many other Papua New Guinea peoples are concerned that the female aspects of their personalities will gain the upper hand, and it seems very likely that the severe rituals they must undergo to assure their masculinity and the need to derogate women so severely reflect such concerns. However, one major reason for the secrecy has to do, as Herdt recognized, with the reluctance to inform the boys that homosexuality was enforced not simply to make it possible for the initiate to become a man, but also to keep adolescent sons from seducing, or being seduced by, their mothers or other married women. Then, at the sixth stage of initiation when a man has one or two children, he is given an important reason and a personal interest in maintaining the homosexual practices to ward off his son's oedipal rivalry with him.

A further reason to keep the myths secret from the boys is the fear the first-stage initiates confided in Herdt (1981); namely, that they could be impregnated by the insemination. They had been reassured it was not possible; but the men are now told that Chenchi had been impregnated orally. Then, too, the homosexuality must be concealed from women because, as one informant told Herdt (1981), if women knew of it they would not marry but say to men that they could just continue copulating with one another.

We may surmise that if the men believe that their wives would copulate with their sons, these men, who as children had been taken away from their mothers so abruptly, never really overcame their oedipal fantasies despite the stringent measures taken by the men's cult. The men believe that if they do not take precautions they could lose their wives to their sons or at least to the son of a covillager. However, it is probably not simply a matter of childhood fantasies or a projection but reflects a real danger. After all, the wives have little, if any, libidinal attachment to their older husbands who not only practice intercourse very guardedly but also dominate, derogate, and beat their wives. It is quite likely that a woman's major erotized attachment is to her sons.

Consider a myth of the Keraki people who live far from the Sambia in the southern part of the island (Williams, 1936). The Keraki also believe that a boy must be inseminated, albeit anally rather than orally, and must stay in the men's hut isolated from women for many years. The Keraki primal ancestors were Kambel and his wife, Yuma. They had a son named Gufa who was a puny little thing. Kambel decided that if he inseminated Gufa anally it might make him grow. This worked so very well that when Kambel left home to hunt, Gufa and Yuma had intercourse. There are various versions. In one, Yuma seduced Gufa, saying, "Your father is too old for me"; in another Gufa made an assignation with her and Yuma could not wait until they had the opportunity. Kambel suspected what happened, bided his time, and caught them in flagrante. Yuma told Kambel, "You were a fool to leave us alone." Kambel then killed Gufa and Yuma wandered off to another part of New Guinea. Men today are not as foolish as Kambel and they keep the boys isolated from any contact with women even before they reach puberty, and then provide them with a homosexual outlet until they have wives.

6 Masculinization

The myth of Numboolyu leaves us in something of a quandary concerning the basic purpose of the initiation rituals and particularly the obligatory homosexuality. Prior to the revelation of the myth it had seemed that the rituals had in a tangible but still symbolic form rid the boy of his mother's womb blood that went into his composition and of her noxious emanations and attributes that prevented his sexual maturation, separated the initiates from the debilitating influences of women, and, in essence, enforced separation and disidentification from the mother with whom the boy had lived so intimately for many years. Then the boy was provided with semen to turn him into a man and concretely internalize a masculine identity. Envy of women's creative and nurturant capacities was countered by the assumption of similar abilities by the men. Oedipal desires for the mother, and indeed for sexual relations with any woman prior to marriage, were countered most strongly by emphasizing women's emasculating characteristics through making women's sexuality mortally dangerous to men, and almost secondarily by direct threats that any man who had extramarital sex within the community would be castrated and killed.

However, the myth of Numboolyu conveys that a central purpose of the rituals is the avoidance of oedipal conflicts. Perhaps the boys are taken and isolated from their mothers and all women before puberty to prevent incest and the seduction of, or by, married women rather than to protect them from female emanations that would thwart growth and weaken them. The insemination is not to turn boys into men, but to provide a socially approved homosexual outlet for youths that keeps them from the married women (and virtually all postpubertal girls are married women), and turns their erotic interest to boys.

The men are, in a sense, like Kambel caught in a bind. They wish for strong sons, fierce warriors to protect the village, but in so doing they risk losing their young wives to their own sons or someone else's son. The danger of conflict between men over women is untenable because of the imperative need for unity among the men in the small hamlet encompassed by enemies. Nevertheless, although important, oedipal conflict is an insufficient explanation of the initiations. There is ample evidence that not only among the Sambia but also among other peoples, the defeminization of boys and turning them into fierce and even heartless warriors are major functions of the lengthy initiations, which also enable them to procreate after having been indoctrinated with a fear of the lethal dangers of women's sexuality.

A main thrust of the initiations seems to be what Harrison (1912) had written about early Greek initiation rituals; namely, to turn a "woman thing" into a "man thing," and that "Manhood, among primitive peoples, seems to be envisaged as ceasing to be a woman" (p. 507). In the eastern highlands and in a number of other localities, the boys' long residence with their mothers with little intervention by the father creates a feminine "core identity" so firm that in Herdt's (1981) words, the men "must rattle the very gates of life and death to effect the desired modifications in even visible masculine gender behavior" (p. 305). Indeed, Poole (1982a), who studied the very brutal and disillusioning rites of the Bimin-Kuskusmin, like Herdt (1981), expressed doubts that the men fully succeed in eliminating the deeply ingrained female core identity. Behind it all lurks the suppressed belief that women are basically more self-sufficient and powerful than men—residua of the little boy's impression of the mother who provides for him and who, he needs to feel, is all-powerful.

Still, in an environment in which a boy may not simply envy women's natural capacities, but may be reluctant to become a man who must repeatedly risk his life in battle, show off his extreme masculinity by assertiveness as well as fighting ability, and risk his health and life in making babies, the Sambia squelch any conscious or unconscious desires to be a woman by placing women in a very subservient and scorned position in the society, while taking over many of her natural capacities through ritual means. To some extent, the woman is treated as if she is a member of a different and lower species to which no boy would wish to belong if he could avoid it.

There is, we believe, a fundamental reason why the process of defeminization and masculinization and the control of oedipal strivings are carried out together and are all aspects of a critical developmental transition. The conflict between a thesis and counterthesis can be resolved through a new synthesis, a deeper insight that we shall suggest in the chapter on psychoanalytic considerations of the masculinization process, after portraying the practices of several other Papua New Guinea peoples.

7
The Forest Lodge

We drew attention to the brief forest lodge ritual of the Sambia, which served primarily to offer opportunities for frequent inseminations of the initiates by bachelors from other communities as well as their own. The prolonged forest lodge ritual found in various other societies fills an important function aside from either fostering inseminations or removing boys and bachelors from women to counter incestuous and endogamous premarital sexual activities; namely, to learn masculine activities and to care for themselves when separated from their mothers.

Psychoanalysts have been aware that boys and young adolescents in Western societies seem to require the experience of managing on their own—or at least with the collaboration of other boys or youths—relatively free from the control and direction of their mothers. Their nascent masculinity requires separation from females, including girls, to enable them to develop masculine characteristics, form firm relationships with agemates who are experiencing similar problems and with whom they can empathize, and to begin to find their place in society by competing with and comparing themselves to other boys. As Sullivan (1953) elaborated, boys tend to form an intense relationship with a *chum* (the word used by Sullivan) who is much like themselves and with whom they can share experiences and support one another. The relationship may include some transient overt homosexuality, but more commonly is only latently homosexual in the sense of the mutual affection of the "chums." A major element of the monosexual aspects of latency and early adolescence lies in overcoming the identification with and dependency on the mother. This involves having a partner or a group of companions facing the same tasks with whom the boy can venture forth into the wider world from the home, and ultimately start to relate to those strange creatures of the opposite sex. The division into monosexual groupings is fostered more by the boys' needs to be independent of females than by girls' avoidance of boys. The divergence is accentuated by the earlier maturation of girls that gives them a temporary superiority in size and sometimes in strength, characteristics in which boys are supposed to dominate.

Although the psychoanalytic literature has paid some attention to the developmental tasks of latency that make it useful if not necessary for boys to separate themselves from girls, such needs have been neglected by those persons in the United States who currently foster the unisexual development of children and the inclusion of girls on boys' athletic teams and in all activities of boys (Lidz, 1976). In some Papua New Guinea societies the opportunity for boys to achieve a firm hold on their masculinity through exploring the world free of the presence of females is fostered ritually.

Life in the forest lodge may also promote the boys' and youths' incorporation into the men's cult, which forms a united front, so to speak, against the power of women that arises from boys' dependence on their mothers and early belief in the mother's omnipotence and omniscience. The initiates are learning to displace their loyalty to the mother and dependence on her with a loyalty to and dependence on the men's cult.

The *Bau A*

The various peoples who inhabit the Great Papuan Plateau facing the southern highlands—Etoro (Kelly, 1976), Kaluli

(Schieffelin, 1976), Onabasulu (Ernst, 1978), and Bedamini (Sorum, 1984)—all emphasize masculinization through insemination with relatively little concern with menstrual contamination or the need to defeminize through bleeding. These people live in long houses containing two patrilineages that tend to intermarry and thus the women remain close to agnates after they marry. However, the sexes live in separate sections of the long house; homosexuality is strongly fostered, whereas heterosexual relations are thought to weaken men. Heterosexual relations are forbidden in or near the long house, whereas homosexuality is permitted. The tribes differ in how they inseminate: the Etoro and Bedamini inseminate orally; the Kaluli, who believe that oral insemination can impregnate a man and thereby kill him as he cannot give birth, inseminate anally; the Onabasulu rub the semen into the (abraded?) skin. Here, too, the boys are thought to lack completely the most critical and essential attribute of manhood, namely, semen, and must acquire their life's supply by being inseminated repeatedly from about the age of ten into their twenties. From Sorum's (1984) account of the Bedamini, it seems that the homosexuality is not hidden from the women. Although the two sexes intermingle freely and the men do not seem greatly to fear contamination by women, they are cautious about the loss of their life force through intercourse with their wives. Kelly (1976) calculated that the Etoro proscribe heterosexual relations for various reasons for between 205 and 260 days a year.

When a man's daughter is about five years old, he arranges for her marriage (among the Etoro and Kaluli preferably a cross-cousin marriage to his wife's brother's son), and obtains or will receive in return his wife's brother's daughter as a wife for his son. Among the Bedamini the proper marriage for a girl is to the son of the husband's sister. Here, too, the father is also selecting the primary inseminator for his son in the daughter's betrothed or husband. Thus, among these peoples more definitely than among the Sambia, the brother and sister are for a time both sexual partners of the same man (Kelly, 1976). At least among the Etoro and Kaluli, even though the society is patrilineal, a couple's daughters' children tend to continue the mother's patrilineage through the semen of the maternal cross-cousin, and a boy is turned into a man by the semen of the mother's patrilineage. Optimally, there is a constant crisscrossing of the semen and blood of two lineages.

After having been inseminated by his selected partner, and perhaps by others, the Etoro and Kaluli boys were initiated into manhood and then became inseminators late in adolescence after they spent approximately 15 months participating in the *Bau A* ceremonial. During this period they were isolated from women at a hunting lodge high on a mountain, where they were inseminated by a number of different older youths and men, some of whom specifically went to the lodge for the purpose.

The *Bau A* is no longer held by either the Etoro or Kaluli. The Kaluli abruptly interrupted the last ceremonial in 1964 when missionaries accompanied by patrol officers moved into the area. The men were not only afraid that outsiders would learn the nature of these very secret practices but would ban them as they had banned cannibalism and homicide. Schieffelin (1982) sought to reconstruct the last *Bau A* from the accounts of various participants. He concluded that the *Bau A* could not be considered an initiation ceremonial, as it was led by a youth, and neither imparted esoteric knowledge nor included initiatory rituals. Indeed, it was greatly enjoyed by the participants, many of whom considered it the high point of their lives.

In the *Bau A* the pederastic practices, though carried out in private, were much freer than in ordinary life; and the acquisition of semen from many different inseminators seems to have been important. The participants considered themselves to be in direct contact with the memul, who, it seems likely, were the primal ancestors or the collectivity of ancestor spirits who usually remain aloof from mankind. The memul originally showed women how to conduct the *Bau A*;[1] but when the women

---

[1] A variant of the myth that women originally held the rituals. The nature of the memul is difficult to grasp. According to Schieffelin (1982), they looked like animals to the Kaluli but were people; whereas the Kaluli looked like animals to the memul.

grew taller than trees through the ceremonials (perhaps through being inseminated), the men decided to prevent the women from holding the *Bau A* and sent the bachelors instead.

The organization and procedures of the *Bau A* were quite complicated, and it does not seem necessary to describe just what transpired. Much of the time was spent hunting in small groups to collect animals for the ceremonial at the termination that was attended by a large number of men, women, and children. A central aspect of the *Bau A* seems to have been to demonstrate that men do not need women—the boys their mothers, or the bachelors women for their sexual needs. Men can be self-sufficient without women who the men believe are the cause of virtually all discord and deplete men's vital essence. The novices are separated from their mothers for a very long time during which they learn to take care of themselves and depend on men, while gaining supplies of semen that will suffice for the remainder of their lives. Further, the entire *Bau A* has something to do with establishing a close relationship with the memul who, by analogy, we believe are essential to the process of transforming boys into men. Even though the *Bau A*, strictly speaking, is not an initiation ritual, it fills an important function in transforming boys into bachelors and in teaching them the role of men in the society.

The Maolima

The importance of sending boys and youths to live for periods in a woman-free world is, in some respects, even more marked among the Ilahita Arapesh, a people who live in the low country in the east Sepik province (Tuzin, 1982). Here, as among many of the lowlands peoples, the dichotomy between males and females is not nearly as marked as in the highlands, and adolescent boys and girls even engage in mild premarital sex play.

Like many Sepik peoples, the Ilahita Arapesh adhere to a tambaran cult in which men, completely covered by elaborately decorated wicker body masks, become tumbuan during initiation and fertility ceremonies. The tumbuan are thought to be incarnations of ancestor spirits by the women and children and may themselves believe that they are possessed by such spirits during the rituals. Here, the first two stages of initiation do not differ greatly from the first stage of the nama cult, except that it is the glans penis that is cut to remove the maternal blood that went into the boy's composition, and the initiates are taught that bullroarers swung by men are the source of the voices of the ancestor spirits. But the rituals are carried out with fierce violence and a cruelty that Tuzin found to contrast sharply with their warm family relations. It is the third stage, the *maolima* that takes place after the boys have become pubertal through the efficacy of the first two stages, that is of particular interest to us.

The initiates are completely secluded from women in a secret forest village for several months. Taken on a preliminary visit to the secret hamlet, they are accosted by cooperating enemy warriors and are rescued by their initiators. They are given clay figurines to hold as their babies. Returned to their homes for a night, they mock their mothers and sisters and tell them that without men they will have to copulate with dogs—an extreme, if not the ultimate, insult. We are reminded of Harrison's (1912) statement about the early Greek initiations, "The Kouretes . . . will hide him for weeks or months in the bush . . . and bring him back . . . his mother's child no more, trained it may be henceforth to scorn or spit at her" (p. 37).

On the following day when the initiates reenter the forest village no one notices them, and they are being mourned at a mock funeral by men, some dressed as women. They see a village complete in its masculinity. Warriors from other villages again attack but soon join the initiators amicably. The novices live in this secluded village for some time, and are transformed into men by severing the ties that have bound them to women, particularly their mothers. Neither homosexuality nor insemination is involved. Rather the boys are stuffed with pork because it is the nature of men to crave pig meat. They learn men can perform women's work as well as men's, and men even pretend that women are not necessary to produce babies.

The initiates learn that their supreme loyalty must be given to the men's cult. They are not simply learning that they can get along without women, but the bonds to their mothers and sisters are being broken. The initiates are taught that they must even be prepared to kill a mother, sister, or child at the behest of the tumbuan. In former times, in the fourth stage of initiation, a man disguised as a tumbuan carried out a ritual murder, and it is said that if the man was unable to find an enemy woman or child, he might even murder his own wife or child. The initiates, in their turn, had to bring back a human victim.

Tuzin (1982) does not mention any practice of insemination, the primary emphasis of the Ilahita Arapesh seems to have been the disidentification from the mother and overcoming the youth's dependency on her, but the power of the men was vividly demonstrated by the violence and cruelty they displayed during all of the initiation rituals.

8
Afek and Yomnok Among the Bimin-Kuskusmin

We have suggested that there need not be any contradiction between the use of initiation rituals to overcome the boy's core identification with his mother, to defeminize and masculinize him, and also to break the erotized aspect of his attachment to his mother. As we shall elaborate in chapter 12, these are all interrelated aspects of the separation-individuation process beyond that described by Mahler and her colleagues (1975). Nevertheless, the Sambia myth of Numboolyu and Chenchi has raised questions because it suggests that the dominant function of the initiations may rather be the avoidance of oedipal conflicts between fathers and sons as postulated by Reik (1946b) and others.

We shall therefore turn to examine the initiation rituals of the Bimin-Kuskusmin people in which the first of the ten stages expressly and definitively seeks to separate boys from their mothers. They are first defeminized and then masculinized and the rituals do not provide youths with homosexual outlets during their prolonged seclusion from women nor are they threatened with death or castration if they have premarital heterosexual relations. We are also interested in the later stages of the initiation and the myths that accompany them because they shed light upon the belief widely held in Papua New Guinea (as well as in the Amazon area and parts of Africa) that the women originally carried out the rituals and possessed the ritual objects which the men took away from them (see also chapter 11). The beliefs and customs of the Bimin-Kuskusmin also bring into focus the paradoxical situation that although in this strongly male dominated society in which the division of the world into masculine and feminine is a most fundamental and pervasive categorization, the men convey an underlying uncertainty concerning their gender identity.

The Bimin-Kuskusmin, who number about a thousand, live in the low mountains about 40 to 50 miles east of Telefomin, among the headwaters of the Strickland River, the major tributory of the Fly River that flows southward into the Gulf of Papua. The region forms the divide between the Sepik and Fly rivers, the two great watersheds of Papua New Guinea, and an area through which cultural influences from the northern and southern coasts flow. The Bimin-Kuskusmin are one of the most eastern of a number of related tribal societies who speak Mountain Ok languages that inhabit a large area that extends westward into the Star Mountains in Irian Jaya. When studied by Poole (1976; 1981a, b; 1982a, b, c; 1983a, b; 1985; 1987; 1988; unpublished) from 1970 to 1972, the Bimin-Kuskusmin contact with any Europeans, including the Australian authorities, had been extremely limited. Although they adhered to the laws pronounced and enforced by Australian patrol officers and no longer killed and ate their enemies, they were still necrophagic, ritually eating portions of dead kin. The Bimin-Kuskusmin prided themselves on their reputation as fierce warriors but also on the intricacies and complexity of their rituals that received their charter, so to speak, from the myths of their two primal androgynous ancestors—the more female Afek who had a vagina in each buttock as well as a penis, and her son/brother/ mate, the more masculine Yomnok—but essentially from the Afek myth cycle.

The Bimin-Kuskusmin have a very different culture from the Sambia; and though it is hazardous to draw inferences from the comparison of such different cultures, there are enough basic similarities in the first stage of initiation to indicate that they both stem from closely related belief systems, even though the first stage of the Bimin-Kuskusmin initiation is more complex as well as both more sophisticated and ruthless. In both, the boys are abruptly taken from their mothers and told they will be killed; the mothers are degraded as defiling and polluting, and the boys deemed thoroughly contaminated by their mothers. The novitiates are bled and forced to vomit to rid them of their mothers' blood and polluting foods; their skin is abraded, apparently to remove skin contaminated by their mothers. They are inseminated, though indirectly among the Bimin-Kuskusmin; reborn as men from men; made privy to a fundamental secret of the male cult, though in a manner that still conceals the core secret; and the rites involve the participation of androgynous ancestor spirits. In both societies, the boys are isolated from all women for many years following the completion of the first-stage ritual.

Poole's initial impression of these people led him to believe that the schism and antagonism between the sexes were even greater than in the highlands proper, with the men not only dominating the women but very contemptuous of them. However, he soon learned that the men were well aware of their need for, and dependence upon, their women, but sought to hide it from them (Poole, 1982b).

The *Ais Am*, the first of the ten stages of the Bimin-Kuskusmin initiation, clearly concerns the transformation of boys from "people of the women's houses" into "becoming new men"; and, in contrast to the Sambia rituals, contains neither threats against incest nor provides homosexual outlets for boys and youths during their lengthy separation from women. The later stages of initiation progressively modify the degradation of women and fears of contamination by them engendered during the *Ais Am* and inculcate a recognition of men's need for women.

The *Ais Am* lasts for three weeks and is not only inordinately complex, filled with overt and even more covert ritual implications, but is appallingly harrowing and brutal. It is as if the Bimin-Kuskusmin recognize that to change the initiate's core gender identity they must force the boys into a state of disorganization through physical and emotional abuse, promote confusion through a series of "double binds" that leaves the initiate deeply depressed and apathetically helpless and creates a sense of profound betrayal that has the intent of firing up an inner rage that will find an outlet in brutality against enemies. We shall present only a rough outline of the proceedings that the leaders properly assert cannot be comprehended cognitively but must be experienced (Poole, 1976, 1982a).

The *Ais Am* contains seven discrete phases: the first half defeminizes and the second half masculinizes, pivoting around critical rituals during the fourth phase. During the one day "Bokhur Pandanus Rite" (named after a female tree and food), the boys are told they will be killed and pigs' blood is poured over them. Their mothers are reviled as polluted and polluting, and the initiates run a gauntlet in which they are severely beaten with switches leaving them bleeding and covered with welts. Then when they are crowded and sealed in a low hut, hidden initiators keep chanting what filthy, putrified, and degenerate creatures they are because of their mothers' contamination. The second phase, the "Sweet Potato Rite," lasts for four days during which the humiliating chant continues, and on each day the novices are forced to eat five different female foods. After eating each food the boys' bruised and bleeding skin is rubbed harshly with nettles and they are forced to vomit. If necessary, they are fed a mixture of pig blood and urine to induce vomiting. The boys' condition becomes increasingly desperate and debilitated as they live amidst the stench of vomit and feces and their filthy bodies are covered with scabrous sores and bleeding wounds. Many boys cannot retain the food they are offered at night and suffer from incontinence. In the third phase, the "Domestic Sow Rite," which lasts for two days, the initiates are likened to sows who foul the hamlets with excrement, and when they are permitted to eat uncooked female parts of dead sows that have been hung in the hut, they are told they must never eat them again but are forced to do so on the following day. The initiators then ask the pigs' ancestors to kill the boys in retaliation for eating the sow meat. The initiates are by now thoroughly perplexed and disorganized. They shrink from those men who seek to comfort them and salve their wounds.

The central phase, the "Great Cassowary and Spiny Ant Eater Rite," lasts for eight awesome and harrowing days[1] At the start, the boys are terrified when the roof of their hut is set afire, but they are led into a neighboring large "forest house," which they enter by passing through the legs of a male initiator (a common symbol of rebirth from males). The next evening the initiates are again reviled and beaten with switches. Their topknots, symbols of the women's house, are now cut. Among the various procedures carried out during the following several days, the umbilicus of each initiate is incised to rid them of menstrual residues; the right forehead is cut to eliminate female influences, while the left forehead is covered with mud to prevent the premature entry of male knowledge, but later is incised to permit its entry. An individual has two navels: the female navel is the umbilicus through which female knowledge enters, and the male navel is the frontal fontanelle, the entry point for male knowledge. Blood from boys of the opposite moiety—which they are told contains menstrual blood that will destroy their penises—is placed on their penises. On the fourth night their nasal septums are suddenly and roughly pierced from the right side with a cassowary dagger, a staggering procedure, and as the blood flows profusely over the boys they are told they are dying. This means of bleeding to rid of maternal contamination is also used by the Kimam-Papuans of Irian Jaya (Serpenti, 1984) and perhaps by other New Guinea peoples as well. The boys are now in miserable condition.

The transition from defeminization to masculinization takes

---

[1] The ritual processes are not held simply to impress the initiates—many facets that are considered vital to the efficacy of the rituals are kept hidden from them. Parts of the Afek myth are recited in an ancient language which the boys, and perhaps the leaders, do not understand. Skulls of former female paramount ritual leaders are hidden from the initiates, as are crystals, the eyes of Afek, capable of "seeing" what goes on in all its complexity, both overtly and within the participants (Poole, 1988).

place on the fifth night. While being treated for their wounds, hot marsupial fat is suddenly poured on their right forearms to raise large blisters. The ancestress Afek is summoned and appears impersonated by two paramount *female* ritual leaders—the presence and importance of the female ritual leaders is kept secret from the boys.[2] These female ritual leaders wear exaggerated breasts and red pandanus fruit as erect penises and are covered with cassowary feathers. Afek is associated with, or represented by, a cassowary, a bird the indigenes believe is androgynous. The boys' blisters are lanced and the serum from them, which is equated with semen, is placed on Afek's phallus for the ancestress to eat. A long recital from the Afek myth cycle tells how Yomnok gained ascendency over Afek and how men took the *Ais Am* ritual from the women. The boys are now given male names and told that they are about to become "new men" but not that severe ordeals still lie ahead.

At dawn, Yomnok appears, actually the female ritual leaders disguised in spiny ant eater (echidna)[3] skins with long bamboo tubes filled with black salt as penises. The boys' blisters are lanced and each initiate is made to eat salt soaked with "semen" of boys of the opposite moiety. Then suddenly their left forearms are scalded, the serum from the new blisters is mixed with salt, and the boys are forced to eat this "semen" of boys from their own moiety to strengthen their male substance. They have thus been inseminated, though indirectly. On the sixth night they are treated more gently, until they are suddenly seized and their nasal septums pierced from the left side. Their

---

[2] The presence of women at an initiation ritual is highly unusual, but they play minor roles in the Marind-anim rituals. The Bimin-Kuskusmin have paramount female ritual leaders, properly two per clan, who are postmenopausal and considered androgynous like the primal ancestors. They have gone through a special ritual ceremony and have high status. Each lives alone in a hut near the men's huts, and they must not and do not convey any of their knowledge of the male rituals and the Afek myth cycle to other women (Poole, 1988).

[3] A monotreme, precursor of both placental mammals and marsupials, found in New Guinea, Australia, and Tasmania. It lays eggs but when the young hatch they feed from milk secreted by mammary glands on the mother's abdomen. The indigenes believe the echidna is also androgynous.

foreheads are again incised as they will be again on the seventh and eighth nights to admit male knowledge. The boys are now too weak to resist. Uncured phallocrypts, which tighten and harden, are placed on their penises, and when the phallocrypts are pulled off, they are thought to stretch the penis. The novices now receive more support; on the final night as the hut is dismantled, their growing maleness is praised. They are led or carried into another hut where they collapse from exhaustion and pain.

The fifth stage, the "Wild Boar Rite," is a reversal of the Domestic Sow Rite. For two days the boys' growing masculinity is praised and strengthened by boar meat which contains the most powerful male essense or "finiik"; the hut is now decorated with boar genitals.[4] The four-day "Taro Rite," the converse of the "Sweet Potato Rite," follows during which they are fed five different cooked male foods each day followed by taro and ginger. The taro, though the boys are not informed of it, has been grown in special gardens, fertilized by tubes of semen, so that the boys are again symbolically ingesting semen; and instead of being rubbed with nettles they are rubbed with soft leaves. During the seventh and final phase, the boys are gathered where they had been assembled on the first day, and praised for their bravery, strength, and growing manhood. Their skin is made to glisten with a mixture of boar fat and white pigment, which they will later learn is also considered an equivalent of semen. They are given switches with which they attack their initiators. After boar blood is poured over the boys, the first stage of initiation is over. Their fathers come to congratulate them and publicly show affection for them for the first time.

The *Ais Am* is not without dangers for initiates have been known to commit suicide or become insane. Such tragic results did not occur during the ceremonies Poole witnessed, though

---

[4]The Telefomin peoples believe that men gain the powerful "finiik" of boars by inserting boar tusks in their noses and wearing boar testicles (Brumbaugh, 1980b).

one father feared his son might commit suicide and two boys remained severely depressed for several weeks.

Poole (1982a) learned, through talks with initiates, that these rituals have a profound effect on the initiates who feel themselves transformed from "people of the women's houses" and with greatly altered dispositions. The boys clearly felt that they had become superior to women, but Poole doubted that the transformation to masculinity was completely fulfilled or would be even after the nine more stages of initiation that took place over the next ten years. Indeed, the next nine stages progressively modify the sharp dichotomy between men and women that the *Ais Am* sought to establish in proportion to the initiates' growing masculinity and increasing ability to tolerate dangerous secret knowledge.

The *Ais Am* differentiates the initiates as males, whereas they had previously been categorized together with the women and girls. As in most cultures in Papua New Guinea, the division into masculine and feminine is among the most basic, and perhaps the most fundamental categorization. However, when we examine some of the Bimin-Kuskusmin beliefs about gender, we find reason to consider that the men's extreme dichotomization of their world into masculine and feminine reflects a reaction formation to their uncertainty about their own gender identity. As a consequence of their ambivalence they exaggerate the boundaries between male and female to offset the lingering belief in the greater natural abilities of women, their desires to be dependent on them, and particularly their identifications with their mothers from whom they had been forced to separate so late in childhood. The primal ancestors are androgynous. The bodies of both men and women are neither totally male nor female, for certain parts such as the brain, heart, skeleton, and hard parts are masculine whereas the stomach, intestines, skin, and soft parts are feminine. Moreover, whether an unborn child will be a boy or a girl is a rather fortuitous matter, for it depends on which aspect of the fetus points toward the vagina at birth, and the position of the fetus can sometimes be influenced up to the time of delivery (Poole, 1981a).

Even more important, a person's essential spirit is composed of both a masculine essence, the *finiik*, and a feminine *khaapkhabuurien*. Finiik is powerful and warlike but concomitantly concerned with ritual and the maintenance of the society whereas khaapkhabuurien is more unfettered, natural, and wild like women who are considered wild, impulsive, sensuous, and ignorant of ritual. Finiik is strengthened by semen and its various equivalents and weakened by menstrual blood and female emanations. Yet both men and women possess both essences; and a baby, male or female, has little finiik and strong khaapkhabuurien which continues to dominate in women, whereas a boy's finiik is strengthened in rituals by semen and male foods. Moreover, though the men teach that Yomnok, the more masculine primal ancestor, gained ascendency over Afek, it is the Afek myth cycle that sets the customs and tradition of the culture, including the initiation rituals.

It is essential for the Bimin-Kuskusmin, as for other warring peoples in Papua New Guinea, to overcome their boys' identification with and dependence upon their mothers because the boys have little input from their fathers for the first eight to 12 years of their lives. The father's aloofness from his son or daughter should not be taken for a lack of interest, concern, and affection. In a society with a high infant and child mortality rate, children are greatly valued. To assist his wife through the dangers and pain of childbirth and to help assure the birth of a live and healthy baby, the father goes through a lengthy and very restrictive couvade. Although he does not participate in the child's care and has limited contact with the child, particularly during the first four years of life, he carries out certain procedures during the *menaak* rites that seek to assure the young child's continued well-being. The rites are particularly important for boys, who are considered more prone to illness and maldevelopment than are girls. It is only after the *menaak* cycle has been completed and the boy's initiation cycle begun that the parents can feel reasonably secure that he will survive.

Prior to the age of two, the baby is completely the mother's child, and the mother is supposed to control the baby's moods properly and assure his salutary development by her ministrations. We have gained the impression that the father's presence may be thought to be harmful to the baby by creating an imbalance between the khaapkhabuurien and finiik, that is, the female and male components of the baby's vital spirit.

At the important juncture when the two-year-old boy is given a "female" name, the father transfuses his son with his own strong male blood either by mouth or through a bone tube connecting their forearms. At times when the small child's life seems threatened by illness, the father may repeat this act; or he may rub his own semen or boar semen on the child's skin (Poole, 1985).

The myth of Turiin, the first Bimin-Kuskusmin child (Poole, unpublished), conveys that traditionally the father watches his son from a distance, but the mother's brother plays with the boy and teaches him. After his son is weaned at about the age of four, his father takes him to have a glimpse into the men's cult house, but then returns him to the mother. Still later, the boy is ceremonially taken into the forest where the men plant a pandanus shoot that will grow along with the boy into a tree that will belong to him when a man; and on a still later occasion the boy is shown how to track the cassowary. Nevertheless, the father remains relatively aloof until the boy is almost ready for the *Ais Am*, when the father takes an active role in teaching his son and preparing him for the coming ordeal.

Among the Bimin-Kuskusmin, the attachment to the mother may be unusually strong and highly erotized because the mothers are taught to stimulate the boy's penis to strengthen it (Poole, 1983b). The child may also play with the mother's breasts, which is erotically stimulating to her; but she is supposed to keep her breasts covered while stimulating the boy's penis to keep him from playing with her breasts at the same time. "Good " mothers follow these injunctions and do not overstimulate the boy, but some "bad" mothers overstimulate the boy's penis for their own gratification and encourage the boy to be lustful toward them. Poole believes this is most likely to occur in young mothers who are angry because they are dominated by older women of the husband's lineage and feel sexually deprived because intercourse is forbidden while nursing, and they are also forbidden to masturbate—the accepted source of relief and sexual gratification prior to marriage—because it will weaken their milk supply. They may also overstimulate the child because they are witches who seek only their own pleasure.

It is of interest that the Bimin-Kuskusmin believe, on the basis of observation, that little boys who have been overstimulated sexually grow into lustful men whose sexual feelings focus on their mother's sexual activities, and become hostile to them. Aggression and lust fuse (Poole, 1983b) and destroy the man's finiik. As the boy becomes older he does not adhere to community values and becomes a marginal person who is impotent and can "sustain an erection only in contexts of aggression" (Poole, 1983b). The belief is a lesson on the origins of "phallic men" and of sadism.

Nevertheless, the emphasis of the *Ais Am* is on disidentification from the mother and the inculcation of a sense of male superiority over women, fierce masculinity, and loyalty to the male cult with minimal attention to countering the boy's oedipal attachment to his mother and incipient rivalry with his father.

Having achieved the desired goal over the next ten years, the elders modify and in some respects almost reverse what they so forcefully indoctrinated during the *Ais Am*.

The reorientation is carried out in two interrelated ways. One is the progressive ritual revelation of the importance of women and of Afek, the more female primal ancestor, together with diminution of fears of the noxious influence of women along with introduction of female foods, even food containing menstrual blood, during the subsequent nine stages of initiation. The other consists of teaching through the exegesis of folk tales about two mythic figures, a male and a female, that Poole (1987) designates as "tricksters." The boys and youths are told tales about the interaction of these figures in a variety of situations, and are required to offer interpretations of these tales that are obscure to them and virtually meaningless to anyone unfamiliar with Bimin-Kuskusmin culture. An elder guides the discussion to an understanding of the story that teaches the initiates correct male behavior and how good women can provide guidance and strength but also how to avoid witches in the guise of normal women, as well as about other dangers. The novices are taught the right "road" for a man to follow in a way that diminishes the fear of the power of women. The female "trickster" often is, or is related to, the hermaphroditic ancestress Afek who is the protectress of the culture and men.

The subsequent nine stages of initiation progressively permit behavior that had been forbidden or deemed dangerous because of female pollution, and gradually reveal men's need for and dependence upon women and the importance of their menstrual blood, particularly in the last three of the ten stages when more explicit information is imparted.

It is not clear to us if the Bimin-Kuskusmin differentiate between "womb blood" that is essential to the composition of the fetus and "menstrual blood" that the Gahuka-Gama and others might consider as "dead womb blood" (Lidz and Lidz, 1977). The Bimin-Kuskusmin believe that the mother's "fertile fluids" derived from the father's semen go into the composition of the fetus—another arrogation of women's capacities by men, but the matter remains ambiguous to us.

In the fourth stage, the initiates' heads and genitals are smeared with a mixture of boar fat and white pigment while the male ritual leaders recite in a "sacred language" incomprehensible to the initiates that the initiates are Afek's children and covered with Afek's semen and glisten with her fat. In the fifth stage, the initiates learn that some of the ancestral skulls in the initiation hut are those of paramount female ritual leaders; and the youths are fed taro covered with black blood—symbolically or supposedly, menstrual blood. In the seventh stage during which the initiates become warriors they are told a segment of the Afek myth cycle that relates how Yomnok would not or could not initiate his son, the taro, so that the hawk and eagle took the taro from him, and hardened (masculinized) the taro by rubbing the tuber with boar fat and white pigment, which, as we have noted, is the equivalent of semen. However, the ritual elders recite the proper version in a secret language; namely, that wild boars made taro masculine by rubbing it with their own semen that posseses powerful finiik.

At the end of the ninth stage, the women ritual leaders bring sweet potatoes and the men bring taro and pork from both sows and boars, all of which are cooked together and eaten by the initiates together with the male and female ritual leaders. Such symbolic acts, as well as others we have not mentioned, indicate the importance of male and female interrelations, that male and female substances are not completely inimical, and also that the initiates are strong enough to partake of female foods together with women. Then the lengthy final *En Am* stage discloses many hidden secrets, "secrets inside the heart," in an amazing fashion, which Poole (unpublished) has described in considerable detail.

The *En Am*, which lasts for ten days, starts in a large hut in a forest clearing near a menstrual hut. The naked initiates destroy the hut and take the ridgepole which is then called Yomnok's penis. Male ritual leaders rub boar fat and white pigment symbolizing semen on one side and end of the pole and female ritual elders smear sow fat and red pigment symbolizing menstrual blood on the other side and end. The initiates slide the pole through the lethal residues in the menstrual hut, coating its red side with them. The female ritual leaders, with genitals covered with bark cloth and wearing phallocrypts which designate them as androgynous, stand over the red end and the male ritual leaders over the white end.

> The initiates slide along the pole through the legs of the women who pour black blood, the idiom for menstrual blood, on them; toward the

middle of the pole they are said to masturbate. In fact, most . . . masturbate privately in the forest and collect the semen in bamboo tubes. They smear the semen over the menstrual debris on the red side of the pole. Finally, they pass between the legs of the male elders, who cut their noses, lips and tongues and let the "red blood"—the idiom for male blood—drip on the young men [Poole, 1988].

The ridgepole is then abandoned. The elders then explain that semen cannot be powerful and fertile without menstrual blood (womb blood?). Finally, after various further ritual acts, the initiates are told the core of the Afek myth cycle that had been hidden from them and which reverses the version taught during the *Ais Am*.

Afek was the first primal ancestor and emerged from a great lizard. Afek impregnated the lizard and Yomnok was born. Yomnok was too weak to inseminate Afek until Afek let him sleep in her vaginas where Yomnok grew powerful. However, when Yomnok left Afek for a long time he became very weak until he put his head in Afek's vaginas and again became strong. He impregnated Afek who gave birth to the cassowary and echidna and "later they brought forth the taro and the sweet potato . . . we [men] are like Afek our mother, like Afek our father, like Yomnok too" (Poole, 1988).

Ritual and myth, like dreams, contain ambiguities, for they convey a multiplicity of messages that emerge from a common theme. The Bimin-Kuskusmin initiation rituals and myths seem to interrelate around the core issue of men's original attachment to, identification with, and envy of their mothers. The *Ais Am* enforced the boys' disidentification with their mothers not only by ridding them of the maternal blood and contamination but by indoctrinating a scorn and disgust for their mothers and the lethal danger of women's genital odor. The *Ais Am* then enforces a rebirth as a man and the strengthening of the masculine finiik by insemination and ingestion of male foods. The men's cult takes over the maternal, protective functions and demands priority over attachments to, and concerns about, mothers and sisters. The later rituals, and particularly the *En Am*, mitigate the messages of the *Ais Am* and reflect the unconscious persistence of the initial core feminine identity and dependency. The *En Am* would seem to symbolize the need for the interdependence of men and women, the need for both semen and womb blood for procreation, and a second rebirth of the initiates, but now from both women and men.

The *En Am* may also serve to offset a belief that semen is the essential in procreation as the beliefs and practices of some peoples along the Gulf of Papua may indicate (see chapter 10). Notable, however, is the conclusion "we men are like Afek our mother, like Afek our father" and then "like Yomnok too" which appears to come to terms with the original feminine identity and subsequent envy of women by emphasizing that men, like Afek, have a major feminine component, and share Afek's fertility.

Despite the earlier teaching that Yomnok supplanted Afek, the more secret myths establish Afek as the first and essential primal ancestor. Though androgynous, Afek is clearly feminine, essentially a woman with a penis who gives birth anally, as some little children imagine their mothers. The men learn that Yomnok gained strength only by entering Afek's womb, and became weak when separated from her, and had to return to her to regain his strength, very much as a child in the rapprochement phase might feel. This may well reflect boys' and men's deeply unconscious and feared wish to return to the protection of the womb, or, at least, their symbiosis anxiety (Stoller, 1974).

The Bimin-Kuskusmin *Ais Am* clearly is concerned primarily with first overcoming the boys' initial identification with and dependence on their mothers, and then forcefully inculcating masculinity with minimal attention to countering the erotic components of the boys' attachments to their mothers. The Bimin-Kuskusmin do not provide the postpubertal youths with a homosexual outlet to prevent incest or endogamy like the Sambia myth of Numboolyu and his son suggests. Like many other Papua New Guinea peoples, the Bimin-Kuskusmin rely on the exclusion of the bachelors from all contact with women other than the postmenopausal paramount female ritual leaders. The defeminization of the boys, for reasons we have explained, must take place before their masculinization, which is essential for the defense of the hamlet against its enemies. It is even more critical than the deerotization of the boy's attachment to his mother that is essential for the maintenance of the inner harmony of the boy and his family, with which the repression of oedipal strivings is concerned. However, as we shall discuss in subsequent chapters, all three processes are critical for the development of the individual as well as for the security of the group, and, we believe, are interrelated aspects of the boy's individuation.

The survival of any society depends on its abilities either to reproduce or recruit. The inculcation of the dangerous characteristics of women have contributed to the need of the Marind-anim to capture or purchase babies from other tribes. The Sambia, as well as others, teach their men when they marry various magic and ritual means of countering their wives' life-endangering libidinal emanations. The Bimin-Kuskusmin, however, progressively modify the teachings of the *Ais Am*, and finally during the *En Am* dramatically let the initiates who are about to attain full manhood learn that they need not fear menstrual blood and women's presence.

The later stages of the Bimin-Kuskusmin initiation not only disclose to the initiates that Afek, who is envisioned essentially as a woman with a penis, is the important primal ancestor who created their world and their culture, but inform us, the outsiders, why the peoples of Papua New Guinea, where the men dominate the women so markedly and where the ancestor spirits of the men and not those of the women are revered, have the belief that the women originally possessed and held the rituals. The secret reliance on Afek indicates that despite the extreme efforts to wipe out the boys' dependency on their mothers, the child's initial awe of the mother's creativity and nurturance and the belief in her omnipotence persists beneath the machismo of the men and further clarifies the men's arrogation of maternal characteristics.

The emergent belief that Afek is, or was, feminine and the primal ancestress who created the people and their world becomes definite in the myths and practices of the tribes in the Telefomin area to whom the Bimin-Kuskusmin are linguistically and culturally related, and whose beliefs we shall examine in the next chapter. The Telefomin myths also serve to clarify the reasons why female goddesses such as Cybele and Astarte have had such a powerful appeal and why the Virgin Mary continues to play an important and sometimes a dominant role in some places in Catholicism today—beliefs and practices for which the strongly patriarchally oriented Freud could not find a place in his writings about religion (Freud, 1913, 1939).

9
Afek at Telefolip

The peoples of the Telefomin and Eliptamin valleys located at the headwaters of the Sepik River, actually close to the divide between the Sepik and Fly rivers, are linguistically and culturally related to the Bimin-Kuskusmin. They too believe that Afek was their primal ancestress. The tribes in the area have a way of life and a belief system similar to those of many other mountain peoples of Papua New Guinea. There is a sharp division between men and women; the men live in cult houses; boys are taken from their mothers by the men to become novitiates in the secret men's cult and go through six further stages of initiation during which they progressively learn the cult's secrets within secrets. The people rely on ancestor spirits to maintain fertility; they raise taro and pigs and hunt marsupials; and prior to pacification, they waged cannibalistic warfare with neighboring groups while at the same time sharing a ritual center at Telefolip and some rituals with them.

Their relative isolation from the world beyond that of the Mountain Ok-speaking peoples was broken by the construction of a military airfield at Telefomin during World War II, and by the presence of a Baptist mission and an Australian government station prior to 1950. Their way of life had changed markedly by the time Brumbaugh (1980a, b) lived among them in 1977 and 1978, but the belief system remained, and insofar as their way of life had altered, the old customs could be reconstructed. However, we shall not discuss the initiation rituals but confine ourselves to customs and myths that add to, and clarify, the beliefs and ways of the Bimin-Kuskusmin and thereby shed light on some puzzling aspects of many Papua New Guinea societies.

In the Telefomin area, Afek is not androgynous but definitely female. Indeed, "Afek" means "Old Woman" and she is referred to as "our Old Mother"; her brother/consort seems to be a rather secondary figure. Afek's sons are the progenitors of the numerous related tribal societies that spread from the Bimin-Kuskusmin and their neighbors the Oksapmin in the east into the Star Mountains of Irian Jaya in the west.

Here, then, we find definite myths about an ancestress who originally possessed the rituals and how men gained possession and control over them; and fairly definite indications of the psychodynamic meaning of the myth.

As in many creation myths, Afek, as the primal ancestress with godlike properties, gave birth to the first people, the animals and birds, and also created various features of the physical environment. It was she, for example, who created the Telefomin valley by flattening the mountains; and it was her menstrual blood that turned the earth red in certain localities. The origin of Afek herself remains obscure. Myths tell that she came from the east, perhaps like the sun. While traversing the area she was raped by the "Old Man," whom she killed, as well as by a great serpent. The Old Man reappears as her brother—according to some versions Afek brought him back to life (Brumbaugh, 1980a). She not only gave birth to sons, but dictated where and how they and their descendants would live. For example, Afek sent the sons whose language was aberrant to the outer fringes of the region. She also determined the attributes of each species of animal. Afek built the first cult house at Telefolip, which the surrounding people still consider the sacred center of their religion. She lived in the cult house in which she gave birth to the progenitors of many species, and hunted simply by calling animals to come to her and then killing them. Her brother, with whom she ate (consorted?), lived in a hut below hers where he raised pigs and taro.

When Afek had finished creating everything, including the bow and arrow and the shield, she knew the time had come to change places with her brother. Until then the meat and taro provided by Afek failed to stick to the stomach and did not relieve hunger. According to one version of the myth, the brother spied on Afek and entered the Ariol, the cult house, and discovered the secret of the pig fat (boar fat?) that she had kept hidden from him.[1] He placed the fat on the taro and pigs after which they satisfied hunger. Thereafter, Afek raised the pigs and taro, and her brother took charge of the Ariol and went hunting. The myth provides an explanation for the reputed reversal of male and female functions, and how men became responsible for the rituals. In another version, the brother fed a white sticky milk sap to a certain type of marsupial and thereafter food kept them from being hungry. Brumbaugh (1980b) notes that the myth is strange as there is no ritual in which marsupials are fed milk sap. It will be recalled that among the Sambia, men replenished their supply of semen by imbibing milk sap. A major secret revealed to boys during the first stage of initiation is that the men eat this specific variety of marsupial in the cult house. We are not informed if the marsupials had previously been fed milk sap, boar fat, or semen. By analogy with the practices of other peoples in Papua New Guinea, it seems likely that it was semen or a substitute for it that made boys grow and become strong, as will become even more apparent when we consider the practices of the peoples of the Gulf of Papua.

The myth appears to reflect the widespread belief that women can nurture little boys and girls but that only men can turn boys into men and do so by feeding them semen or rubbing it into their skins. Men can become free of their need for their

---

[1] According to a related myth, Afek killed her brother because he secretly entered her cult house; and now in retribution women are killed if they enter the men's cult house (see chapter 11 for analogous Amazon Indian myths).

mothers when they come to believe that semen is not only the equivalent of breast milk but can even accomplish what breast milk cannot.

The Telefomin creation myth has Afek, a female, give birth to all things, for it is Woman who creates and nurtures, and there is a sacredness to her creativity as well as a mystery. The attachment to the mother and a sense of the mother's omnipotence remains in Everyman. It may be hidden beneath the anger at the mother because she ceases to provide nurture and protection. Well, who needs a mother? Men created their own mystery of rebirth that was hidden from women, and men could nurture the boys with their semen that was more powerful than breast milk. It is, of course, possible and even probable that the transition came with the knowledge that semen was essential for procreation. Some aboriginal peoples in Australia, and also the Trobriand Islanders (Malinowski, 1929), do not believe that conception is related to sexual intercourse.

Freud, raised in a society with strong patriarchal sentiments, was unable to find room for female goddesses—Earth Mothers and Magna Maters—that he knew had existed, and he traced the belief in God to the desire for a supernatural protector in the image of an omnipotent and omniscient father. In Papua New Guinea we can follow a transition from belief that a female primal ancestress created the people and gave them their way of life and their implements to a belief in a male primal ancestor—a precursor of a male god. However, in Papua New Guinea, as in many other places in the world, myths persist that the women originally controlled the rituals; and in the Telefomin area the primacy of an ancestress and the transfer of her power to the men's cult are made explicit.

We have noted the belief among the Bimin-Kuskusmin that some parts of the bodies of both men and women are male and other parts female; and that the essential spirit of both men and women consists of finiik and khaapkhabuurien, a masculine and feminine essence. Among the Telefomin peoples, the dual masculine and feminine composition of people, at least of men, is even more explicit. The masculine "arrow" aspect is unbridled aggressive and sexual lust, and some men can only give vent to sexual impulses in conjunction with hostility and aggression—a fusion of sex and aggression as psychoanalysis postulates occurs in the dual instinct theory of sadism. The "taro" aspect has to do with the home and family, clearly a feminine side of the men. Thus, men's identification with the mother persists, and in Telefomin societies, should persist in all men. Under peaceful circumstances the proper man balances the "arrow" and "taro" sides of his makeup; but if he cannot rouse the "arrow," aggressive part when appropriate and is too passive, he is not a real man. On the other hand, a man who manifests the "arrow" side of his nature consistently or inappropriately cannot be a proper member of a community. (It is worth noting the analogy to the Bimin-Kuskusmin beliefs mentioned in the previous chapter.)

Every cult hut contains two fireplaces: one is "consecrated," so to speak, to the arrow ancestor, and the other to the taro ancestor, and a different descent group or patrilineage is responsible for each of the fires; but both are encompassed within the single cult hut as they also should be within each man.

Among the Telefomin peoples the initial bond between the mother and small child is unusually intense. The very young child cries uncontrollably if the mother is not in sight so that the mother may be able to leave only when it becomes dark and the child will not note that another woman is being substituted for the mother. The shift to the men's cult is particularly traumatic when the boys are beaten and must renounce their mothers and live collectively in a boys' hut. The beatings have the specific purpose of instilling "arrow" character in the boys. They do not accept the beatings with Spartan stoicism but go into a "convulsion of rage," screaming and crying. The men say that a feeling of rage is created that never goes away and, as among the Bimin-Kuskusmin, must be suppressed but remains inside ready to take over in combat or when challenged. It also emerges in sexual excitement, for the "arrow" attribute is considered a single inner "heat" that emerges as belligerence or sexual excitement according to the circumstances.

During the initiations, however, some men serve as male "mamas" who comfort the boys and seek to protect them. These men are utilizing their "taro" character and would seem to be identifying with the mothers they had supposedly renounced. As among the Sambia and other groups, it is one way of assuming maternal characteristics, or of compensating for what had been renounced. In another sense, the men, according to Brumbaugh (1980b), demonstrate that they can be better mothers and that the men's cult forms a self-sufficient social system without women.

Brumbaugh (1980b) believes the "enemies" represent the fathers with whom the initiates are engaged in oedipal rivalry, and the "mamas" the oral narcissistic attachment to the mothers—concepts that follow early psychoanalytic theory, and particularly Roheim's conceptualizations. We are back to the question raised by the Sambia myth of Numboolyu and Chenchi. Does the initiation with its beatings strive to counter incestuous oedipal strivings, or does it seek to instill and foster aggression that is essential to a man? We might consider, as we have previously, that marshaling the boys' aggression can present a grave danger to the fathers rather than suppress their sons' hostility to them that is aroused by rivalry for the mother.

As psychoanalysts have recognized, the small "preoedipal" child can become disillusioned and hostile to the mother when she withdraws her nurturant care, particularly when she actually more or less abandons the child, and may turn to the father. Here the mother who hands the child over to the initiators becomes the "bad" mother who, among these peoples, as in many other localities, is replaced by a "good" mothering father figure—a concept we shall consider in the next chapter.

Reik (1946a) in "The Puberty Rites of Savages," a work that, as we have noted, has been critical to the psychoanalytic understanding of initiation rituals, commented on the dualism of the initiating men. He considered the attributes of fathers toward sons to be both hostile and affectionate. His general approach to so-called "puberty rites" was that the most common feature was the symbolic death and rebirth of novitiates, in which they were often told they were to be devoured by a monster. The fathers showed their hostility by dragging the boys off to be devoured, and their affection by their attempts to protect the boys from the monster. He interpreted the attitude of affection as a means of concealing the hostility engendered by the fear their sons would eventually seek to kill them as they had wished to kill their own fathers. While his theory has pertinence, it takes into account neither the central significance of changing "women things" into "men things" by means of the rituals nor the fact that among many societies in Papua New Guinea as among the Telefomin anthropophagi, the threat to the boys that they will be eaten presents a very realistic danger, nor that circumcision is not part of the initiation in these areas.

Among the Telefomin area peoples, it seems particularly apparent that the boys are, in contrast to Western cultures, "twice born"—not just in the sense of being reborn into a religious belief—but from a feminine thing given birth by their mothers and then reborn as a man into the male cult with its control of the rituals and its "religious" cult belief system. They are born of women, nurtured by them for many years, and they identify with and, to some degree, internalize their mothers; and then they are reborn in a way that forcefully changes their gender identity which is imbued with fierce "arrow" masculinity. Still, during the initiations, as when engaged in peaceful domestic pursuits, men can express a more feminine "taro" side of their natures. (It is somewhat perplexing that the "taro" aspects of their makeup is the more feminine side, for taro is elsewhere a male food, and in a sense, symbolic of masculine hardness and strength.) As a result of the sequential and very different types of nurture, the men acquire something of a dual character. We might consider a "layered" personality in which masculinity overlays a feminine core which, despite the extreme efforts taken to repress or destroy it, still finds outlets for expression, even if it is disguised as an acceptable type of male behavior.

It is of considerable interest that the initiate's protective sponsor in many Papua New Guinea societies is the mother's actual or classificatory brother. He is, in a sense, a representative of the mother and a protector of the rights the mother's lineage has in her children: a right in many places to have her children marry their maternal cross-cousins by an exchange of daughters. The situation is even more complex where, as we have seen, the boy's sister's husband is his primary inseminator; and still more involved where, as among some peoples along the Gulf of Papua, the maternal uncle not only inseminates but fills very much of a paternal role.

10

The Papuan Gulf

We now turn to consider several cultures of the Gulf of Papua, primarily those of the Marind-anim and Kimam-Papuans of southeast Irian Jaya, but with references to the Kiwai, Keraki, and Elema of the Trans-Fly region of Papua New Guinea, all of whom share beliefs and customs. We do so with considerable reluctance, for although they help clarify the myths and beliefs we have been presenting, they differ from the cultures we have been discussing in fundamental ways. Many of their practices were eradicated by missionaries and government authorities generations ago, so that much of what is known depends on reconstructions of practices from descriptions elicited from older inhabitants. We must admit, despite our efforts to view matters from the indigenes' perspective, we find aspects of much of what we must relate, however run-of-the-mill to the natives, rather repugnant. We shall confine the presentation to particularly salient aspects of these cultures because the extremely complex rituals and myths of the Marind-anim collated by van Baal (1966) in his monumental but difficult book *Dema* and many years earlier by Wirz (1922–1925) are difficult to grasp and sometimes of uncertain validity, as well as the studies of the Kimam-Papuans by Serpenti (1984). However, some beliefs and practices demand attention for they are highly pertinent to the topics we have been scrutinizing.

As we shall present, the primal forebears of the Marindanim and the Kimam-Papuans are believed to be neither male nor androgynous but clearly female; and among the Marindanim, if not also elsewhere, are split into a "good" and a "bad" maternal figure. Here, we do not find myths of sons eating their father as posited by Freud (1913) in *Totem and Taboo*, but rather according to some myths, they ate the primal mother. There is evidence that a woman representing the primal mother or an ancestress related to her was eaten ritually at regular intervals. Among the peoples of the region, the men do not fear the noxious and debilitating qualities of vaginal secretions, but nevertheless suffer severe inhibitions of heterosexual relations because of the fears of castrating women or castrating vaginas— in essence, in contrast to early psychoanalytic theory, because of fears of a castrating mother rather than a castrating father.

Here, too, multiple inseminations are required both to form a baby and to foster maturation, not just of boys but also of girls. Male homosexuality is neither concealed from women, nor limited to ritual inseminations, but, it seems, may be preferred to heterosexuality. Rather than the husband alone, his patrilineal kin collectively inseminate a man's wife, at least on certain occasions. Here, interestingly, the mother's brother not only assumes many paternal functions for his nephew as in matrilineal societies (Malinowski, 1929) but is also the boy's primary inseminator.

As we have already noted, it has been known for almost 100 years that sodomy was widely practiced in the region for Beardmore (1890) reported that "sodomy is regularly engaged in." However, Landtman (1927) not only reported that among the Kiwai who live on an island in the Fly River delta, the women were treated almost as equals by the men and that couples were commonly affectionate and protective of their children, but also that vaginal secretions were considered beneficial rather than dangerous. Thus, to help her son obtain a wife, a mother would rub her vaginal secretions on her son's drum to make it sound more attractive to girls, or anoint him with her secretions mixed with an aromatic herb or with her husband's semen. Van Baal considered that the Marind-anim did not have discrete male and female cultures because the girls went through initiations similar to those of the boys, sometimes together with them; because women participated in the boys' initiations, though in secondary roles; and because women accompanied the men on headhunting expeditions.[1]

Among the Marind-anim and Kimam-Papuans, the absence of fear of women's vaginal secretions and the better social position of women did not leave the men free of dread of vaginal intercourse. Marind-anim myths are replete with tales of "dema," ancestors trapped in intercourse, and of dema who were castrated by mothers of girls with whom they had intercourse or whom they had sought to seduce.

The nature of dema, who play a central role in Marind-anim myths, folklore, ritual, and everyday life, is far from clear, not only to us but to van Baal, Wirz, and Verschueren who studied the Marind-anim. We gather that they are thought of as giant ancestor spirits who lived in mythic times. In one way or another they created many landmarks and traditions, as well as creating fire and teaching how to carry out various instrumentalities. In some respects they fill the functions that the primal ancestors fill in other New Guinea cultures, but there are a multiplicity of dema. They are no longer present, but their habitat is often marked by a stone, commonly by a phallic-shaped stone. Rituals keep their power and tradition going. As the Marind-anim, just as most other New Guinea societies, have no sense of the depth of the past, some dema are thought to have existed in recent times. In another sense, anything very large or very old may be considered a dema, perhaps because it seems supernatural (e.g., a beached whale was called a dema as was a very old man). However, we are referring to dema in the sense

---

[1] The different status of women and the absence of fear of vaginal secretions among the Marind-anim and some other groups may be related to the absence of warfare with neighboring groups or the taking of wives from enemy groups; but it may well be that these coastal cultures had different relations between men and women than did those in the interior.

of some type of ancestor spirit with supernatural powers (van Baal, 1966).

We should note that the Huli people who live in the southern highlands far from the Marind-anim, despite very marked differences in the cultures, have some customs and beliefs that seem to us to be similar to those of the Marind-anim. The Huli also have a primal ancestress; and figures called *dama* who, like the dema, form something of a host of demidivinities, one of whom had no phallus, but was deemed to have great power.

A central rite of the first stage of the boys' initiation in the eastern part of the Marind region is called the sosum ritual. *Sosum*, which is also the word for the phallic-shaped bullroarer, was a dema whose penis was cut off by his partner's mother when entrapped in copulation. A giant effigy of his penis is venerated by the men, who dance around it, and at the termination of the ceremony subject the novitiates to promiscuous anal intercourse. Phallic worship is common in many parts of the world, but a ritual that takes place around an amputated penis seems unusual. It seems to symbolize the dangers of vaginal intercourse and why men prefer anal intercourse with boys.[2]

A central Marind-anim myth, to which we shall return, concerns the origin of fire (Wirz, 1922–1925). A male and female dema entrapped in intercourse were eventually freed when another dema twisted and turned them. The friction caused fire to shoot out of the vagina and set fire to a large area.[3] The Kimam men believe that a woman or witch named Kone who has no husband seeks to seduce men when their wives are away fishing, and when she succeeds she amputates the man's penis

---

[2] There is also a folk tale that tells of a dema with an extremely long penis who molested a girl in her mother's presence and the mother cut off his penis.

[3] Although the Huli do not have a similar myth of the origin of fire, according to their mythology, their primal ancestress, Honabe, cooked her food by the heat of her genitals (Glasse, 1968). Günter Grass (1977) in his novel *The Flounder* emphasizes men's dependence upon a primal mother figure and their longing to be nurtured by her, with great emphasis on cooking and food. He narrates how the primal mother hid the coals she stole from the wolf god in her vagina.

with her vagina. She is now supposed to live behind a certain tree which no man will pass when alone lest he be raped and lose his penis.

It seems likely that the fears of being entrapped and castrated are expressions of an ambivalent wish/fear to be a female that is a residue of the identification with the mother, but perhaps the myths provide a defense against the regressive longing to be permanently fused with a woman. The Sosum Dema could no longer have heterosexual intercourse after losing his penis, and therefore could only be passively penetrated like a woman. It is particularly noteworthy that men do not fear castration by a father figure, as posited in psychoanalytic theory, but by a woman. Here, then, is it that the mother protects her daughter, or that the mother is too strong and forbidding; or as encountered in the analysis of men in Western countries and, very notably in Japan, too engulfing and thereby castrating?

The Marind-anim and the related Kimam-Papuans deem a mother figure to be the primal ancestress, who, as among the Telefomin peoples, is called the "Old Woman" or "our Old Mother." However, there are two such figures. The Marind-anim have two major rituals: the "mayo" cult with its ritual center in the eastern coastal area, and the "imo" cult with its center in the central or western coastal area. The mayo cult centers around a more or less benevolent figure, the Mayo Woman, about whom there is an aura of mother-son incest, and who, according to some reports, is eaten at the end of the ritual. The myth and ritual may reflect the unconscious desire to incorporate the mother rather than be incorporated by her. There is also an important myth that she fled with her son to the region of the imo cult where they were both captured, raped, and eaten.

In the mayo cult initiation both boys and girls are carried into an enclosure by a man dressed as the Old Mayo Woman and adorned. The boys are given a shell and the girls an apron to cover their genitalia (van Baal, 1984). They receive foods mixed with semen for several days. The semen is obtained by a rite termed "otiv-bombari" in which many men have serial intercourse with several women and the semen and vaginal fluids are collected as they drip from the women's vaginas, which indicates that the vaginal fluids are not deemed dangerous to men. The myths are confusing: in one version the woman representing the Mayo Woman is burned and in another she emerges from the ceremony as the great python with her children, the new initiates.[4]

Van Baal felt certain that the Mayo Woman, presumably a woman who represented her, was not actually killed at the end of the ceremony (van Baal, 1984). However, Wirz who studied these people much earlier, even before 1922, sought to learn about the Rapa cult ceremony that was related to the mayo ritual and took place in Sendar. According to his account, Wirz managed to gain entrance to the cult house. He learned that men who had been initiated into the cult raped a young woman of their own lineage, then killed her and pierced her body with fire-drilling sticks to start a large fire onto which they threw her corpse, and then roasted a pig on the coals. They made an opening in the pig's abdomen through which came a jet of steam and hot fat which they set afire. The women watching from a distance exclaimed that the fountain of fire was the Rapa Dema. The young woman's corpse was then cut up and eaten. The woman's bones were buried next to coconut palms to increase their fertility and one bone was placed with bones of previous victims in the cult house. The ritual clearly commemorates and, in a sense, repeats the myth of the origin of fire, and is at the same time a fertility rite (Wirz, 1922–1925). Van Baal, however, believes Wirz was misled and does not believe the woman was eaten.

The imo ritual connected with pig killings and headhunting is very different. The boys' initiation is harsh and cruel. The Imo Woman is not at all motherly and is called the "Bad Woman" or the "Excrement Woman." The novices are dragged by their hair into her enclosure where their faces are smeared with a mixture of feces and semen, and they must lie there until maggots appear in the excrement, after which they are bathed and

---

[4]The belief that ancestor spirits exist in the form of a python will be discussed in a subsequent work.

cleansed. Apparently little is known about the ritual (van Baal, 1984), but it includes or ends with a fertility rite in which sexual promiscuity with women takes place—the men copulate freely with any woman except kin in an orgiastic night that the missionaries sought to halt.

The Mayo Woman and the Imo Woman, both creators of the Marind-anim world and their customs, would seem to represent the splitting of the primal ancestress into "good" and "bad" mother figures. As child analysts have observed, very young children who have not achieved sufficient object constancy to keep their mothers unified and are not yet capable of ambivalent feelings toward the same object are likely to believe they have a "good" mother and a "bad" mother, an extension of the Kleinian concept of a "good" and a "bad" breast. The "good" mother is the early "preoedipal" nurturant mother, and the "bad" mother the restrictive, controlling, and bowel training mother. (In the psychoanalytic literature, however, the preoedipal mother is sometimes deemed the "bad" mother.) The splitting is a defense against the child's recognition that the mother cannot always satisfy needs and always be properly nurturant.

The division of the primal mother into a good and bad mother may have a more profound significance. Children, particularly those whose mothers have been overly protective and who constantly seek to provide nurturance, can, as we have already noted, become disillusioned and hostile to their mothers when they are no longer so protective and the child, most commonly the boy, is expected to manage in the world without his mother, or even begin to fill mother's needs to have a successful son.

Okonogi (1978, 1979) has described this situation that is, or was, common in Japan in his articles on the Ajase complex, which helps explain the split between men and women in traditional Japanese families, and the men's reactive misogyny when their expectations that their dependency, or Amaeru (Doi, 1973), is no longer met by their mothers.

In Papua New Guinea a boy has very tangible reasons to

turn against his mother who, as we have discussed, abandons him to the men's cult.

Among various peoples along the Gulf of Papua, semen, as we have noted, has tremendous importance and is used to make girls grow as well as make boys mature and become strong, to fertilize plants, and also as a panacea to heal wounds, cure illnesses, and protect against danger on headhunting expeditions. It is not clear to us if the people believe that semen alone forms babies within the uterus (as do the Amazon Indians; see chapter 11), or if they simply consider it to be the quintessential fertilizing and healing agent.

Among the Kimam-Papuans, and probably among other peoples in the area, semen is utilized lavishly to masculinize boys and make them mature and grow strong. The Kimam boys are initiated some time between the ages of ten and 14, and the initiation begins at the time of a funeral ceremony. The boy's rebirth or birth as a man must be balanced by death. At the final feast for the deceased, promiscuous intercourse with the participating women takes place. The next morning the initiate's face is painted like the dead person's and, like the corpse, he is placed on a raft piled with food topped by a pig on which the boy is placed. The initiate's female relatives and particularly his mother wail and sing songs of mourning. A mourning hood is thrown over the boy; symbolically he has died. Serpenti (1984) suggests that women produce life that ultimately leads to death, but then the men ritually produce life out of death and turn boys into men. It seems likely though that the start of the initiatory rebirth at the time someone has died reflects the belief that a balance between life and death must be maintained. The cannibalistic, headhunting raid at the termination of the series of initiation rituals may be considered essential to balance the rebirth of the new initiate by killing a person whose blood and flesh enter into the initiate when eaten.

The initiate is taken directly from the raft to the bachelors' hut. Here, too, the boys must remain secluded from women for a long time and must not see or be seen by women while their transformation into men goes on abetted by several types of insemination.

When a boy enters the bachelors' hut, his betrothed moves into his parents' house where she is under the aegis of the boy's father. She puts herself at the disposal of his male relatives who have serial intercourse with her—according to reports, as many as ten to 15 men in succession—to collect sufficient semen to rub into the incisions that are being made in the initiate's skin by his mentor. The semen is essential to make him mature and become strong and vigorous. The girl is prepubertal and according to old mission reports sometimes as young as eight. It is an ordeal that makes the youth indebted to his future wife, and gives the girl a powerful investment in her betrothed.

The boy is also placed under the charge and guidance of a mentor who serves as his adoptive father and who properly is his mother's actual or classificatory brother. The mentor becomes the boy's inseminator (Serpenti, 1984). The Marind-anim have a similar practice. Here the mentor is termed the boy's *binahor* and "feeds" him with semen anally to make him grow. The Marind-anim boys and youths live in a shed some distance from the village and avoid women, but each sleeps with his binahor in the men's house. The boy does not have sexual relations with any other men except during the sosum ritual when he is available for promiscuous intercourse with other men. The binahor has obligations to the boy. He not only gives him his first penis shell and a finely decorated bow and arrow but may even trade his daughter in exchange for a wife for the boy. Van Baal (1966) believes it likely that the sexual relationship ceases when the boy receives the penis shell, but a close relationship continues between them; the boy assists in his binahor's garden and brings his wife game he has hunted. The binahor's wife fills something of a maternal role, preparing the boy's meals and helping with his complicated hairdo. Among the Kimam-Papuans a joking relationship exists between the boy and the mother's brother who is his mentor: they play pranks on one another and the boy shows little respect for his uncle, a situation reminiscent of the relationship between the wau (classificatory maternal uncle) and laua (nephew) among the Iatmul that Bateson (1958) described in *Naven*.

The initiates are also fed semen in foods, at least when they enter the bachelors' house; and in some places their skin is covered with a mixture of charcoal and semen that may not be washed off for a long time. During the last stages of initiation, the initiate's body is again covered with semen just before another symbolic rebirth when he wriggles through a narrow opening, assisted by his mentor. The youth is then ready for marriage.

There is, however, another major aspect to the youths' initiations among the Kimam-Papuans, and also among the Marind-anim and other tribal groups in the region. They are obligated to bring back the head of a person killed in a raid on a village of another tribe. In contrast to tribal groups in most other areas of Papua New Guinea, the Marind-anim, who are scattered over a very large area, do not engage in war or make raids on other Marind-anim hamlets. The headhunting raids are carried out against distant, unrelated tribes.

Among the Kimam, promiscuous intercourse between the men and young girls again takes place on the night before the raiding party sets out in order to obtain semen to anoint the novice hunters to protect them from being killed. The gruesome proceedings of the headhunt and the ensuing rites do not concern us here. The uncle/mentor is the actual headhunter and presents the head to his youth. On their return the hunters again engage in intercourse with the fiancées of the novices and the collected semen is smeared on the severed heads which are prepared to be hung in the bachelors' house. The remainder of the victim's body is eaten.

Insofar as we have been able to determine, it is not clear that a woman's husband is involved in her children's conceptions. As we have described, the husband's patrikin not only have serial intercourse with his betrothed to obtain the semen needed to make him grow, but also before a husband and wife consummate their marriage. They apparently believe, as in many places in Papua New Guinea, that multiple inseminations are required to form a fetus and they all chip in, so to speak, or they may consider it a matter of fostering growth. The husband then continues to have intercourse with his pregnant wife in order to feed the fetus, or perhaps fertilize it and make it grow. It seems probable that the serial inseminations by the husband's patrikin are thought to bring about conception, for when the wife is ready to become pregnant again—when she again starts to menstruate—the male patrikin again have serial intercourse with her. The child, then, is an offspring of the patrilineage rather than of the husband alone.

The ways of the Marind-anim and Kimam-Papuans leave us with the impression that their cultures have, in some respects, remained more primordial than most of the other Papua New Guinea cultures we have been considering. We are left to ponder whether these cultures are closer to some original state of the Papuans which then became modified in various ways in other sections of the island; or if these are simply variations of characteristics that underlie the other cultures.

We now use our prerogative as psychoanalysts and theoreticians to move into the realm of conjecture.

The question we have already broached of whether a true nuclear family exists in Papua New Guinea is particularly pertinent to these societies. Of course, there is a family of father, mother, and children but the husband does not live with his wife; the husband's patrikin inseminate his wife; the mother's brother not only inseminates the son to make him a man but fills various other paternal functions; the boy sleeps in his uncle's cult house, helps in his garden, and provides game for his wife. The maternal uncle passes on his masculine spirit via his semen which is semen of the mother's and not the father's patrilineage, and serves as an educator and protector, as well as the killer who takes the head for the initiate on the headhunting expedition. He may fill this role of binahor, the inseminating mentor, for several of his sister's sons.

The family, then, has a different meaning and different functions than in most cultures. Although there is a husband and father, he plays a rather minimal role either as husband or father other than economic. He has relatively little to do with his children's development and education and the protection he provides is largely as a member of the protecting collectivity of men. The family seems to be at a stage in the emergence of a true nuclear family. Perhaps it is an intermediate stage in the shift from a matrilineal to a patrilineal family, a stage in which the mother is the central figure, the parent whose relationship to her children is apparent. It may be that it is a family in which the child belongs to her lineage, though to her patrilineage and not her matrilineage; and with the mother's brother the boy's mentor and guardian and to some extent the mother's protector as in matrilineal societies.

The family and the mythology here are obviously very different from Freud's "primal horde" with its all-powerful father who usurped all of the females for his own lust,[5] which Evans-Pritchard (1965) irreverently but properly termed *a just-so story*. There is in Papua New Guinea, as elsewhere, no indication that the individual father ever exerted such powers, or that sons revolted as a group and killed and ate the primal father, for the youths are controlled by the collectivity of "fathers."[6] Even more striking, Marind-anim myth conveys that here it was the primal mother who was eaten, if not raped, killed, and eaten.

Of course, we might argue that it is not only a man's, or at least a boy's, repressed wish to have intercourse with his mother, but a deeply repressed wish to incorporate her orally and thus possess her forever; or by incorporating her, become

---

[5] However, the Chief of the Big Nambas people on Malekula island in Vanuatu (New Hebrides), it is said, claims any girl or boy who strikes his fancy for his sexual use (Allen, 1984).

[6] Consider the Greek myths of Uranos and Kronos, as well as the failed filicide of Laius and Oedipus, and of Abraham and Isaac, and more locally the western Enga folk tales recorded by Meggitt (1976). In one (pp. 78–79) a man orders one of his wives to kill her newborn if it is a son; she pretends to do so, but hides it in the hollow of a tree and secretly feeds the child who miraculously grows up rapidly. In another (p. 80), the son, whom the mother hides, grows up and like Oedipus unknowingly kills his father, but unlike Oedipus marries his half-sister and not his mother. Or we may realize that Jesus was the son, whom His omnipotent Father let be crucified.

free of her. In any case, the men's revolt against their mothers and subjugation of them may be fundamental to the belief that is not only omnipresent in Papua New Guinea but found along the Amazon as well as in parts of Africa that the women originally possessed the rituals and ritual objects. While such myths probably do not convey a historical reality, they reflect the need of the boy in growing up to overcome the dominance of his mother and his dependence on her. We believe that a critical aspect of the myth of Oedipus is that by solving the riddle of the Sphinx, namely, that a man can get along without a mother,[7] he

[7]There are analogies with early Greek societies in which the dominant supernatural figures, both feared and venerated, were female earth spirits of various types (Harrison, 1912). The mythology of Thebes, which has very ancient roots, seems to focus on the denial of the mother. Cadmus follows a cow in search of Europa and arrives at Thebes where he sacrifices the heifer. The Spartoi were born from dragon's teeth without a mother. Cadmus' daughter Semele, pregnant by Zeus, insisted she see Zeus in his natural form and was destroyed by his lightning, but Zeus snatched the fetus from her womb and placed it in his thigh. Dionysius, the twice born (like Papua New Guinea initiates), the god of the double door, is thus born from Zeus, not from a mother. Agave, mother of Pentheus who was King of Thebes when Dionysius returned, tore her son asunder when he, dressed as a woman, spied on the Bacchanal. Next Zeus impregnated Nycteus, daughter of the regent of Thebes, and she (unmotherlike) exposed her twin sons on Mount Cytherean but they, like Oedipus, were rescued by shepherds and later overthrew the regent. When Labdacus, the King, died, his son Laius fled to the court of Pelops, while Amphion and Zethus, the motherless sons of Nycteus, built the city of Thebes. Laius fell in love with and abducted Pelops' son Chrysippas, which caused Pelops to place a curse on Laius. Laius, it is said, introduced sodomy to Attica. The curse was that Laius would be killed by his son. When he married Jocasta, the Queen Priestess of Thebes, Laius would not have intercourse, supposedly because he feared the birth of a son who would kill him. Hera, the protectress of the hearth and family, sent the Sphinx to isolate Thebes because Jocasta, the earth priestess, was not fertilized. Jocasta made Laius drunk to induce him to have intercourse and she became pregnant. When Oedipus was born, Jocasta was willing to forgo motherhood and let Laius expose Oedipus on Mount Cytherean. He was rescued and eventually unknowingly killed his father, Laius, and then solved the riddle of the Sphinx. He alone could solve the riddle and overcome the Sphinx, the strangler—the strangling mother—because he knew that man can get along without a mother. Oedipus had crawled on all fours as a baby (four legs in the morning) and now walked on two legs as a mature man, and prophetically would walk on three, with a cane, when a blind, old man. The Sphinx killed herself when Oedipus did away with the need for a mother. He married Jocasta, and in taking her as a wife denies that she is a mother. Oedipus then ruled as king—the end of matriarchy and matrilineage (Lidz, 1988).
There are other turns and twists to the Theban myth cycle, but we have here sought to indicate how it reflects a denial of motherhood and covertly recounts how matriarchy came to an end in Thebes.

overcame the power of the strangling, incorporating mother whom the Sphinx personified, and became free of the need/fear of women. In our contemporary Western societies, adolescents commonly revolt against parental domination and perhaps even more against their projected desires to be dependent on their mothers, and find ways of distancing themselves from their mothers, often by becoming defiant or daring to do what had been forbidden. In Papua New Guinea where the boys' dependency on their mothers is extreme and in some cultures the mothers are overly engulfing, the boys need to be "rescued" by the men. In fear of the reincorporating or castrating qualities they project onto the mother, they turn to male groups for protective strength and to male sexual outlets.

It is at least feasible to consider that the nuclear family developed through a stage such as exists in Papua New Guinea. It is possible that the sons could not gain manhood in a family dominated by a mother and with a father who filled a very secondary role. Among the Marind-anim, we find the primal mother divided into a "good" and a "bad" mother, much like the child does before acquiring the capacity to recognize that the mother who nurtures and gives and the mother who restricts and denies is the same person. It is a state that psychoanalysts currently observe in so-called borderline or anaclitic patients who continue to seek a "good mothering" object with whom they can form a permanent, dependent attachment. The negative aspect of the mother can readily gain predominance in Papua New Guinea when the boy becomes bitterly resentful when the mother who had been very protective suddenly abandons him to the harsh masculine world and the cruelty that is an inherent part of the first stage of initiation rituals.

Boys in Western societies commonly form all-male groups in their efforts to overcome dependency on mothers and share experiences in venturing beyond the home. In Papua New Guinea the men form cults that exclude women and not only assert masculine superiority but require that the men place loyalty to the cult above their attachment to their mothers and sisters.[8] The woman's allegiance, in contrast, is toward her children who have been part of her and whom she nurtures. The men, better suited by the evolutionary process for combat and unencumbered by pregnancies and babies, need to form an alliance to protect the women and children, and, as we have seen, compensate for what they do not possess naturally by means of ritual, reaction formation of contempt for women, and arrogation of female creative capacities.

Among the Marind-anim and Kimam-Papuans the large amounts of semen needed for the numerous anointments and for mixing with food gives the men a position of superiority. However, it is collected largely by means of serial coitus with girls and women whose vaginal secretions are not considered detrimental to the initiate's growth or to men's health. The men's reluctance to have heterosexual intercourse and preference for homosexual sodomy derive, according to myth and ritual, from fears of being trapped in the woman's vagina, and fears of the "dentate" or castrating vagina; both fears, as we have commented, may be fears of ambivalent wishes. Whether the fears of castration are precursors of the fears in other regions of Papua New Guinea of vaginal emanations and the female libido, or a regional equivalent to such fears, both would seem to derive from fears of the desire to remain attached to the mother and the need to disidentify from her.

Here, as among the Telefomin area societies, the belief that the primal "ancestor" or "ancestors" who created much of their world and established the way of life the people follow were ancestresses—maternal, creative, and nurturant figures who

---

[8] It is important to recognize what Vanggaard (1972) has examined and summarized in his book *Phallòs*, namely, that sociosyntonic homosexuality and bisexuality have been present in many societies, including Greece and Rome at the height of their cultures. In ancient Greece it was an honor for a boy to be chosen as the homosexual partner, the *erómenos* of a noble *erastés* whose virtues and nobility of spirit, his arete, he gained via his mentor's semen. The Sacred Band of Thebes, which was the "backbone of the Theban army that conquered the Spartans at Leuctra in 371 B.C." (Vanggaard, 1972, p. 41), was comprised of pairs of lovers who fought side by side, each of whom would die heroically rather than appear cowardly to his partner.

could also be overpowering and devastating. These primal ancestresses interacted with various dema who were probably their offspring who became demigodlike ancestors. In contrast to most other Papua New Guinea cultures, here the ancestors are not fused into a collectivity of ancestor spirits who control fertility and defend the cultural traditions given the people by the primal ancestor but form something akin to a pantheon of figures who bestowed various techniques on the people such as the creation of fire, the knowledge of how to build homes, how to eat coconuts, and so forth. All these primal figures have disappeared but their contributions are remembered in rituals, and the continuation of the rituals seems essential to the preservation of what they gave. We shall elsewhere examine the importance of ancestors in the formation and preservation of all Papua New Guinea cultures; here we are noting and emphasizing the importance, as among the Mountain Ok–speaking peoples, of primal ancestresses who are akin to deities who have little if any place in most Papua New Guinea male-dominated societies. The importance of the primal ancestresses, we believe, furthers both our understanding of the reactive domination of the men and of the longings of people in various parts of the world for maternal goddesses, but also why more cognitive religions such as Judaism and most forms of Protestantism turned away from the worship of maternal figures.

11
The Myth of Matriarchy

The myths that women originally possessed the rituals, ritual objects, and cult houses originally seemed peripheral to our interest in the rituals, in Papua New Guinea that defeminize and masculinize the boys. However, as we sought to understand the men's fears of the engulfing and emasculating powers of women, the existence of beliefs in these male-dominated societies that the women in primordial times carried out men's tasks and controlled the men gained increasing importance in our search for an understanding of the masculinizing rituals.

Aware that myths and beliefs existed in Africa and South America, that women originally controlled the rituals and the men, and were reflected in the worship of goddesses in many parts of the world, we thought we might gain further insight by comparing such beliefs and practices in societies unrelated to those of Papua New Guinea that we have been presenting and analyzing.[1] We decided to sample the myths and cultural

[1] The Greek myths of the Amazon women in Asia Minor with whom the great mythic heroes Theseus and Hercules fought and who aided in the defense of Troy do not seem to relate to the myths of Papua New Guinea—although the Sambia believed that a tribe of women who went naked and who killed any man who might come upon them inhabited a distant valley (Herdt, 1981). Cybele and other female deities in Asia Minor, variants of the Great Mother, or the Priestess Queen representative of the earth, were worshipped by peoples with high cultures, and as noted in an earlier chapter, represented men's desires to regain the protection of a mother, and perhaps also to regain an identification with her.

patterns of some peoples dwelling in the rain forest along tributaries of the Amazon in Brazil. The river had gained its name because one of the earliest explorers of the region, Francisco de Orellana, had believed the stories he was told of tribes in which women ruled, hunted, and waged war while the men carried out the domestic tasks.

Myths of the original dominance of women are actually widespread in South America and are not limited to the remote reaches of the Amazon. The Yomana Indians of Tierra del Fuego have not only believed that the women originally possessed the cult house, but that the men were subservient to them and did "women's work" because the women, by wearing masks and painting themselves, had tricked the men into believing they were spirits. Sunman (a primal ancestor) eventually discovered the hoax and a battle ensued in which the women were killed or transformed into animals, after which the men were dominant but continued the rutial practices previously carried out by the women (Bamberger, 1974). The Selk'man Indians who also live near the southern tip of the continent believe that women gained or maintained the subjugation of men through witchcraft, and although the men possessed bows and arrows, they believed themselves powerless in the face of the witchcraft that could make them ill or kill them. Eventually, when the women's oppression became too great, they revolted and murdered all the women. Then to keep the girls from regaining power when they grew up, the men inaugurated a secret cult of their own, banished women from the cult house on pain of death, and kept the women subjugated by posing as spirits (Bridges, 1948).

Along the Amazon, similar myths exist among the Mundurucu (Murphy and Murphy, 1974) and the Mehinaku (Gregor, 1985), as well as elsewhere. The Mundurucu myths tell how the women gained ascendency when three women caught three musical fish that turned into trumpets—sacred objects containing spirits that conferred power on their possessors.[2] In those

---

[2] The Mundurucu horns supposedly originated from fish. Bullroarers, as have been noted, are shaped like fish. The flutes are made of bamboo. All have phallic significance, and carry an implication that women originally possessed penises. However, as the

days women lived in the cult house and forced the men to stay in the dwelling huts and perform domestic tasks. However, the trumpets had to be fed meat to satisfy the spirits and as women could not hunt, they agreed to hand over the trumpets and the cult hut to the men. On the last night of their power, the women forced the men to have intercourse with them through the entire night. Thereafter, in retaliation, if a woman were to enter the cult hut or see the sacred trumpets, she would be gang raped by all of the men of the village.

The Mehinaku, as other groups of Xingu Indians, tell that originally the men lived like animals and the women left them and went to build a village much like they now have with a house for the spirits, and that the women possessed the spirits' flutes. The men found out what the women were doing and attacked the village swinging bullroarers that frightened the women whom they chased and subjugated. (The Dogon people of Mali have a similar myth of the use of bullroarers to frighten and subjugate women [Parrinder, 1967].) The women hid in their houses and that night the men raped them. Here, too, women are forbidden to enter the cult hut or see the flutes and will be gang raped if they do, but they peer through holes in their huts and witness ceremonies in which bullroarers are whirled (Gregor, 1985).

The Amazon Indians, whose myths, like those of the various tribal societies in Papua New Guinea, tell of the initial dominance of the women because of their control of the ritual objects, have a number of other beliefs and customs that are strikingly similar to those of Papua New Guinea peoples. The Mehinaku, like various tribal societies in Papua New Guinea, used both flutes and bullroarers in their rituals, shared meat with the spirits of the flutes, had a sacred men's cult that kept

---

Murphys (1974) have discussed, the fishlike horns are hollow, and have a connotation of penis-swallowing or engulfing objects; and in some ways convey the same fear as that of the enveloping and swallowing anaconda (all women are anaconda) (Gregor, 1985) or of castrating alligators or piranhas. The Mehinaku believe that menstruation is caused by a tiny piranha in the vagina that bites every month (Gregor, 1985).

the ritual objects hidden from women in a cult hut in which the men usually slept. They isolated boys from prolonged periods during puberty during which sexual intercourse was forbidden because it would weaken them. During this period they learned to hunt and gained other masculine skills, culminating in an ear-piercing ceremony in which the bleeding from the ear was treated ritually in the same way as a girl's first menstrual period.

These Amazon tribes also believe that women are inherently lustful and promiscuous and must be controlled by men. Here, too, men run the danger of encountering bewitched women (rather than women witches) who try to seduce and drain every man they meet. Like the Marind-anim and various Trans-Fly peoples, the men have a notable fear of the castrating vagina, which seems to be more powerful than any penis envy in women. Before the Brazilian authorities abolished warfare and headhunting, the Mundurucu were fierce warriors who, like the Marind-anim, went on headhunting raids to far places and were greatly feared. The raiders, like the Marind-anim, captured small children whom they raised as Mundurucu—perhaps, not just to supplement the children born into the tribe, as we have considered in discussing the Marind-anim and Kimam-Papuans, but as an arrogation of the maternal ability to provide children for the community. The assumption of maternal or female characteristics by the men does not seem to be as widespread as among various Papua New Guinea societies, but the men follow a rather prolonged couvade practice. According to myth, their ear ornaments first came from the pubic hair of the primal ancestress (Gregor, 1985) while the headdress worn at the ear-piercing ceremony originated from the labia (of a bat).

These societies, like those in Papau New Guinea, do not have laws but are governed by customs handed down from primal ancestors; and ancestor spirits are fed meat as an essential aspect of their rituals. Here, too, the societies are essentially egalitarian, and though they have chiefs, the chief, like the Papua New Guinea Big Man, cannot command but only lead and persuade as "the first among equals." As among the indigenes, the men have a primary loyalty to the men's cult that collectively reaches decisions for the community, but the women seem to be more able to assert themselves than in New Guinea societies.

There are, however, notable differences between these Amazon societies and those of Papua New Guinea. There is neither a period of ritualized homosexuality nor the use of semen or its substitutes in the initiations of the boys. The men apparently do not fear women's secretions and emanations other than menstrual blood, though their myths and joking remarks clearly indicate a fear of both the castrating and engulfing vagina. Though husbands properly reside in their cult hut, they frequently sleep in their wives', or some other woman's, hut and even in the woman's hammock. Thus, they do not avoid their young children from fear of the child's contamination by the mother.

Though these are patrilineal societies, they are uxorilocal, and the huts in which the women and their young children live are those of their female agnates. The women have the security of remaining in their mother's home surrounded by female relatives, whereas the husband remains something of an outsider or guest. Although couples from the same village can marry if they come from opposite patrilineal moieties, here the husband rather than the wife is likely to come from another village. The men's cult is thus, to some extent, an alliance of men from different villages who are visitors in homes that belong to the women.

Perhaps the most striking difference of the Mehinaku from virtually all of the peoples of Papua New Guinea is their sexual promiscuity, despite the men's fears of women and particularly their anxieties about sexual intercourse that were very apparent to Gregor (1985), and women's fears of the pain and dangers of childbirth. Among the Mehinaku, though not among the Mundurucu, having a mulitplicity of sexual liaisons at the same time seems to have been a major activity and challenge. Gregor (1985) found both men and women to be very open about their sexuality and sexual affairs and he had little trouble in collecting the statistic that there were 150 possible extramarital pairings between the 37 adults in the village if incest taboos, in-law avoidance, and respect of older persons were taken in account. Eighty-four of the potential 150 extramarital liaisons were actually being carried on. Women who refused men's advances were considered niggardly and were apt to be disliked. Even though most women were reluctant to have sexual relations after they had several children, only a few consistently refused extramarital sexual advances. Although newly married men were apt to resent the seduction of their wives, the resentment did not lead to attempts at vengeance, and a husband soon came to acept his wife's affairs for he would be having sexual relations with other women. Sexual relations were an essential aspect of courting and a girl could not expect a young man to move into the home in which she lived, that is, to marry her, unless she engaged in a sexual relationship with him; and in contrast to the situation in Papua New Guinea, the sexual seduction of married women by adolescent youths was not only accepted but looked upon with amused tolerance.

These Indians, like the indigenes, believe that multiple inseminations are required to form a fetus, but they consider that a child can have multiple fathers. As the husband believes he had done most of the inseminating, he usually assumes that he is the primary father. Here, in contrast to the beliefs of most peoples of Papua New Guinea, but perhaps like the Marind-anim and Kimam, only semen is thought to enter into the formation of the fetus. Some believe that a minute "Grandmother Spirit" that lives just outside the uterus shapes the semen into a boy or girl (Gregor, 1985).

The role of the father in rearing young children among these Amazon tribal societies differs from child rearing in Papua New Guinea in essential ways. Though the father does not formally live with his wife but in the men's hut, he spends a good deal of time with her, and has sexaul relations in her home as well as in the forest. He does not overtly manifest fear of her sexual secretions or imbue sons with such fears. Though the mother is subservient to her husband, she is not dominated or beaten for, surrounded by agnates, she has considerable security. For the children, the home is their mother's domain and a secure shelter provided essentially by women.

The relationship between the mother and small child is highly symbiotic. The Mehinaku mother and child are almost never separated during the first two years of the child's life, much as we have described for the Bimin-Kuskusmin. The mother and baby sleep together naked in the mother's hammock, and infants are nursed whenever they indicate discomfort for at least the first two years and after the first year, the child goes everywhere with the mother, carried on her hip. When slightly older, the child may be placed briefly in the care of a sister, but until shortly before the mother produces another baby, children can feel that their mothers belong to them.

Shortly before giving birth to another baby, a mother weaves a hammock for her child and, at first, places the child in it only after rocking it to sleep in her own hammock. She starts to wean the child gradually and gently, and may let the child nurse occasionally after the birth of a sibling.

Nevertheless, the separation from the mother is usually a very traumatic experience for the child who goes through a fairly lengthy period during which there are episodes of sobbing, rage, and temper tantrums that can bring the mother to the verge of despair and cause her to lose patience and become punitive. Gregor (1985) writes that:

> The key to Mehinaku masculinity is the extraordinarily intense and sensual period of intimacy with the mother during the first years of life. At a time when male children in most cultures have discovered the differences between themselves and their mothers, a Mehinaku boy is still basking in an undiminished maternal warmth. With the arrival of a new sibling, he is evicted from the mother's hammock, and given (at best) second place at the breast . . . anger and dependency are generalized to all women [p. 182].

The boy, and later the man, must guard against regressive urges and tends to fear sexual intimacy with its dependency upon a woman and a reunion with her. The adolescent boys and girls are secluded within their homes for a period, and the boys are warned that sex can stunt their growth, that women emasculate, and those who are most difficult to resist are the most dangerous (Gregor, 1985). The initiations are not as painful and terrifying and do not inculcate the derogation of women and grave fear of sexuality as in many Papua New Guinea societies.

We may consider that the promiscuity of both the men and women may be a resultant of the early symbiotic closeness to the mother that is not countered by severe ritual separation from the mother and the inculcation of fears of women's sexuality prevalent in Papua New Guinea, or derailed by enforced homosexuality. The Mehinaku, despite their anxieties, may be driven by a narcissistic or anaclitic need to regain the admiration and possession of a woman to fill the emptiness left by their mothers' seeming desertion of them.

The Murphys (1974) recognize, as we have, that there is a universal and existential flaw in the male role. Men "are born of women, nurtured and loved by women, protected and dominated by women, yet must become men" (p. 226). Aside from the young child's relationship to his mother being charged with sexuality, the mother provides the child's earliest source of identification, "his first breakthrough from his primary narcissism . . . a terrible bond . . . not easily broken" (p. 226). We do not consider the child's earliest state to be "narcissistic" or even "autoerotic" but symbiotic, but the essential concept is the same. They also note that the boy's transition to masculinity is tenuous, for powerful forces press to reverse the developmental process to a return to passivity. The mother figure is "a destroyer as well as a giver of life" (p. 226), for the ultimate goal of regression is the return to the womb. The Murphys (1974) state the core of the matter, and note the great importance not only of the child's initial dependence upon the mother and erotized attachment to her that psychoanalysts have studied, but also the child's identification with her. They also discuss the fundamental conflict between a desire or instinctual drive to experience life, that Freud termed *Eros* and tended to equate with the pleasure principle, and a return to a protected state of dependency, and even a return to the womb that is simultaneously desired and feared, and which might be termed the "Nirvana principle" that has both similarities and notable differences from Freud's *thanatos* or death instinct.

Freud had, for a time, accepted and used the term "Nirvana principle," essentially as an instinct to get away from stimuli and tensions, or maintain a constrained level of excitation. The many problems in accepting Freud's (1920) death instinct, to which he attributed aggressive, destructive impulses, cannot be considered here. The opposition between the desire to experience and grow into life as against the regressive pull back to total dependency seems to us a more fundamental and universal problem of humankind.

The Murphys (1974) considered that the Mundurucu men's cult concealed the men's fragility and vulnerability from themselves and the women. "They are transients in their houses and their communities, their own sense of unity is uneasily maintained" (p. 226) and gives rise to an even stronger unity among the women. The men banded together in their cult as a major defense against their fear and desire to regress.

Neither the Mundurucu nor the Mehinaku, however, have a society with as marked a division between the sexes as in Papua New Guinea that requires similar strenuous measures to transform little boys into men, or in which the men manifest such severe and divisive fear of the female libido as in many Papua New Guinea societies.

It is, of course, of great interest that the Murphys, anthropologists and not psychoanalysts, had prior to the studies of Herdt and the psychoanalytic commentaries on the initiation rituals in Papua New Guinea (Lidz and Lidz, 1977, 1984; Stoller and Herdt, 1982), found in their material the critical importance of the boy's identification with, and dependency upon, his mother as well as his libidinal attachment to her. Moreover, they emphasized the fears of castration and engulfment by the mother rather than fears of castration by the father that has been prominent in psychoanalytic theory, and also recognized the cardinal conflict between the need to separate from the mother and gain masculine independence and the magnetism of the desire to regain her protection and nurturant comfort.

The parallels between the Amazon and Papua New Guinea cultures are striking. They include, for example, the belief that women originally possessed or invented the rituals and ritual objects; the secret men's cults with their cult houses from which women are rigidly excluded on pain of death or gang rape; the residence of the men in the cult house separate from their wives and children; the ritual use of bullroarers and flutes that designate or contain ancestor spirits; the belief that multiple inseminations are required to form the fetus; the men's anxieties about having heterosexual relations; the bleeding of the boys and their isolation as part of their initiation into the men's cult; the belief that female witches or bewitched women attract in order to drain a man sexually and thereby kill him. Closely related beliefs and practices are also found in Africa (among the pygmies [BaMbreti] in the Congo [Turnbull, 1962], the Kowo of Guinea, and in the mythology of the Poro societies of Sierra Leone, Guinea, and surrounding regions [Parrinder, 1967], for example) though not as clearly and as explicitly as in Papua New Guinea and the Amazon.

The similarities can be attributed to dispersion or to homology which are related concepts; to analogy, the separate origin due to similar circumstances; or to a "collective unconsciousness" transmitted by Lamarckian evolution as Carl Jung believed; or as a few seem to propose, to common structural characteristics of the brain that give rise not simply to common syntactical structures in different languages but to common ideas throughout mankind (Chomsky, 1978).

The attribution of the similarities of New Guinea and Amazon cultures to dispersion or homology, that is, an origin from a common root, seems very unlikely. According to current concepts they both would have derived from Asia, and the connection between Amerindian and Asiatic cultures goes back 25,000 years when a land bridge connected Siberia and Alaska. While it is possible that a more recent linkage between Africa and New Guinea may have existed for Melanesians, who migrated from southeast Asia into the Pacific in several waves, though still many thousands of years ago, and may have previously migrated to Asia from Africa; it is unlikely that there could have been such connections between New Guinea and South America. Whereas it is possible, and even probable, that Polynesians reached South America, there has been no indication that Melanesians made such extensive migrations across the Pacific. Aside from their Fijian outpost, all of the islands they occupy are part of a chain from Asia in which the next island is actually or virtually visible. Bamberger (1974) even doubts that peoples as widely separated and living in such different climes as the equatorial Amazon and frigid Tierra del Fuego attained similar beliefs about the primal dominance of women through cultural diffusion. It is unlikely, but not impossible, for the extent of origins of customs by diffusion or homology may be difficult to imagine. For example, Wasson (1985), the distinguished ethnomycologist, has found that both the Mayans and the people of India in Vedic times believed that the mushroom, *Amanita muscaria*, was the product of lightning striking Mother Earth, and that the belief crossed from Asia into the Americas over 25,000 years ago. Perhaps, the major reason to discount a homologous origin for the Papua New Guinea and Amazon myths, rituals, and customs is that they are so very similar, whereas one would anticipate much greater divergence after 25,000 years and such lengthy migrations. Even the relatively proximate cultures of Papua New Guinea that clearly arose through homology from one or more root cultures show much greater divergencies.

Whereas the attribution of the marked similarities to analogous origins also seem unlikely, less idiosyncratic, similar living patterns that arose virtually everywhere arose by analogy such as the division of life's tasks between men and women due to the nature of the structure of men and women. Women are tied to the birth and nurture of children, and men have evolved into larger and more muscular beings.[3] The degree to

---

[3] The women's liberation movement can lead us to forget that the traditional social roles of men and women were established before the evolution of homo sapiens, and that equivalent capabilities for many occupations became possible only with reliable contraception, disposable menstrual pads (circa 1917), baby food formulas, and the mechanization of some occupations.

which very different branches of the evolutionary process can develop similar physical characteristics by analogy becomes apparent by a comparison of the animals and birds of Australia with those of Eurasia and the Americas (Gould, 1982, 1986). It has been apparent that the marsupials of Australia developed species very similar to the placental mice, bear, and wolves, though these two evolutionary branches of animals arose from an extremely remote common ancestor that did not resemble either line, probably from monotremes (egg laying animals such as the echidna and platypus) as an intermediary form between them and reptiles. The analogous but unrelated species arose in response to similar environments.[4] More surprising is the evolution of the Australian birds. Many species closely resemble European and Asiatic species, and had long been thought to be variants of them, descended from birds that had flown in—much like the divergence of finches in the Galapagos. However, molecular biological studies (Sibley and Alquist, 1981, 1985) have proved that the Australian warblers, thrushes, fly catchers, and so on, are unrelated to the similar species in Eurasia and the Americas but developed into similar species by analogy. Of course, in contrast to biological forms, the differentiation of cultural homology from cultural analogy cannot be made through the study of biological markers and can be confused by migrations and the influences of contiguous but analogous cultures.

For example, Fiji, the outpost of Melanesian cultures, has been influenced by its Polynesian neighbors, particularly by an invasion from Tonga. Still, the transition from Polynesian to Melanesian cultural characteristics can be noted on the small islands between the two groups. However, for reasons we have presented, it is fairly certain that the Papua New Guinea and

---

[4] When South America was joined to Australia it was also inhabited by marsupials, whereas North America had none. However, when the land connection between the northern and southern American continents formed, mammals replaced the South American marsupials, aside from the opossum—a marsupial that survived and migrated into North America.

Amazon cultural characteristics we have been considering arose through analogy.

We find that the anthropologists who have studied the Mendurucu and Mehinaku, like their counterparts in Papua New Guinea, do not give credence to the idea that the myths transmit a reality that had once existed. Such beliefs reflect rather the young child's identification with the mother, and the boys' dependency and attachment to mothers who, during the men's childhood, controlled and protected the child and provided a sort of "golden age" in which an ever-flowing breast nurtured and satiated, and the warmth and odor of the mother's body furnished security and a union with an all-caring and providing person that would never be found again.[5]

When we consider, then, the myths of primordial matriarchies are not without a foundation in reality. In these societies the home in which the child lives for the first six to 12 years of his life is essentially matriarchal, even though the larger society is strongly patriarchal. In many Papua New Guinea societies, the father has little if any place in the mother's hut. Along the Amazon the societies are uxorilocal, and the early mother-child relationship is intensely close, and although the father plays more of a role in the small child's life than in Papua New Guinea, he is an outsider, a visitor in the matrilineal home, who gains security and dominance by uniting with other husbands, many of whom are also outsiders, into the men's cult.

Although it is very unlikely that these societies were ever matriarchal, it is quite likely that they were once matrilineal and have not fully changed to patrilineality. We have noted the profound importance of the mother's brother to the mother and her children in many Papua New Guinea societies, and particularly along the Papuan Gulf in the Trans-Fly region. Among the Marind-anim and Kimam-Papuans, the child's paternity remains obscure because numerous patrikin participate in inseminating

[5] Günter Grass in *The Flounder* imagines how in the Stone Age the women "suckled their men until . . . they were all . . . sated. Never again, never in the future that dawned later on, were we so sated. We were suckled and suckled. Always superabundance was flowing into us. . . . It was always suckling time. . . . There were no fathers. Matriarchy held sway. It was a pleasantly historyless age" (pp. 19–20).

the mother. Among the Mehinaku marital promiscuity is so common that they believe in multiple paternity. Among such peoples it is a wise mother who knows the child's father. The identity of the mother is apparent and thus matrilineal descent can take precedence over the patrilineal.

It is extremely unlikely that women would have invented the rituals that give rebirth to boys to turn them into men, but they may have conducted, as many still do, rituals for girls at their menarche, and the men followed their example and produced ceremonies relating to pubertal development in boys.

The women could have originally possessed the flutes either to mark their patrilineage or matrilineage, particularly when they live among their husband's patrilineage. The Sambia refer to the sound of the flutes as the "female hamlet spirit" and, as we have remarked, the sex of the flutes is often ambiguous. A large flute or wooden horn is called "the mother of the flutes" and would seem to mark the unity of the various patrilineages in a village or phratry. The different tunes played by each set of flutes represent the song of a bird that marks the patrilineage, and the bird may also represent the ancestors of the lineage, in accord with the belief, particularly prevalent among the various peoples of the Great Southern plateau, that when a person dies, his or her essential spirit is transformed into a bird that flies away. They are thus filling two functions attributed to "totems"—as a symbol of the group and as an object or animal (here a bird) that contains the ancestor spirits and therefore is sacred and must be fed.

Lévi-Strauss (1962) in *Totemism* seems to us to confuse matters by designating three different usages of the term *totem*, pointing out quite correctly that nowhere are the three usages filled. His analysis does not consider that the term has sometimes been misused, and that a basic meaning exists that relates to beliefs that animals or objects are, or contain, dead ancestors that will be reborn—as in parts of Australia—and thereby are sacred to the group and also designate the essence of the group.

The need for women to have markers of their patrilineage is

greater than the men's need in patrilineal societies, but the men may have arrogated the flutes, symbolic of their masculinity. In the Mundurucu myth, the musical fish that turned into their sacred horns have the shape of bullroarers. Murphy and Murphy (1974) suggest that the horns represented the women's phalluses, but they are also hollow tubes, and "In their cavities dwell the ancestral spirits, just as the real cavities of women contain the regenerative potential of the people and the clans" (p. 94). Men here jokingly refer to the vagina as "the alligator's mouth," so that although these instruments are a male possession they have a female significance.

It is essential that boys overcome their identification with their mothers as well as their attachment to them and dependence on them, but the process can unfold in various ways. It is apparent that it will be and must be very different in the settings in Papua New Guinea and along the Amazon that we have been describing from the process in nuclear families in which the parents form a coalition in relating to their children. We are suggesting that the striking similarities between the myths and rituals of various Papua New Guinea and Amazon societies can be understood as analogies that developed because in both areas the children are raised in the mother's home, a little matriarchy within a patriarchal society, and in which the boys, who received lengthy and strongly erotized nurturance from the mother, gained a core feminine identity from her in the absence of a paternal figure to interpose himself between the boy and his mother and provide a masculine figure to emulate. Under such circumstances the transformation of the boy into a man requires rituals of defeminization and masculinization and the initiation into a male cult with mysteries that serve to offset women's natural procreative and nurturant capacities.

Closely similar though less intense problems exist for the development of males in other societies, and as becomes apparent to heedful psychoanalysts, leave residues of varying degrees of longings for reunion with the mother, uncertainties concerning gender identity; anxieties concerning sexual relationships; a need to escape female guidance and protection during midadolescence, at least; a desire for masculine figures with whom to identify and a wish for membership in a male group to provide strength to counter the regressive pull toward dependence upon women. The existence of several of these problems, or at least the reason for them, has been so hidden, so deeply repressed, that they had not been apparent to psychoanalysts until recently.

12

Masculinization in Papua New Guinea and Its Impact on Psychoanalytic Theory

The different ways boys grow up and develop into men in Papua New Guinea than in the countries in which psychoanalysis developed, particularly the very conscious and concrete ways in which they are defeminized and masculinized in contrast to the almost unnoted and virtually unconscious manner in which these processes occur in modal Western families, requires reconsideration of some critical psychoanalytic tenets. Still, when we examine the processes of masculinization in both Western cultures and in Papua New Guinea, we find that despite the vast differences, some basic aspects of male development noted by psychoanalysts and child development specialists are utilized in masculinizing boys in Papua New Guinea.

The human condition is such that babies everywhere are born of women and live in a dependent symbiosis with their mothers during the first year or two of their lives, gradually differentiate and individuate from the mother, and become seriously disturbed if separated from her unless properly prepared to accept a suitable substitute.[1]

---

[1] The seminal work of Mahler et al. (1975) may exaggerate the problem because a

Children gradually develop boundaries between themselves and their mothers, and in the process gain an image of their own bodies, in part by reciprocal interaction with the mother and through reversing roles with her in play. They internalize the mother and her ways and thus gain a core identification with her. The attachment between mother and child is fostered by various inborn factors that have been examined by Bowlby (1969), and as we have noted, by the attraction of mother's pheromones. As the child forms boundaries, the symbiosis breaks down into a dependent (anaclitic) love for the mother that is strengthened by the erotic aspects fostered by the sensuous nature of the maternal care, and into an identification with her as the child develops in a close relation to her and takes in her ways.

The development into a boy or girl obviously differs, and the differentiation starts at a very early age, and in some respects before birth. Freud, whose attention was focused primarily on libidinal development, paid little attention to the child's primary identification with the mother, at least until he wrote "Inhibitions, Symptoms and Anxiety" (1926). As we have commented, he considered that girls have a more difficult developmental task than boys because a girl has to shift her attachment from the mother as the primary love object to the father, as well as because of feelings of inferiority and deprivation due to her lack of a penis. Freud did not consider that the achievement of masculinity constituted anything of a problem for the boy—unless his innate bisexuality was weighted to femininity. The boy's possession of a penis made him superior (or at least feel superior), and Freud did not recognize that the need to overcome the primary identification with the mother could create grave developmental difficulties. The exploration of the complexities of the boy's disidentification with the mother and the need to gain a male identity was left to other analysts. To

---

considerable part of their studies was carried out at a nursery school rather than in the familiar setting of the home, and little attention was given the fathers or the relationships between the parents. However, the effects of the lack of mothering have been well documented by Spitz (1962) and others; and the withdrawal from the mother by Bowlby (1960), Provence and Lipton (1962), Ainsworth (1962), and others.

Freud, the crucial problem for the boy lay in the resolution of his oedipal complex—overcoming his erotic attachment to his mother and the anxiety (castration anxiety) engendered by the projection of his rivalrous wishes to be rid of his father.[2]

We believe that it will be useful to review with some arbitrary brevity the current complex concepts of how boys gain a masculine identity, particularly some psychoanalytic findings and theories—a developmental line of male gender identity (Tyson, 1982)—to be able better to compare it with what transpires in Papua New Guinea and to elucidate how some current analytic theories require modification to apply to all of humankind.

The genesis of a male rather than a female infant depends upon the presence of a Y chromosome in the fertilizing spermatozoa. The development of testes that secrete androgens in utero not only directs the further development of internal and later external male genital organs, but it has become reasonably certain that the male hormone acts on the fetal brain to switch on certain circuits that promote male behavior (Diamond, 1965; Young, Goy, and Phoenix, 1964).[3] While it is unlikely that such hormonal influences on the fetus induce patterned male behavior, they might well influence males and females to learn behaviors and emotional patterns appropriate to their genders (Hamburg and Lunde, 1966; Green, 1974).

[2] Freud's chapter on Identification in "Group Psychology and the Analysis of the Ego" (1921) is rather puzzling and even perplexing. It is difficult to understand how in view of his awareness of the infant and young child's intense relationship to the mother, he could write:

Identification is known to psycho-analysis as the earliest expression of an emotional tie to another person. . . . A little boy will exhibit a special interest in his father . . . [and] takes his father as an ideal. . . . It fits in very well with the Oedipus complex, for which it prepares the way. . . . At the same time . . . or, a little later, the boy has begun to develop a true object-cathexis toward his mother, according to the attachment (anaclitic) type [p. 105].

[3] In chimpanzees, at least, such influences direct males from birth to more active and aggressive play, and females to an interest in infants and a greater interest in grooming behavior (Goodall, 1963, 1965, 1986). Girls of mothers who during pregnancy were given progestins, which have an androgenlike effect, tend to be tomboys (Money and Erhardt, 1972).

The allocation of a male or female identity at birth is clearly important. Parents tend to relate to boys and girls differently even in early infancy, and rather continuously convey a childhood gender to the child. A number of factors have been noted by analysts and others interested in early child development. Babies manifest an interest in their genitalia, and commonly stimulate them during the second half of the first year of life—boys usually earlier than girls (Kleeman, 1965, 1966; Roiphe, 1968; Roiphe and Galenson, 1981). All children start life in a symbiotic relationship to the mother, and genital stimulation, like thumb sucking, may alleviate periods of separation from her by what we might term *transitional self-gratification* that antedates the dependence on transitional objects. Roiphe (1968) believes that the early erotic play suggests that an "anal-genital stage" antedates the boy's phallic stage; that is, that genital erotism occurs earlier than classic analytic theory assumed. The term "anal-genital" may be inappropriate, but it is apparent that many boys (as well as some girls) gain pleasure from playing with their genitalia very early in life. The integration of the male genitalia with an image of the self or body image proceeds more slowly than that of the thumb and toes (Kleeman, 1965). The reciprocity that takes place between the child and mother when the child is between 18 and 24 months plays an important role in the child's attainment of a firm body image, as Greenacre (1921, 1950) emphasized. Roiphe and Galenson (1981) place boys' inclusion of their genitalia into their body image at an even earlier age, and the boy may seem puzzled at the change in his penis with erection. Fenichel (1945) noted that very little boys may become intrigued by the father's urinary stream as well as the size of his penis. Urinating from a standing position may be a decisive marker in a boy's distinguishing himself from girls.

Boys are usually more active than girls even in infancy. A mother often relates more actively with a son than with a daughter (M. Cohen, 1966) and her pride in having created a son may bolster the boy's self-pride or "narcissism." Fathers are apt to interact more roughly with little boys than with girls, and from very early in a boy's life usually seek to counter feminine characteristics (Goodenough, 1957). Kleeman (1971) noted that by about 12 months a girl behaved in a coy, flirtatious manner with her father but not with her mother. It is difficult to know if such behavior demonstrates an innate characteristic or a response to fathers' tendencies to feel freer to show affection and softness to a daughter than to a son. Erikson (1959) considers that the boy, because of his penis, tends to be intrusively active, whereas the girl because of the nature of her genitalia develops feelings of an inner space that influences her feelings about herself and her ways of relating that are receptive and can even be ensnaring.

Clearly the establishment of a firm gender identity is complex, subject to a multiplicity of influences. Neither purely genetic nor purely environmental explanations of the origins of gender roles and orientations are adequate. Some time before the age of three, a more general factor comes into play. Children have by then deduced what male and female behavior is supposed to be and seek to adhere to the stereotypes they have formed (Kohlberg, 1966), and as they grow older appreciate more and more complex aspects of maleness and femaleness. Money, Hampson, and Hampson (1957) established, largely on the basis of studies of children with anomalous genitalia that led to erroneous gender allocation at birth, that by the age of two-and-a-half the child's identity as a boy or girl is well ingrained in the child's conscious and subconscious awareness and behavior. Efforts to change (i.e., to correct) a child's gender assignment after that age are likely to create serious problems for the child.

Children know whether they are boys or girls, but not necessarily that they will remain male or female when they grow up. They know what they are but not what they might become; and a boy's wishes to become like his mother, or a girl's envy of her brother's penis can turn fantasies into a belief in the possibility of changing gender. There is ample evidence that many inconsistencies in the little child's self-concept are important developmentally. Freud (1909) noted that "Little Hans" would fantasy "he was a mother and wanted children with whom he could repeat the endearments he had experienced himself"

(p. 93). Jacobson (1950) not only drew attention to the boy's wish to have a baby but suggested that male analysts had neglected or overlooked the preoedipal boy's pregnancy fantasies because of their own reaction formation to such childhood wish/fantasies. Lidz (1976) also considered such problems in the boy's achieving a stable gender identity. Loewald (1951) not only emphasized the boy's fear of, and wish for, reengulfment by the mother as a critical developmental problem, but also noted the possibility that fears of castration by either parent could reflect a wish for a female identity and not simply a fear of the father.

The father clearly is important to the boy's developing masculinity even before the oedipal stage, as he provides an image for identification that fosters the boy's separation-individuation from the mother, and can also be a love object who provides an alternative to the boy's erotic attachment to the mother. Indeed, as Freud (1921) commented, "The father can be taken as . . . an object from which the sexual instincts look for satisfaction" (p. 106); and as Tyson (1986) has noted a boy can have transient fantasies of marrying a man when he grows up that derive from his love for his father. In contrast, the father's jealous hostility to a son can presage a difficult oedipal transition. Then, too, the father's emotional support and the sexual gratification he provides his wife clearly abet the mother's ability gradually to withdraw her erotized interest in her son and the sensuous gratification that accompanies her nurturant care.

There are, in brief, many preoedipal influences affecting a boy's emerging masculinity. We are focusing particularly on the boy's need to rescind his identification with his mother and not simply on how the erotic aspect of his love for her and attachment to her is resolved or repressed. Both are essential to his individuation, but overcoming his identification with her is central to the attainment of a masculine identity—and to some degree to the avoidance of the later choice of a male love object. The love includes both an erotic aspect and an anaclitic love of the nurturing, protecting parent, i.e., a differentiation often overlooked by psychoanalysts. The deerotized love for the mother properly develops into and remains a cardinal object relationship. We have, however, not only considered the difficulties in the way of achieving a masculine identity brought about by the initial identification with the mother, but also by the envy aroused in boys when they recognize that whatever the advantages of possessing a penis, they lack women's natural creative and nurturant capacities.

A renewed interest has arisen in men's initial identification with women and envy of them because of Greenson's (1966, 1968) and Stoller's (1966, 1968, 1974, 1985) analyses of transvestite and particularly transsexual men; from Bettelheim's (1971) recognition that boys envy girls' genitalia and attributes just as girls show penis envy, and from the Lidz and Lidz (1977) study of "male menstruation" in Papua New Guinea. As we presented in chapter 5, Bettelheim (1971) studied the subincision rites of some Australian aborigine tribes, and came to reject the concept that the practice was imposed by adult males to increase the boy's castration anxieties, but rather it helped overcome conflicts concerning gender identity. He believed that to understand such rituals it is necessary to consider the child's preoedipal experiences, including both boys' and girls' close attachment to the mother, "and the ambivalences of boys and girls originating the pre-genital fixations about accepting their prescribed sexual roles" (p. 19).

We can assume that many of these preoedipal influences observed in Western cultures also apply in Papua New Guinea—notably, the biologic influences, the gender allocation at birth, the mother's pride and sense of fulfillment in having a son, the different treatment of baby boys and girls, the boy's incorporation of his genitalia into his body image, the initial dependent symbiosis with the mother and its change into an identification with her and an erotic investment of her, the parents' different interaction with a son than with a daughter, and the little boy's greater activity and movement into masculine play with other boys whereas girls tend to remain more closely associated with the mother.

There are, though, some important differences even in these earliest years. In Western societies the processes of disidentification with the mother and early identification with the father, despite resistances and regressive trends, are essential precursors of the transitions of the oedipal stage (deGroot, 1952). Freud (1921) commented that idealization and identification with the father were prerequisites to the oedipal phase, and Greenson (1968) warned that a prolonged symbiosis with the mother and identification with her can impede and even preclude movement into the oedipal phase and thereby the boy's attainment of a masculine identity. In most Papua New Guinea societies the identification with the mother is prolonged; the father enters the picture late and then not as a primary parent; and often unloved and even unwelcome by the mother, he does not so readily provide a male figure with whom the child can identify. Moreover, in some Papua New Guinea societies, such as the Bimin-Kuskusmin, the mother intensifies the symbiotic phase by the strength of her erotic relationship with her little son. The boy remains essentially his mother's son and is even categorized with the female half of these very dichotomous societies long beyond the time of the oedipal transition in Western culture. The little boy may become angered at the mother's withdrawal of nurturance because of the birth of a sibling, and more clearly by his mother's desertion of him when he is initiated into the male cult, and not because he feels replaced by his father or through envy or rage over his parents' sexual relations, which do not take place in the home. The radical differences in the masculinization process, however, come later.

Despite the attention to the preoedipal influences in the boy's masculinization, virtually all psychoanalytic theories consider them as precursors to the climactic occurrences in the oedipal or phallic stage of (libidinal) development, which is placed somewhat nebulously between the ages of three and five, or by some between three and six.

Freud's discovery of the oedipal conflict and its resolution has been considered, particularly by psychoanalysts, as a landmark in man's struggle to understand himself; and it stands as a cornerstone of psychoanalytic theory though with considerable modification in the thinking of many psychoanalysts.

It may seem unnecessary and even boring to present again the "classic" concepts of the boy's transition through the oedipal phase that is so well known that it has virtually become part of our cultural heritage, but a consideration of some of its modifications and some of its questionable if not untenable aspects will open the way for the understanding of the very different way the oedipal transition occurs in Papua New Guinea.

Freud, as we have discussed, took the boy's masculine identity and his initial identification with his father as a given, that is, as inherent (except in boys with anomalous innate bisexuality). Freud became convinced that children develop an intense sexualized love for the parent of the opposite sex with the shift in the investment (cathexis) of libido from the anal area to the genitals at the phallic stage of childhood. The child desires and seeks sexual gratification with the parent of the opposite sex and wishes to marry the parent. We shall confine our considerations to the boy, for as Freud came to realize, the girl's oedipal situation is not, as he originally believed, the converse of the boy's. The boy who has identified with his father now becomes his rival for the mother and wishes to be rid of his father. He not only projects his hostility onto his father, but as he becomes aware of the connection between his erotic fantasies about his mother and his genital sensations may fear that his father will settle matters by cutting off his penis. Such "castration anxiety" has been deemed the source of almost all anxiety, including anxiety about dying, despite the rather obvious precedence of separation anxiety. Unable to tolerate the anxiety, the boy renounces his sexual desires for his mother, and takes on father's real or imagined prohibition against such wishes, and instead seeks to become a man like his father who can gain a wife like the boy's mother. Thus, in renouncing or repressing his sexual desires for his mother, he gains a superego by internalizing the paternal veto and, at least, begins to become capable of controlling his instinctual drives. In the process, he reaffirms his identification with his father and consolidates his masculinity.

It has been believed that with the resolution of the oedipal complex the boy enters a new phase—either because of a biological subsidence of libidinal impulsions or because of their repression—a *latency period* when he is relatively free from conflict-producing libidinal drives until the onset of puberty.

There is no evidence that the child experiences an upsurge of libido during the oedipal period, in the sense of increased sexual drive such as takes place at puberty. Efforts to detect an increase in hormones that might be pertinent have failed. Gonadotrophic hormones are not detectable, nor are steroids that are considered to reflect the secretion of androgens. Estrogen secretion measured by bioassay is negligible (Hamburg and Lunde, 1966). The events can be explained in other ways, notably by how the child comes to terms with his feelings toward his parents and settles into his place as a male childhood member of his family and identifies himself as a member of a specific family.

Many analysts no longer tend to separate the oedipal period from the preoedipal as distinctly as was formerly the case. There has been a steady increase in designating various preoedipal origins of psychopathology. The popularity of the concepts fostered by both Kohut (1971) and Kernberg (1975) may well relate to their focus on narcissistic problems—perhaps more correctly stated, on difficulties arising during a child's movement away from the symbiosis with the mother. The studies of Mahler and her coworkers (1975) on the separation-individuation process—in a sense on the child's earliest steps toward individuation or the attainment of an "ego identity"—have served to release psychoanalysts from explaining psychopathology primarily in terms of libido theory and dislocations of the oedipal phase, concepts which they have not been able to discard readily because so much of psychoanalytic theory depends on them.

Cultural questions are also involved. Psychoanalysis had its origins in a strongly paternalistic Europe where fathers were not only dominant, but whose interactions with their small children were often formal and rather limited. The father was often regarded by small children, and particularly by sons, as a feared, punitive intruder.[4] Earlier in this century, actual castration threats made to stop the child's masturbation that was believed to weaken both body and brain, indeed, to be a major cause of insanity, were common. Times have changed. In the United States, and we believe increasingly in Europe, the father does not dominate his wife and children, though he may retain an "instrumental" role while he, out of necessity, but also because of changed concepts of masculinity, shares many nurturant functions with his wife.

Of course, there are fathers who tyrannize the home and may physically express their jealousy of their sons, and fathers who spend little time in the home, or desert their families; and there are mothers who use a son to complete their lives that have been frustrated because they are women, and others who reject a child who ties them to an unwanted marriage. The variations are infinite; and attempts to stereotype the course of the oedipal transition have sometimes led psychoanalysts astray. However, if we are to generalize about the oedipal transition and the oedipal period for boys in the United States, we would suggest the following considerations.

All children need to overcome the intense, and usually erotized bonds to their mothers that were essential to their preoedipal development. They do so for reasons that may or may not include fear of the father. The mother properly gradually frustrates her child's attachment by diminishing the

---

[4] The difference between European and American giants—symbolic of father figures—is notable. Grimm's and other European giants are fearsome and often cannibalistic figures whom the heroic boy overcomes. American giants are heroic, grandiose figures: Paul Bunyan, John Henry, Finn McCool, Popeye, Superman, etc.— whom the boy would like to emulate.

physical care she provides as the child becomes increasingly competent. Knowingly or unknowingly, she creates boundaries between herself and the child, a process fostered and required if she has another child. The boy has wished to marry his mother, and may have thought he had pleased her when he confided: "I'm going to marry you when I grow up." Now, he realizes that she has not shared his wish. She loves his father who has very important prerogatives denied the boy, such as sharing a bed with mother, and often enough the boy knows that his father has sexual relations with her. He realizes that when he is old enough to marry, his mother will be as old as his grandmother. Now as he becomes aware of his separation from his mother, and also something of his parents' limitations in their ability to protect him, he becomes aware of his vulnerability. Nightmares may accompany the anxieties that come with his growing independence or reflect his own hostility to one or both parents or a sibling, and not simply a fear, real or projected, of his father. Mahler (1971) did not attribute the child's increased effort to remain close to the mother during the rapprochement phase of development to an increase in libido at the start of the so-called phallic phase, but to heightened awareness that the mother was a separate person.

The child is gaining the ability to sort reality from fantasy, and the need to come to terms with his relation to his parents is a crucial aspect of coming to grips with reality. The blow to the boy's narcissism and sense of security can be severe; and the child's resentment toward his mother because of her imagined rejection of him can be extreme, and even reach matricidal proportions when actually rejected. It is at this juncture in life that the boy develops a defensive pattern, and not simply some mechanisms of defense, to prevent recurrence of the insecurity and loss of self-esteem that might again provoke untenable anxiety, an unbearable sense of loss and emptiness, or the depression that accompanies hostile resentments.

One such defensive pattern is that described by Freud as engendered by the boy's projection of his own hostile feelings toward the father. However, when the father desires the son and gains pleasure and pride in having him, feels secure of his wife's affection, participates in the child's care, and plays and shares with him, he becomes a source of pleasure and security to the child. Thus, any hostile impulses are apt to be short-lived. Indeed, the boy appreciates that having a father has its advantages. He identifies with his father, whom his mother loves, in order to retain his mother's love and eventually to become a man who can attain a love object like his mother; and in so doing gains a masculine model to follow into adulthood. He gains self-esteem by his identification with a man whom his mother respects and admires. Then, too, if he identifies with his father, who he feels is benevolent, he regards his own achievements as extensions of those of his father, rather than rivalrous efforts to supplant him, and is less likely to be inhibited by fears of hubris, an outcome of the metaphorical castration anxiety.

There are, as we have commented, many other ways in which a boy can seek to defend from the anxieties and depressive feelings that follow his sense of loss of primacy with his mother. The alternatives are many, both before and during the oedipal period and the differences do not seem to depend primarily on innate characteristics of the boy, or simply upon how either parent relates to the child, but also upon how the parents relate to one another, and the nature of the family transactions as a whole. Indeed, we may contemplate the entire situation from a different perspective. It has to do with the dynamic structure of the family. A child properly needs two parents, one as a primary love object and the other as an object for identification. Stated very briefly, in most societies it is important for the mother and father to form a parental coalition in which both parents adhere to their respective gender linked roles and maintain adequate boundaries between the parental and childhood generations (Lidz, 1963). Though these requisites may sound simple, they are not readily achieved. To illustrate our meaning: if the parents form a unity, the child's efforts to win one parent or the other for himself, or to insert himself between them are frustrated; if they maintain their gender-linked roles, the child is guided into a proper gender identity; and if the parents maintain boundaries between the generations, the boy does not experience competition for the mother from the father, nor is he misled by the mother's need to have him complete her life or fill her erotic desires (Lidz, 1963, pp. 45–75; Lidz, 1976, pp. 239–240). The child is thus guided into the proper position of being a boy or girl member of the childhood generation. In the process the child overcomes an egocentric, or as some might say, "narcissistic" orientation, and finds and accepts a place as a member of a family, a mutually protective unit, with which he identifies and is identified.

The boy in Western societies has, through one of the ways presented or suggested, gained a masculine identity, but the process is still incomplete. What psychoanalysts have termed the *latency period* is not so latent. Just as there is no evidence of increased hormonal impulsions during the oedipal phase, there is no evidence of their subsidence to furnish a hiatus between the erotic conflicts of the phallic or oedipal phase and the hormonally motivated upsurge of growth just prior to puberty and the urgent sexual drives of adolescence. However, the child moves beyond the family into the world of playmates, schoolmates, and teachers. The boy usually seeks to play with other boys and avoids females both to overcome their importance in his life, because boys are more active and aggressive, and to solidify his maleness. He begins to find his place and his worth in comparison with his peers which may differ on the playground and in school. In a disturbing contrast to his home where, optimally, he has been cherished and accepted simply because he is his parents' child, he finds himself evaluated on the basis of achievement and personality by both teachers and agemates, an evaluation that usually, but perhaps unconsciously, includes judgments of his maleness. Then, too, the boy often forms an intimate relationship with another boy, his "pal" or "special friend" with whom he shares adventures and secrets, and with whom he gains the courage to face his increasingly expanding universe. The relationship is not usually erotically charged consciously but some homoerotic play may occur and does not connote that the boy is becoming homosexual unless it becomes a fairly consuming preoccupation or activity.

During adolescence, if not earlier, the predominance of heterosexual fantasies if not activities consolidates the youth's sense of his masculinity. Some will seek and need to have early heterosexual relations, and even to make a girl pregnant to prove their shaky masculinity to themselves and perhaps even more to others. We shall not here consider the importance of marriage and parenthood as an important indication that a person has become a man—a circumstance that, as we have already noted in chapter 6, has particular importance among some Papua New Guinea peoples, and perhaps among all.

The processes by which boys gain a firm male identity in Papua New Guinea are obviously very different from the psychoanalytic concepts based primarily on analyses and observations in Western societies. In Papua New Guinea the achievement of masculinity is a far more overt process that is conscious and purposely fostered by the adult men of the community. Although many of the problems of attaining a secure masculine identity that have been noted by analysts and child development experts are also found in Papua New Guinea because they are inherent in the human condition, attention to how boys are turned into men in Papua New Guinea can clarify some aspects of male development that have remained obscure and rather peripheral in psychoanalytic theory.

It is essential to note that in comparing the boy's development in Papua New Guinea with psychoanalytic concepts, we cannot discuss his defeminization and masculinization in terms of preoedipal, oedipal, and latency periods because in Papua New Guinea there is no oedipal *period*, because the oedipal transition transpires very differently; and moreover in many societies the boy's later childhood is highly erotized.

Throughout Papua New Guinea the family situation is very different and neither the resolution of the boy's erotized relationship with his mother nor his defeminization and masculinization occur prior to the age of five or six. Indeed, the major aspects of these essential processes are induced by a series of rituals that start no earlier than the ages of six or seven, and usually considerably later though prior to puberty. The initial rituals are, as we have emphasized, a means of inducing puberty, which the men believe will not occur naturally as it does in girls. After the many years under the mother's aegis, categorized as a person of the women's houses, with minimal care and direction from the father, the boy is abruptly taken from his mother and initiated into the men's cult. Although it is essential to offset the boy's dependence on his mother that has lasted for so many years, and deerotize his attachment to her, the need to insure the boy's defeminization and masculinization takes precedence. As the very existence of the hamlet or parish depends on its warriors, the men simultaneously seek to inculcate a burning hostility that can later be discharged against enemies.

We have documented how, in most Papua New Guinea societies, the processes of defeminization, masculinization, and deerotization of the boy's oedipal attachments are interrelated, and are not part of a gradual transition, but a sudden and often violent disruption of the boy's earlier attachments, identifications, and life patterns. Here, the intent is not simply to repress the boy's erotic object relationship to his mother, but to eradicate his entire object attachment to her as well as his identification with her, and replace it with a loyalty to the men's cult.

The forcible removal of the boy from his mother into a masculine world, the rituals that tie boys together, and the provision of older youths to admire and even love and with whom the boys can identify are all forceful measures that have less obvious counterparts in Western cultures. We have noted the need of school-age boys to associate primarily with other boys, to find chums, to be judged by peers and elders on the basis of personality and achievement, to follow and learn from older boys, to look upon youths with admiration and even have crushes on an adolescent hero.

In Papua New Guinea the boys are not only separated and

isolated from women but the separation is enforced by repeated warnings of the polluting characteristics of women that have prevented the boy's maturation and the emasculating qualities of women's sexual emanations and secretions. In some areas they spend months or years in a "forest lodge"—in an artificial community devoid of women, but which may include men in female garb, where they learn that men do not need women. The threats of castration if they seduce or are seduced by married women concern the future. When repeated during rituals at puberty they seem a secondary matter, though they may reinforce the taboo against sexual activity with mothers and sisters and against adultery. Indeed, in later life the danger of adultery generally lies in the belief that the woman's husband will take vengeance by sorcery rather than by physical action. The men are not fabricating threats to make the boys stay away from women, but are expressing their own beliefs and fears. It is their duty to protect the boys from women's emanations and, in places such as among the Marind-anim, from their castrating vaginas. It is not the father figure who will castrate but the women.

Depending on the culture, the novitiates are subjected in one way or another with the ideas that they have been contaminated by their mothers, that they cannot develop into men unless their mother's blood that went into their composition is "washed away"; the contaminated foods they have been fed are eliminated; and their defiled skin abraded; that women's sexual emanations will weaken them; that sexual intercourse deprives them of the semen that is the essence of their masculine spirit; that they can be impregnated during intercourse and will die for they have no way of giving birth; that some women are witches who will seek to drain them of semen, or have castrating vaginas; that their penises can become entrapped in the vagina and may have to be cut off. The men in Papua New Guinea have been thoroughly indoctrinated with such fears, but some of these beliefs occur in boys and men in Western societies and their origins have been explored psychoanalytically. These concerns are most likely to occur in boys and men who have had overly possessive, intrusive, and engulfing mothers whose metaphoric embrace is difficult to escape. They must unconsciously utilize strong reaction formation against their own wishes and fears of reincorporation into the mother and of remaining feminine. In Papua New Guinea the boy's prolonged intimate relationship with his mother, and the mother's libidinal investment in her son that is often greater than with her husband, promotes such fears. The men do not need to protect their interests in their wives by threats of castration; the boys are taught that the danger comes from women, as it does when the father does not provide "a paternal veto against the libidinal relationship with the mother. Against the threat of maternal engulfment, the paternal position is not another threat or danger, but a support of powerful force" (Loewald, 1951, p. 14).

The Sambia men, it will be recalled, continue to believe that were it not absolutely forbidden by their primal ancestor, mothers would gladly have sexual relations with their sons—we believe because the men's libidinal desires for their mothers have not been resolved in childhood but rather had been suddenly disrupted.

The belief in, or the unconscious tug of, the power of the mother is reflected in the omnipresent myth that the women originally created the rituals and the ritual objects, and that the men's cult arose in the process of taking possession of the rituals, flutes, and bullroarers that now must be hidden from the women, as well as in the belief of some societies that they did not have a primal ancestor but an ancestress; or, at least, that the pair of ancestors were hermaphroditic, one of whom became male whereas the other was deprived of a penis.[5]

We have commented that boys in Western cultures may become antagonistic to a mother when she withdraws her nurturant care, or when they feel that she has been unfaithful to

---

[5] We might even be led to speculate that the institutions that led to the formation of societies arose from men's needs to counter the attractive power of women, and to move away from women's primary interest in the family to formulate rituals and traditions that would integrate a society—in the sense that religions serve to integrate the ethos and mores of a group (Durkheim, 1915; Evans-Pritchard, 1965; Geertz, 1973).

12 Masculinization in Papua New Guinea and Its Impact on Psychoanalytic Theory 191

them. In Papua New Guinea the first-stage initiates who are treated cruelly by the men have good reason to feel abandoned and deceived by their mothers and develop a misogyny, abetted by the initiators' teachings that women are degraded, polluting, dangerous, and castrating.

The novitiates taken from their nurturant mothers and subjected to severe torment feel lost and regress. They are provided with a sponsor who, when feasible, is the mother's real or classificatory brother who tries to support the boy during the ordeals. Further, among some groups, the boy is taught to suck the bachelors' penises, which among the Sambia are called a "breast nipple" as well as a "glans penis" and the semen is considered identical to breast milk. Some little boys in Western societies will, as noted, because of their identification with their mothers as well as their attachment and love for their fathers, express their fantasy of marrying their fathers, perhaps as a replacement for the desire to marry and be protected by their mothers. In Papua New Guinea the boys may form a strong libidinal attachment to a particular young man. Among the Marind-anim and the Kimam, the boy is virtually married to his binahor (see chapter 11) who properly is his mother's brother.

Although the bachelors' sexual use of the prepubertal boys helps keep the unmarried youths from incest and sexual relations with the women in the community, the insemination of the boys, in many places without sexual relations and through the use of substitutes for semen, is deemed essential to turn the boys into men and provide them with a store of semen. In Western societies when fathers are absent or aloof, or when boys are separated from their parents at an early age and raised in a predominantly male environment, some will develop a compulsive need to be inseminated, and a homosexual relationship serves their needs as well as those of the inseminators. In Papua New Guinea in those societies in which the boys are subjected to oral or anal insemination, just such conditions exist.

Whereas little boys in Western societies may envy their mothers' nurturant and creative capacities, and the breasts and vagina that make these capacities possible, in Papua New Guinea the prolonged symbiotic attachment and identification seem to heighten such desires to have maternal capacities. They are met in various ways. The men believe that whereas women give birth to babies, only men can give birth, or rebirth, to men. They can feed the boys with semen instead of the milk mothers feed babies; and they not only equate semen with milk but consider it more powerful. The Sambia, and probably others, believe that the wife's milk is the husband's transformed semen that she has ingested. Some peoples believe that the woman's vital womb fluids that enter into the conception of a baby derive from her father's semen. Envy of women's natural ability to purify themselves by menstruating is countered by teaching men to menstruate artificially by bleeding themselves. The practice is clearly not a substitute for castration, as men carry it out on themselves and feel strengthened by the procedure. Perhaps, the most important arrogation of creative attributes by the men is their belief that through the possession of the rituals and the ritual objects, they possess the power to influence, and in some areas, control, the ancestor spirits who, in turn, control the fertility of the women, pigs, and soil. Thus, the men through their rituals are responsible for the well-being and productivity of the group, as well as for the group's protection through their abilities as warriors.

Nevertheless, underneath the flamboyant power of the men, and the central significance of the men's cult, we can note not only an envy of women, but a recognition of the basic creative capacities of women and the need for their nurturant care. It is manifest in the belief in the power of the primal ancestress among the Bimin-Kuskusmin and the other "min" peoples who radiate out from Telefomin, and among the Marind-anim and Kimam-Papuans.[6]

We commented in the introductory chapters that the universe of the people of New Guinea was dichotomized into masculine and feminine. We hazard that when the boy-child's

[6] It is prominent in the various religions that worshipped goddesses representative of the earth mother and her nurturant fecundity, and in the centrality of Mary in Catholicism.

separation from his mother and boundary formation from her remains indefinite, and men are not quite certain of their masculine gender, they retain a need to accentuate the difference between masculine and feminine, even to the extent of dividing everything, animate and inanimate, into male and female.

The attainment of a superego is a major factor in strengthening a boy's masculinity. According to conventional analytic theory, the boy develops a superego when he internalizes the paternal prohibitions that terminate the oedipal period, but analysts have recognized that aspects of the superego develop earlier, and that the superego does not arise fully armored like Pallas Athena but takes shape and properly gains strength over many years (Kohlberg, 1963, 1964). Although in Papua New Guinea boys assume some degree of self-control prior to their initiation, they tend to act impulsively and disregard reprimands. Their fathers or father figures, at least among the Sambia, threaten that they will regret their disobedience when they are initiated, but do little else to control the boys (Herdt, personal communication). Then, during the first stage of initiation the boys are punished harshly and forced to be obedient. Major elements of the superego are progressively inculcated over some years when initiates are taught that the mores and ethos of the culture must be maintained to retain the good will of the ancestor spirits.

The material we have been considering indicates that all men, born of women and nurtured by women, have some core feminine component in their makeup—something that the Bimin-Kuskusmin appreciate in the belief that a female "khaap-khabuurien" spirit exists in all children, but a male "finiik" spirit gains prominence in men through the initiation rituals with the transfer of "semen" to the initiates. Even the phallic masculinity that is so prominent in Papua New Guinea, as we might expect from psychoanalytic theory, overlies a core female identity which is not fully overcome by the intense rituals to which the initiates are subjected, by their isolation from women, or by the marked male domination in these societies,[7] as both Herdt and Poole (1982) came to believe. Freud, of course, considered bisexuality inherent to the human makeup because of the nature of genital differentiation in the fetus. We are considering, rather, an orientation that depends upon the nature of the human condition—a psychodynamic orientation. The orientation further indicates that gender identity problems are not, or are not always, related to problems of libidinal drives, but rather to the family structure and transactions.

It is also striking that in many Papua New Guinea societies, much as in some ancient Greek cultures, homosexuality is the road to masculinity and is fostered by the fathers. Despite the strong embedding of homosexuality in boys and bachelors adult men are essentially heterosexual. Among the Sambia, for example, adult homosexuality is uncommon. Although it has been argued that the oral and anal insemination forced upon the young initiates is not truly homosexual but simply a means of providing boys with the semen they are believed to require in order to mature, Herdt found that among the Sambia the relationship between a boy and his inseminator can be strongly erotized. However, in various Papuan Gulf societies men have prolonged homosexual relationships with boys, and apparently prefer homosexual sodomy to vaginal intercourse.

---

[7]The same developmental problems exist for boys in the southern and western highland societies in which obligatory initiation rituals do not exist. However, among the Huli in the southern highlands, about half of the boys voluntarily (?) go through initiation to become members of the "bachelors club" and pay an entrance fee to do so. They are secluded for about two years during which they are taught various types of magic and to be self-reliant and to disdain physical discomfort, and thereafter spend another year when they appear only on certain ritual occasions (Glasse, 1968). Beliefs concerning female contamination are very prominent. Among the Mae Enga and Kyaka of the western highlands, the initiation may not be as formal as among the tribal societies we have discussed, but boys are encouraged to move into the men's hut when around six, and in adolescence they participate in extensive rituals to undo the contamination by women which includes a period of seclusion in isolated huts (Meggitt, 1965). Here, too, the men are extremely fearful of female sexual pollution and consummate their marriages only after learning the magic that protects them from their wives' menstruation. When a man finally has intercourse he mentally utters a spell to prevent the loss of his vital juices through the ejaculate, and supposedly continues to use such copulation magic either for a year or until the birth of his first child (Meggitt, 1965).

* * *

There are a number of similarities in the way in which indigene boys are raised to family situations that have been noted to lead to homosexuality in Western societies. It seems likely that in many parts of Papua New Guinea the homosexuality is sociosyntonic and fostered because of inclinations that derive from the family structure. We do not intend to pursue in detail the nature of these similarities, or to consider just how the examination of the conditions in Papua New Guinea may clarify our understanding of various types of homosexuality in our own society, but rather to comment on several aspects that may help explain why some men become homosexual.

Homosexuality is a term that encompasses a spectrum of activities and fantasies. We believe that the understanding of the various practices in Papua New Guinea serves to accentuate the recognition that three factors that are commonly interrelated enter into the etiology of homosexuality: confusion of gender identity; homoerotic object investment (cathexis); and fear of, or hostility to, women.

We have discussed the Papua New Guinea boy's prolonged identification with his mother that leaves him with a core feminine identity. In our society a mother who identifies her son with herself and keeps him symbiotically attached to her; the absence of a father or an aloof father who fails to insert himself between the boy and his mother and to supply a male figure with whom to identify; and a mother's contempt for the boy's father, are likely to foster a boy's continuing identification with his mother and may be a factor in the etiology of homosexuality. The boy in Papua New Guinea also has a strong libidinal attachment to a mother who provides affection, protection, and nurturance which may well guide the youth back to heterosexuality even when he has passed through a lengthy period of homosexuality. Freud believed that a major factor in the etiology of homosexuality was the inseminator's desire to nurture the boy as he had wished to be nurtured. Similarly, we have considered that when a youth gives a boy his penis to suck, he is identifying with his mother in using his penis as a breast, and counters his envy of women's nurturant capacities by the belief indoctrinated in Papua New Guinea that he possesses a more powerful, masculinizing milk in his semen.

Kolb and Johnson (1955), in line with the Johnson and Szurek (1952) hypothesis concerning "acting-out" in general, believe that when homosexuality occurs in Western societies, one or the other parent unconsciously, or not so unconsciously, encourages it; for example, when a father hands over the son to act out his own homosexual impulses toward a man, or the mother prefers to keep her son from a sexualized attachment to any other women. In Papua New Guinea societies that inseminate orally or anally, the boy does not initially choose a male sexual object. The homosexual activity is forced upon him by father figures and only after he has been forced into the practice does he erotize specific persons. Regressed after his abrupt separation from his mother, and forced to live among men who, at first, treat him brutally, the boy may welcome a nurturant older male and the semen he provides as a replacement for the mother's nurturant breast and food. In Western societies some boys are led into homosexuality through seduction by an important father figure whose authority leads the boy to believe the activity is proper, or whose power forces him to accept it. Then, too, when boys are separated from nurturant women at an early age and placed in an all-male boarding school, as has been the practice in middle- and upper-class circles in Britain, some boys are readily seduced into homosexuality because of their need for some protective figure.

In Papua New Guinea the semen is presumed to masculinize by promoting sexual muturation and instilling the masculine spirit or essence that boys lack. In Western societies some homosexual boys and men compulsively seek out men to inseminate them in order to gain masculinity from them, usually, if not always, if they lacked a father figure with whom they could identify. Some homosexuals in our society compulsively seek to be repetitively inseminated in their need for "masculinization." The passive partner in anal intercourse may, at the same time, identify with the mother in being penetrated by a penis of a dominant male, and some male homosexuals think of the anus as a "dirty vagina." The active partner avoids fear of a castrating or incorporating vagina, and perhaps the fears engendered by the woman's genital odor that had once helped tie him to the mother from whom he must now escape.

The conviction that women's genital secretions are emasculating or that their vaginas are castrating, and that sexual intercourse can be life endangering is indoctrinated into the Papua New Guinea initiates very forcefully. Psychoanalytic studies have found that many men, but particularly homosexual men in Western societies, have similar beliefs. The beliefs are apt to arise in reaction formation to desires to be reincorporated into a mother to whom they had been closely attached; or to a fear of being overwhelmed by a noxious, "castrating" mother.

Thus, although homosexuality is sociosyntonic in many tribal societies in New Guinea, and there serves important functions in masculinizing boys, the underlying origins of the homosexuality are in many respects similar to the etiology of homosexuality in Western societies. The study of the practices in New Guinea can, as Stoller and Herdt (1982) have elucidated in part, confirm and broaden our understanding of male homosexuality and the importance of the family transactions in its etiology. We have dealt with the topic rather sketchily because it has not been a central issue in our studies which focus primarily on the importance of defeminization and masculinization in male development.

Now, although the developmental process in Papua New Guinea that we have sought to outline differs greatly from our own, but as we hope we have made clear, it takes into account the same essential developmental needs of the boy in becoming a man as does our own process. If we recognize that the very different ways of rearing boys in Western cultures and in Papua New Guinea serve to accomplish the same ends, it may not be proper to formulate the oedipal transition as strictly as in analytic theory and certainly not primarily in terms of libidinal stages of development. We may rather consider the oedipal transition, which has been a major focus of psychoanalytic theory as inherent in the human condition, as but one aspect of a necessary continuation of the separation-individuation process after the mother-child symbiosis is overcome, a process that still has a long way to go before the youth achieves true "individuation," and, in Erikson's (1959) terms, an "ego identity," or in terms of libido theory, attains "genital sexuality"—a concept that has remained vague and uncertain.

The studies from Papua New Guinea indicate that there can be very diverse ways of carrying out these tasks that are consequences of the human condition; ways that are very different in Papua New Guinea and Vienna, and to a lesser extent from turn-of-the-century Vienna to the contemporary United States, and from family to family in the United States.

The family configuration in most societies in Papua New Guinea in which the father does not live with his wife and young children and, in general, is not loved or admired by a wife he derogates and misuses illustrates the importance of family structure on children's developmental processes as well as on the structure of the society. The problem, at least what from our standpoint we consider a problem, is circular. Men's fear of female pollution keeps them from living with their wives and young children, which leads, in turn, to boys living under the aegis of their mothers for the first seven to 15 years of their lives. Stringent rituals are then required to defeminize and masculinize the boys into strong warriors, but they nevertheless reactively fear the power of women and must counter their strong ties to and identification with their mothers by avoidance of women's attraction for them in very radical ways. The inculcation of a fear of the incorporative and emasculating qualities of women, and in some places, even a marked hostility toward them perpetuates the cycle and prevents the formation of a true nuclear family. The failure of men and women to unite properly in a marriage that is mutually gratifying for them and the children has not prevented the formation of a workable, enduring society, but it leaves both men and women bereft of the emotional relationship and sexual satisfaction that alleviate life's tribulations for many persons in other societies.

The developmental process in Papua New Guinea leads to a very different outcome than in the modal contemporary Western family; an outcome that brings into focus the critical issue of masculinization of boys, the force of men's envy of women's natural creative capacities, commonly termed *womb envy*, the importance of men's fears of reincorporation or castration by women that can interfere with heterosexual intercourse, and other related matters that we have discussed. As single-parent families are becoming increasingly common in the United States, both because of divorce and the large number of children born to adolescent unmarried mothers, and in which fathers fill a minimal and sometimes a negative place in the boy's early life, the situations encountered in Papua New Guinea become increasingly pertinent to our own society.

References

Ainsworth, M. S. (1962), Deprivations of maternal care: A reassessment of its effects. Public Health Papers No. 14. Geneva: World Health Organization.
Allen, M. (1967), *Male Cults and Secret Initiations in Melanesia*. Melbourne, Australia: Melbourne University Press.
—— (1984), Homosexuality, male power, and political organization in North Vanuatu: A comparative analysis. In: *Ritualized Homosexuality in Melanesia*, ed. G. Herdt. Berkeley: University of California Press.
Bamberger, J. (1974), The myth of matriarchy: Why men rule in primitive society. In: *Women, Culture and Society*, ed. M. Z. Rosaldo & L. Lamphere. Stanford, CA: Stanford University Press.
Barth, F. (1975), *Ritual and Knowledge among the Baktaman of New Guinea*. New Haven, CT: Yale University Press.
Bateson, G. (1958), *Naven*, 2nd ed. Stanford, CA: Stanford University Press.
Beardmore, E. (1890), The natives of Mawat, Daaudi, New Guinea. *J. Royal Anthropol. Inst.*, 19:459–466.
Berndt, R. M. (1965), The Kamano, Usurufa, Jate and Fore of the eastern highlands. In: *Gods, Ghosts and Men in Melanesia*, ed. P. Lawrence & M. J. Meggitt. Melbourne, Australia: Oxford University Press.
Bettelheim, B. (1971), *Symbolic Wounds*, rev. ed. New York: Collier Books.
Bjerre, J. (1964), *Savage New Guinea*. New York: Tower Publications.
Boelaars, J. (1950), *The Linguistic Position of Southwestern New Guinea*. Leiden: E. J. Brill.
Bowlby, J. (1960), Grief and mourning in infancy and early childhood. *The Psychoanalytic Study of the Child*, 15:9–52. New York: International Universities Press.
—— (1969), *Attachment and Loss*, Vol. 1. New York: Basic Books.
Bridges, E. L. (1949), *Uttermost Part of the Earth*. New York: Dutton.
Brown, P. (1978), *Highland Peoples of New Guinea*. Cambridge, UK: Cambridge University Press.
—— Buchbinder, G., eds. (1976), *Man and Woman in the New Guinea Highlands*. Publication No. 8. Washington, DC: American Anthropological Association.
Brumbaugh, R. C. (1980a), *A Secret Cult in the West Sepik Highlands*. Doctoral dissertation. Department of Anthropology, State University of New York, Stony Brook.
—— (1980b), Models of separation and a Mountain Ok religion. *Ethos*, 8:332–348.

Buchbinder, G., & Rappaport, R. A. (1976), Fertility and death among the Maring. In: *Man and Woman in the New Guinea Highlands*, ed. P. Brown & G. Buchbinder. Publication No. 8. Washington, DC: American Anthropological Association.
Burton, R. V., & Whiting, J. W. M. (1961), The absent father and cross-sex identity. *Merrill-Palmer Quart. Behav. & Develop.*, 7:85–95.
Butler, S. (1872), *Erewhon*. New York: Lancer Books, 1968.
Chomsky, N. (1978), A naturalistic approach to language and cognition. Presented at Meeting of the American Psychoanalytic Association.
Cohen, M. B. (1966), Personal identity and sexual identity. *Psychiatry*, 29:1–14.
Connolly, B., & Anderson, R. (1987), *First Contact*. New York: Viking.
Cowan, B. (1980), The serpent's coils: How to read Caroline Gordon's later fiction. *Southern Rev.*, 16/2:281–298.
Daly, C. (1928), Der Menstruationskomplex. *Imago*. 14:11–75.
deGroot, L. (1952), Reevaluation of the role of the Oedipus complex. *Internat. J. Psycho-Anal.*, 33:335–342.
Diamond, M. (1965), A critical evaluation of the ontogeny of human sexual behavior. *Quart. Rev. Biology*, 40:147–175.
Doi, T. (1973), *The Anatomy of Dependency*. Toyko: Kodansha International.
Durkheim, E. (1915), *Elementary Forms of the Religious Life*. New York: Free Press, 1965.
Erikson, E. (1959), Growth and Crises of the "Healthy Personality." *Psychological Issues*, Vol. 1. No. 1, Monograph No. 1. New York: International Universities Press.
Ernst, T. M. (1978), Aspects of meaning and exchange and exchange items among the Onabasulu of the Great Papuan Plateau. *Mankind*, 11:187–197.
Errington, F. K. (1974), *Karavar*. Ithaca, NY: Cornell University Press.
Evans-Pritchard, E. E. (1965), *Theories of Primitive Religion*. London: Oxford University Press.
Fenichel, O. (1945), *The Psychoanalytic Theory of the Neuroses*. New York: W. W. Norton.
Ferenczi, S. (1924), *Thalassa*. Albany, NY: Psychoanalytic Quarterly Inc., 1938.
Festinger, L. (1957), *A Theory of Cognitive Dissonance*. Stanford, CA: Stanford University Press.
Fortune, R. F. (1963), *Sorcerers of Dobu*, rev. ed. London: Routledge & Kegan Paul.
Freud, A. (1965), Normality and Pathology in Childhood, Vol. 6, *Writings of Anna Freud*. New York: International Universities Press.
Freud, S. (1909), Analysis of a phobia in a five-year-old boy. *Standard Edition*, 10. London: Hograth Press, 1955.
———— (1910), Leonardo da Vinci and a memory of his childhood. *Standard Edition*, 11:63–137. London: Hogarth Press, 1957.

——— (1911), Formulations of two principles of mental functioning. *Standard Edition*, 12:218–226. London: Hogarth Press, 1958.
——— (1913), Totem and Taboo. *Standard Edition*, 13:1–161. London: Hogarth Press, 1953.
——— (1915), Instincts and their vicissitudes. *Standard Edition*, 14:117–140. London: Hogarth Press, 1957.
——— (1920), Beyond the pleasure principle. *Standard Edition*, 18:7–64. London: Hogarth Press, 1955.
——— (1921), Group psychology and the analysis of the ego. *Standard Edition*, 18:69–143. London: Hogarth Press, 1955.
——— (1924), The economic problem of masochism. *Standard Edition*, 19:159–170. London: Hogarth Press, 1961.
——— (1926), Inhibitions, symptoms and anxiety. *Standard Edition*, 20:87–172. London: Hogarth Press, 1959.
——— (1927), The future of an illusion. *Standard Edition*, 21:5–56. London: Hogarth Press, 1961.
——— (1939), Moses and monotheism. *Standard Edition*, 23:7–137. London: Hogarth Press, 1964.
Geertz, C. (1973), Thick description: Toward an interpretive theory of cultures. In: *The Interpretation of Cultures. Selected Essays by C. Geertz*. New York: Basic Books.
Gewertz, D. (1982), The father who bore me: The role of Tsambunwuro during Chambri initiation ceremonies. In: *Rituals of Manhood*, ed. G. Herdt. Berkeley: University of California Press.
Gillison, G. (unpublished), The moon is our first husband: Menstruation as a symbol of incest among the Gimi of Papua New Guinea, 1984.
Glasse, R. M. (1968), *The Huli of Papua*. Paris: Mouton.
——— (1969), *Pigs, Pearlshells and Women*. Englewood Cliffs, NJ: Prentice-Hall.
Godelier, M. (1982), Social hierarchies among the Baruya of New Guinea. In: *Inequality in New Guinea Highland Societies*, ed. A. Strathern. Cambridge, UK: Cambridge University Press.
Golson, J. (1982), The Ipomorean revolution revisited: Society and the sweet potato in the upper Wahgi valley. In: *Inequality in New Guinea Highland Societies*, ed. A. Strathern. Cambridge, UK: Cambridge University Press.
Goodall, J. (1963), My life among wild chimpanzees. *Nat. Geographic*, 124:272–308.
——— (1965), New discoveries among wild chimpanzees. *Nat. Geographic*, 128:802–831.
——— (1986), *The Chimpanzees of Gombe*. Cambridge, MA: Harvard University Press.
Goodenough, E. W. (1957), Interest in persons as an aspect of sex differences in the early years. *Genet. Psychol. Monographs*, 55:287–323.

Gould, S. J. (1982), Darwinism and the expansion of evolutionary theory. *Science*, 216:380–387.
——— (1986), Evolution and the triumph of homology, or why history matters. *Amer. Scientist*, 74:60–69.
Grass, G. (1977), *The Flounder*. New York: Fawcett Crest Books, 1979.
Green, R. (1974), *Sexual Identity Conflict in Children and Adults*. New York: Basic Books.
Greenacre, P. (1921), Penis awe and its relation to penis envy. In: *Emotional Growth*, Vol. 1. New York: International Universities Press, 1953.
——— (1950), Special problems in early female sexual development. *The Psychoanalytic Study of the Child*, 5:122–136. New York: International Universities Press.
Greenson, R. (1966), A transvestite boy and a hypothesis. *Internat. J. Psycho-Anal.*, 47:396–403.
——— (1968), Dis-identifying from mother. *Internat. J. Psycho-Anal.*, 49:370–374.
Gregor, T. (1985), *Anxious Pleasures*. Chicago: University of Chicago Press.
Hamburg, D., & Lunde, D. (1966), Sex hormones in the development of sex differences in human behavior. In: *The Development of Sex Differences*, ed. E. Maccoby. Stanford, CA: Stanford University Press.
Hampson, J. L., & Hampson, J. G. (1961), The ontogenesis of sexual behavior in man. In: *Sex and Internal Secretions*, Vol. 2, 3rd ed., ed. W. C. Young. Baltimore: Williams & Wilkins.
Harrison, J. (1912), *Themis*. New York: Meridian Books, 1969.
Herdt, G. (1977), The shaman's "calling" among the Sambia of New Guinea. In: *Folie, Possession et Chaumanism en Nouvelle-Guinée*; special volume of *Journal de la Société des Oceanistes*, ed. B. Juillerat. 56–57:153–167.
——— (1980), Semen depletion and the sense of maleness. *Ethnopsychiatrica*, 3:79–116.
——— (1981), *Guardians of the Flutes*. New York: McGraw-Hill.
———, ed. (1982), *Rituals of Manhood*. Berkeley: University of California Press.
———, ed. (1984), *Ritualized Homosexuality in Melanesia*. Berkeley: University of California Press.
——— (1987), *The Sambia: Ritual and Gender in New Guinea*. New York: CBS College Publishing.
——— Poole, F. J. P. (1982), Sexual antagonism: The intellectual history of a concept in the anthropology of New Guinea. In: *Sexual Antagonism, Gender and Social Change in Papua New Guinea*, ed. F. J. P. Poole & G. Herdt. *Social Analysis* (Special Issue), 12:3–28.
Hogbin, I. (1970), *The Island of Menstruating Men*. Scranton, PA: Chandler.
Horney, K. (1932), The dread of women. *Internat. J. Psycho-Anal.*, 13:358–360.

Hutchins, E. (1980), *Culture and Inference*. Cambridge, MA: Harvard University Press.
Inhelder, B., & Piaget, J. (1958), *The Growth of Logical Thinking from Childhood to Adolescence*. New York: Basic Books.
Jacobson, E. (1950), Development of the wish for a child in boys. *The Psychoanalytic Study of the Child*, 5:139–153. New York: International Universities Press.
Jaffe, D. S. (1968), The masculine envy of woman's procreative function. *J. Amer. Psychoanal. Assn.*, 16:521–548.
Johnson, A. M., & Szurek, S. A. (1952), The genesis of antisocial acting-out in children and adults. *Psychoanal. Quart.*, 21:323–343.
Kelly, R. C. (1976), Witchcraft and sexual relations: An exploration in the social and semantic implications of a structure of belief. In: *Man and Woman in the New Guinea Highlands*, ed. P. Brown & G. Buchbinder. Publication No. 8. Washington, DC: American Anthropological Association.
Kernberg, O. (1975), *Borderline Conditions: Pathological Narcissism*. New York: Jason Aronson.
Kleeman, J. (1965), A boy discovers his penis. *The Psychoanalytic Study of the Child*, 20:239–266. New York: International Universities Press.
―――― (1966), Genital self-discovery during a boy's second year. *The Psychoanalytic Study of the Child*, 21:358–392. New York: International Universities Press.
―――― (1971), The establishment of core gender identity in normal girls: I. a) Introduction; b) Development of the ego capacity to differentiate. *Arch. Sexual Behav.*, 1:103–116.
Kohlberg, L. (1963), The development of children's orientations toward a moral order. I. Sequence on the development of moral thought. *Vita Humana*, 6:11–33.
―――― (1964), Development of moral character and moral ideology. In: *Review of Child Development Research*, ed. M. L. Hoffman & L. W. Hoffman. New York: Russell Sage Foundation.
―――― (1966), A cognitive developmental analysis of children's sex role concepts and attitudes. In: *The Development of Sex Differences*, ed. E. Maccoby. Stanford, CA: Stanford University Press.
Kohut, H. (1971), *The Analysis of the Self*. New York: International Universities Press.
Kolb, L. C., & Johnson, A. M. (1955), Etiology and therapy of overt homosexuality. *Psychoanal. Quart.*, 24:506–515.
Landtman, G. (1927), *The Kiwai Papuans of British New Guinea*. London: Macmillan.
Lawrence, P. (1964), *Road Belong Cargo*. Manchester, UK: Manchester University Press.

Leach, E. (1964), Anthropological aspects of language: Animal categories and verbal abuse. In: *New Directions in the Study of Language*, ed. E. H. Lenneberg. Cambridge, MA: MIT Press.

Lévi-Strauss, C. (1962), *Totemism*. Boston: Beacon Press.

——— (1966), *The Savage Mind*. Chicago: University of Chicago Press.

Levy-Bruhl, L. (1923), *Primitive Mentality*. New York: AMS, 1976.

——— (1926), *How Natives Think*. Salem, NH: Ayer Publishing, 1979.

Lidz, R. W., & Lidz, T. (1977), Male menstruation: A ritual alternative to the oedipal transition. *Internat. J. Psycho-Anal.*, 58:17–31.

Lidz, T. (1963), *The Family and Human Adaptation*. New York: International Universities Press.

——— (1975), *Hamlet's Enemy: Madness and Myth in Hamlet*. New York: Basic Books.

——— (1976), *The Person*, rev. ed. New York: Basic Books.

——— (1988), The riddle of the riddle of the Sphinx. *Psychoanal. Rev.*, 75:35–49.

——— Lidz, R. W. (1984), Oedipus in the Stone Age. *J. Amer. Psychoanal. Assn.*, 32:507–527.

——— ———, & Burton-Bradley, B. (1973), Cargo cultism: A psychosocial study of Melanesian millenarianism. *J. Nerv. & Ment. Dis.*, 157:370–388.

Lindenbaum, S. (1976), A wife is the hand of man. In: *Man and Woman in the New Guinea Highlands*, ed. P. Brown & G. Buchbinder. Publication No. 8. Washington, DC: American Anthropological Association.

Loewald, H. (1951), Ego and reality. In: *Papers on Psychoanalysis*. New Haven, CT: Yale University Press, 1980.

Low, B. (1920), *Psycho-Analysis*. New York: Harcourt, Brace.

Mahler, M. (1971), A study of the separation-individuation process. *The Psychoanalytic Study of the Child*, 26:403–424. New York: Quadrangle Press.

——— Pine, R., & Bergman, A. (1975), *The Psychological Birth of the Human Infant*. New York: Basic Books.

Malinowski, B. (1922), *Argonauts of the Western Pacific*. New York: Dutton.

——— (1929), *The Sexual Life of Savages in North-Western Melanesia*. New York: Harcourt, Brace & World.

Mead, M. (1928), *Growing Up in New Guinea*. New York: William Morrow.

——— (1968–1971), *The Mountain Arapesh*, 3 vols. Garden City, NY: Natural History Press.

Meggitt, M. J. (1965), The Mae Enga of the western highlands. In: *Gods, Ghosts and Men in Melanesia*, ed. P. Lawrence & M. L. Meggitt. Melbourne, Australia: Oxford University Press.

——— (1970), Male-female relationships in the highlands of Australian New Guinea. In: *Cultures of the Pacific*, ed. T. Harding & B. Wallace. New York: Free Press.

——— (1976), A duplicity of demons: Sexual and familial roles expressed in western Enga stories. In: *Man and Woman in the New Guinea Highlands*, ed. P. Brown & G. Buchbinder. Publication No. 8. Washington, DC: American Anthropological Association.

Mikloucho-Maclay, N. (1871–1883), *New Guinea Diaries*. Madang, Papua New Guinea: Kristen Press, 1975.

Money, J. (1965), Psychosexual differentiation. In: *Sex Research: New Developments*. New York: Holt, Rinehart & Winston.

——— Erhardt, A. (1972), *Man and Woman, Boy and Girl*. Baltimore: Johns Hopkins University Press.

——— Hampson, J. G., & Hampson, J. L. (1957), Imprinting and the establishment of gender roles. *Arch. Neurol. & Psychiat.*, 77:333–336.

Murphy, Y., & Murphy, R. (1974), *Women of the Forest*. New York: Columbia University Press.

Newman, P. (1965), *Knowing the Gururumba*. New York: Holt, Rinehart & Winston.

——— Boyd, D. J. (1982), The making of men: Ritual and meaning in Awa male initiation. In: *Rituals of Manhood*, ed. G. Herdt. Berkeley: University of California Press.

Norbeck, E., Walker, D., & Cohen, M. (1962), The interpretation of data: Puberty rites. *Amer. Anthropol.*, 64:463–485.

Okonogi, K. (1978), The Ajase complex of the Japanese. No. 1. *Japanese Echo*, 5:88–105.

——— (1979), The Ajase complex of the Japanese. No. 2. *Japanese Echo*, 6:104–118.

Parin, P. (1972), Der Ausgang des odipalen Konflikts in drei verschiedenen Kulturen. In: *Das Elend mit der Psyche:* II. *Psychoanalyse*. Wagenbach: Kursbuch Verlag.

Parrinder, G. (1967), *African Mythology*. London: Paul Hamlyn.

Parsons, T. (1954), The incest taboo in relation to social structure and the socialization of the child. *Brit. J. Sociol.*, 5:101–117.

Piaget, J. (1926), *The Language and Thought of the Child*. New York: Harcourt Brace.

——— (1952), *The Origins of Intelligence in Children*. New York: International Universities Press.

——— (1970), *Structuralism*. New York: Basic Books.

Poole, F. J. P. (1976), *The Ais Am*. Doctoral dissertation. Department of Anthropology, Cornell University, Ithaca, NY.

——— (1981a), Transforming "natural" women: Female ritual leaders and gender ideology among Bimin-Kuskusmin. In: *Sexual Meanings*, ed. S. B. Ortner & H. Whitehead. Cambridge, MA: Cambridge University Press.

——— (1981b), Taman: Ideological and sociological configuration of "witchcraft" among Bimin-Kuskusmin. *Social Anal.*, 8:58–76.

——— (1982a), The ritual forging of identity: Aspects of person and self in

Bimin-Kuskusmin male initiation. In: *Rituals of Manhood*, ed. G. Herdt. Berkeley: University of California Press.

―――― (1982b), Symbols of substance: Bimin-Kuskusmin models of procreation, death and personhood. Presented at meeting of the Association for Social Anthropology in Oceania.

―――― (1982c), Couvade and clinic in a New Guinea society: Birth among the Bimin-Kuskusmin. In: *The Use and Abuse of Medicine*, ed. M. W. deVries, R. L. Berg & M. Lipkin, Jr. New York: Praeger Scientific.

―――― (1983a), Cannibals, tricksters and witches: Anthropophagic images among Bimin-Kuskusmin. In: *The Ethnography of Cannibalism*, ed. P. Brown & D. Tuzin. Washington, DC: Society for Psychological Anthropology.

―――― (1983b), Folk models of eroticism in mothers and sons: Aspects of sexuality among Bimin-Kuskusmin. Presented at annual meeting of the American Anthropological Association.

―――― (1985), Coming into social being: Cultural images of infants in Bimin-Kuskusmin folk psychology. In: *Person, Self, and Experience: Exploring Pacific Ethnopsychologics*, ed. G. M. White & J. Kirkpatrick. Berkeley: University of California Press, pp. 183–242.

―――― (1987), Morality, personhood, tricksters, and youths: Some narrative images of ethics among Bimin-Kuskusmin. In: *Anthropology in the High Valley. Essays on the New Guinea Highlands in Honor of Kenneth E. Read*, ed. L. L. Langness & T. E. Hays. Novato: Chandler & Sharp.

―――― (1988), Veils of illusion, kernals of truth: Secrecy and revelation in Bimin-Kuskusmin ritual. In: *Ritual Secrecy*, ed. D. W. Jorgensen & E. G. Schwimmer. Toronto: University of Toronto Press.

―――― (unpublished), Rites of childhood: Images of the child as person in Bimin-Kuskusmin society.

Pospisil, L. (1978), *The Kapauku Papuans of West New Guinea*, 2nd ed. New York: Holt, Rinehart & Winston.

Provence, S., & Lipton, R. D. (1962), *Infants in Institutions*. New York: International Universities Press.

Rappaport, R. (1984), *Pigs for Ancestors*, rev. ed. New Haven, CT: Yale University Press.

Read, K. E. (1952), Nama cult of the central highlands, New Guinea. *Oceania*, 23:1–25.

―――― (1954), Marriage among the Gahuka-Gama. *South Pacific*, 7:864–871.

―――― (1965), *The High Valley*. New York: Charles Scribner's Sons.

―――― (1984), The nama cult recalled. In: *Ritualized Homosexuality in Melanesia*, ed. G. Herdt. Berkeley: University of California Press.

Reay, M. (1959), *The Kuma*. Melbourne, Australia: Cambridge University Press.

Reik, T. (1946a), The puberty rites of savages. In *Ritual: Psycho-Analytic Studies*. New York: Farrar, Straus.

―――― (1946b), *Ritual: Psycho-Analytic Studies*. New York: Farrar, Straus.

Roiphe, H. (1968), On an early genital phase. *The Psychoanalytic Study of the Child*, 23:348–365. New York: International Universities Press.
—— Galenson, E. (1981), *Infantile Origins of Sexual Identity*. New York: International Universities Press.
Salisbury, R. F. (1965), The Siane of the eastern highlands. In: *Gods, Ghosts and Men in Melanesia*, ed. P. Lawrence & M. J. Meggitt. Melbourne, Australia: Oxford University Press.
Sapir, E. (1949), *Selected Writings of Edward Sapir in Language, Culture and Personality*. Berkeley: University of California Press.
Schieffelin, E. (1976), *The Sorrow of the Lonely and the Burning of the Dancers*. New York: St. Martin's Press.
—— (1982), The *Bau A* ceremonial hunting lodge: An alternative to initiation. In: *Rituals of Manhood*, ed. G. Herdt. Berkeley: University of California Press.
Serpenti, L. (1984), The ritual meaning of homosexuality and pedophilia among the Kimam-Papuans of South Irian Jaya. In: *Ritualized Homosexuality in Melanesia*, ed. G. Herdt. Berkeley: University of California Press.
Sibley, C. G., & Alquist, J. E. (1981), The phylogeny and relationship of the ratite birds as indicated by DNA-DNA hybridization. In: *Evolution Today*, ed. G. Scudder & J. L. Reveal. Proceedings of the Second International Congress on Systematic Evolutionary Biology. Hunt Institute for Botanical Documentation, Pittsburgh.
—— —— (1985), The phylogeny and classification of the Australo-Papuan pauerine birds. *The Emu*, 85:1–14.
Sinclair, J. (1971), *The Highlanders*. Milton, Queensland: Jacarando Press.
Socarides, C. W. (1973), Sexual perversion and the fear of engulfment. *Internat. J. Psychoanal. Psychother.*, 2:433–449.
Sorum, A. (1984), Growth and decay: Bedamini notions of sexuality. In: *Ritualized Homosexuality in New Guinea*, ed. G. Herdt. Berkeley: University of California Press.
Spitz, R. (1962), Autoerotism reexamined. *The Psychoanalytic Study of the Child*, 17:283–315. New York: International Universities Press.
Stoller, R. (1966), The mother's contribution to infantile transvestite behavior. *Internat. J. Psycho-Anal.*, 47:384–395.
—— (1968), A further contribution to the study of gender identity. *Internat. J. Psycho-Anal.*, 49:364–368.
—— (1974), Symbiosis anxiety and the development of masculinity. *Arch. Gen. Psychiat.*, 30:164–172.
—— (1985), *Presentations of Gender*. New Haven, CT: Yale University Press.
—— Herdt, G. (1982), The development of masculinity: A cross-cultural contribution. *J. Amer. Psychoanal. Assn.*, 30:29–59.

Strathern, A., ed. (1982), *Inequality in New Guinea Highland Societies*. Melbourne, Australia: Cambridge University Press.
Sullivan, H. S. (1953), *The Interpersonal Theory of Psychiatry*. New York: W. W. Norton.
Turnbull, C. (1962), *The Forest People*. New York: Simon & Schuster.
Tuzin, D. (1982), Ritual violence among the Ilahita Arapesh: The dynamics of moral and religious uncertainty. In: *Rituals of Manhood*, ed. G. Herdt, Berkeley: University of California Press.
Tyson, P. (1982), A developmental line of gender identity, gender role, and choice of love object. *J. Amer. Psychoanal. Assn.*, 30:61–68.
—— (1986), Male gender identity. Early developmental roots. *Psychoanal. Rev.*, 73:1–21.
van Baal, J. (1966), *Dema*. The Hague: Martinhus Nijhoff.
—— (1984), The dialectics of sex in Marind-anim culture. In: *Ritualized Homosexuality in Melanesia*, ed. G. Herdt. Berkeley: University of California Press.
Vanggaard, T. (1972), *Phallós*. New York: International Universities Press.
Vicedom, G. F., & Tischner, H. (1943–1948), *Die Mbowamb*, 3 vols. Hamburg: de Gruyter.
Vygotsky, L. S. (1962), *Thought and Language*. New York: John Wiley.
Wasson, R. G. (1985), In pursuit of mushrooms. *Discovery* (Yale Peabody Museum), 18/2:9–15.
Webster, E. M. (1984), *The Moon Man*. Berkeley: University of California Press.
Werner, H. (1964), *Comparative Psychology of Mental Development*, rev. ed. New York: International Universities Press.
White, J. P., & Allen, J. (1980), Melanesian prehistory: Some recent advances. *Science*, 207:728–734.
—— O'Connell, J. F. (1979), Australian prehistory: New aspects of antiquity. *Science*, 203:21–28.
Whiting, J. M. W., Kluckhohn, R. C., & Anthony, A. (1958), The function of male initiation ceremonies at puberty. In: *Readings in Social Psychology*. 3rd ed., ed. E. Maccoby, T. Newcomb, & E. Hartley. New York: Holt, Rinehart & Winston.
Whorf, B. L. (1956), *Language, Thought and Reality: Selected Writings of Benjamin Lee Whorf*, ed. J. Carroll. New York: MIT Press and John Wiley.
Williams, F. E. (1936), *Papuans of the Trans-Fly*. London: Clarendon Press.
Wirz, P. (1922–1925), *Die Marind-anim von Holländisch-Sud-Neu-Guineu*, 4 vols. Hamburg: L. Friederichsen.
Young, W., Goy, R., & Phoenix, C. (1964), Hormones and sexual behavior. *Science*, 143:212–218.

Name Index

Ainsworth, M. S., 174, 201
Allen, J., 22, 210
Allen, M., 70, 71, 152, 201
Alquist, J. E., 168, 209
Anderson, R., 21, 202
Anthony, A., 69, 210

Bamberger, J., 158, 167, 201
Barth, F., 27, 201
Bateson, G., 4, 43, 150, 201
Beardmore, E., 94, 142, 201
Berg, R. L., 208
Bergman, A., 14, 206
Berndt, R. M., 64, 201
Bettelheim, B., 50, 69, 71, 72, 179, 201
Bjerre, J., 40, 201
Boelaars, J., 43, 201
Borsuch, H. D., ix
Bowlby, J., 174, 201
Boyd, D. J., 63, 207
Bridges, E. L., 158, 201
Brown, P., 32, 53, 201, 202, 205, 206, 207, 208
Brumbaugh, R. C., ix, 121, 133, 134, 135, 138, 201
Buchbinder, G., 32, 46, 201, 202, 205, 206, 207

Burton, R. V., 70, 202
Burton-Bradley, B. G., ix, 4, 5, 45, 206
Butler, S., 7–9, 202

Carroll, J., 210
Chomsky, N., 166, 202
Cohen, M. B., 69, 176, 202, 207
Comte, 41
Connolly, B., 21, 202
Cowan, B., 10, 202

Daly, C., 67–68, 202
deGroot, L., 180, 202
deVries, M. W., 208
Diamond, M., 175, 202
Doi, T., 147, 202
Durkheim, E., 14, 18, 190, 202
Dwyer, M., 24

Erhardt, A., 175, 207
Erikson, E., 177, 198, 202
Ernst, T. M., 109, 202
Errington, F. K., 39, 202
Evans-Pritchard, E. E., 152, 190, 202

Fenichel, O., 176, 202
Ferenczi, S., 76, 202

Festinger, L., 202
Fortune, R. F., 4, 202
Fraser, J. G., 18
Freud, A., 14, 202
Freud, S., 18, 40, 42, 53, 71, 73, 75, 77, 82, 131, 136, 142, 152, 164, 165, 174, 175, 178, 180, 184, 194, 195

Galenson, E., 176, 209
Geertz, C., 43, 190, 203
Gewertz, D., 64, 203
Gillison, G., 66, 67, 203
Glasse, R. M., 144, 203
Godelier, M., 28, 83, 203
Golson, J., 22, 203
Goodall, J., 175, 203
Goodenough, E. W., 177, 203
Gould, S. J., 168, 204
Goy, R., 175, 210
Grass, G., 144, 169, 204
Green, R., 175, 204
Greenacre, P., 176, 204
Greenson, R., 49, 50, 71, 74, 75, 179, 180, 204
Gregor, T., 158, 159, 160, 161, 162, 163, 164, 204

Hamburg, D., 175, 182, 204
Hampson, J. G., 177, 204, 207
Hampson, J. L., 177, 204, 207
Harding, T., 206
Harrison, J., 57, 58, 104, 112, 153, 204
Hartley, E., 210
Hays, T. E., 208
Herdt, G., ix, 10, 26, 32, 41, 50, 51, 53, 55, 57, 58, 83, 84, 85, 86, 87, 88, 89, 90, 91, 92, 93, 94, 95, 96, 100, 101, 102, 104, 157, 165, 193, 194, 197, 201, 203, 204, 208, 209, 210
Hoffman, L. W., 205
Hoffman, M. L., 205
Hogbin, I., 60, 61, 62, 204

Horney, K., 74, 204
Hutchins, E., 1, 38, 205

Inhelder, B., 1, 42, 205

Jacobson, E., 178, 205
Jaffe, D. S., 50, 205
Johnson, A. M., 196, 205
Jung, C., 166

Kelly, R. C., 98, 108, 109, 205
Kernberg, O., 182, 205
Kleeman, J., 176, 177, 205
Klein, M., 147
Kluckhohn, R. C., 69, 210
Kohlberg, L., 177, 193, 205
Kohut, H., 182, 205
Kolb, L. C., 196, 205

Lamphere, L., 201
Landtman, G., 142, 205
Langness, L. L., 208
Lawrence, P., 4, 201, 205, 206, 209
Leach, E., 206
Leary, M., 24
Lenneberg, E. H., 206
Lévi-Strauss, C., 42, 43, 170, 206
Levy-Bruhl, L., 43, 206
Lidz, R. W., 45, 50, 126, 179, 206
Lidz, T., ix, 45, 50, 68, 69, 74, 76, 108, 126, 153, 178, 179, 185, 186, 206
Lindenbaum, S., 33, 46, 64, 206
Lipkin, M., Jr., 208
Lipton, R. D., 174, 208
Loewald, H., 71, 74, 76, 178, 190, 206
Low, B., 206
Lunde, D., 175, 182, 204

Maccoby, E., 204, 205, 210
Mahler, M., 14, 71, 115, 173, 182, 184, 206

Name Index

Malinowski, B., 4, 19, 95, 136, 142, 206
Mead, M., 4, 14, 19, 206
Meggitt, M. J., 25, 30, 33, 79, 83, 95, 152, 194, 201, 206, 209
Mikloucho-Maclay, N., 21, 207
Money, J., 175, 207
Murphy, R., 158, 159, 164, 165, 171, 207
Murphy, Y., 158, 159, 164, 165, 171, 207

Newcomb, T., 210
Newman, P., 26, 39, 51, 58, 60, 63, 77, 207
Norbeck, E., 69, 207

Okonogi, K., 147, 207
Ortner, S. B., 207

Parin, P., 73, 207
Parrinder, G., 159, 166, 207
Parsons, T., 74, 207
Phoenix, C., 175, 210
Piaget, J., 1, 38, 42, 44, 207
Pine, R., 14, 206
Poole, F. P., ix, 10, 26, 31, 32, 44, 46, 50, 64, 84, 104, 116, 117, 118, 119, 120, 121, 122, 123, 124, 125, 126, 127, 128, 194, 204, 207
Pospisil, L., 21, 44, 208
Provence, S., 174, 208

Rappaport, R., 26, 46, 202, 208
Read, K. E., 4, 26, 27, 34, 50, 51, 52, 53, 84, 208
Reay, M., 31, 208
Reik, T., 68, 69, 115, 138, 208
Reveal, J. L., 209
Roheim, 138
Roiphe, H., 176, 209
Rosaldo, M. Z., 201

Salisbury, R. F., 64, 78, 209
Sapir, E., 43, 45, 209

Schieffelin, E., 26, 27, 30, 33, 44, 109, 110, 209
Scudder, G., 209
Serpenti, L., 33, 57, 63, 64, 78, 119, 141, 148, 149, 209
Sibley, C. G., 168, 209
Sinclair, J., 24, 209
Socarides, C. W., 49, 74, 209
Sorum, A., 109, 209
Spitz, R., 174, 209
Stoller, R., 49, 50, 74, 75, 76, 129, 165, 179, 197, 209
Strathern, A., 210
Sullivan, H. S., 107, 210
Szurek, S. A., 196, 205

Tischner, H., 25, 26, 210
Turnbull, C., 166, 210
Tuzin, D., 10, 35, 63, 112, 113, 208, 210
Tyson, P., 50, 175, 178, 210

van Baal, J., 33, 57, 78, 79, 97, 141, 143, 144, 145, 146, 147, 149, 210
Vanggaard, T., 155, 210
Verschueren, 143
Vicedom, G. F., 25, 26, 210
Vygotsky, L. S., 42, 210

Walker, D., 69, 207
Wallace, B., 206
Wasson, R. G., 167, 210
Webster, E. M., 21, 210
Werner, H., 42, 210
White, J. P., 22, 210
Whitehead, H., 207
Whiting, J. M. W., 69, 70, 202, 210
Whorf, B. L., 43, 45, 210
Williams, F. E., 66, 94, 98, 102, 210
Wirz, P., 141, 143, 144, 146, 210

Young, W., 175, 204, 210

Subject Index

Aborigines, 17, 40, 49, 69, 136, 170, 179
  ritual subincision of, 71–72
Accidents, beliefs about, 39
Acculturation, freedom from, 17
Adolescence
  adultery and, 162
  heterosexual fantasies and, 187
  seclusion from females and, 90–91, 107–140, 148
  unmarried mother and, 199
Adultery
  Amazonian versus New Guinean society and, 161–162
  dangers of, 90
  pig indemnification and, 35
Afek
  myth cycle and, 46–47
  at Telefolip, 133–140
  Yomnok and, 115–131
Age
  marriage and, 34
  perception of, 40
Aggression, overstimulation by mother and, 125
Agnate
  contact with, 32–33
  importance of, 109

Ajase complex, 147–148
Amazon Indian, 159–163
  New Guinean society and, 166–172
  matriarchy and, 157–161
Anal intercourse, 144. *See also* Sodomy
Ancestor
  lifestyle and, 40–41
  primal, 39
  female, 142, 155–156
  spirit and, 28–30
  fertility and, 133
Androgen, 182
Androgyny, 46
  Bimin-Kuskusmin and, 129
Animal-vegetal boundary, 46
Astarte, awe of mother and, 131
Australia
  animals and birds of, 168
  geography of, 22–23
  law and, 26, 116

Baby purchase and capture, 130
Bad mother, Kleinian theory and, 147
Battle, matrilineal and affinal ties and, 33. *See also* Warfare

215

Bau A, 108–111
Big Man, definition of, 28, 30
Bimin-Kuskusmin, 115–131
   Afek-Yomnok myth, 128–131
   Ais An (first stage initiation), 117–127
      bleeding and indirect insemination, 119
      brutality and rage in, 125
      dangers of suicide and insanity and, 121–122
      Great Cassowary and Spiny Ant Eater rite, 119
      role of women ritual leaders in, 117–131
   androgynous primal ancestors, 116–117
   En Am (tenth stage), 127
      ritual bleeding, 127
   fourth to tenth stage, 126–127
   initiation, ten stages of, 117–131
   location of, 116
   masculine and feminine essences, 122–124
   similarities to Sambia, 117
   Telefomin and Eliptamin valleys and, 133–140
Birth. *See also* Rebirth
   fantasy, anal, 129
   father and, 123
   myth about origin of, 100–101
   rate of, 79
Bleeding. *See also* Menstruation
   forced, 49–54
   maternal contamination and, 119
   nose, 87–89, 98–99
   penile, 63–64
   ritual, 52–54, 65–79, 160, 192
   of tongue, 62
Bleeding rituals, psychoanalytic concepts of, 75–95
Blood
   destructive power of, 119
   healing power of, 124
   menstrual. *See* Menstrual blood
Bonding of males, 107–140
Breast, mother-child eroticism and, 124–125
Breast milk
   postpartum sexual taboo and, 56
   semen and, 91, 99, 136
Bride, menarche and, 98–99
Bride-wealth, 36
Brother-sister relationship
   incest, 95
   safety of, 33
   trust and, 95
Brutality, 191
   Bimin-Kuskusmin and, 117–122
   Ilahita Arapesh and, 63, 111–113
   nose bleeding ritual and, 88–90
Bullroarer
   ancestor spirits and, 112, 159
   definition of, 55
   dema and sosum ritual and, 144
   myth and, 66
   secret of, 92
   subjugation of women and, 158–159

Cannibalism, 26, 31, 139, 148
   Australian ban on, 26
   headhunting and, 148–150
   ritual, 35
   ritual murder and, 146
   threat of, 139
   warfare and, 133
Castration
   anxiety and, 68–70
   fear of, 71–72, 144–145
      mother engulfment and, 165
      vagina and, 160
   masculine identity and fear of, 181–182

menstrual blood and, 65–79
non-threat of, 115–116
oedipal theory and, 183
vaginal secretions and, 142
Catholicism, awe of mother and, 131
Causality
concepts of, 39
indigenes and, 42–47
magical, 9
sorcery and, 39
Child. *See also* Adolescent; Infant
as bride, 98–99
capture of, 160
detachment from mother and, 183–184
development theories and, 13–16, 173–199
eroticism with mother and, 124–125
female
male child versus, 14–16
value of, 31
gender identity of, 175–177
latency period and
forest lodge ritual and, 107–140
oedipal transition and, 14–15
peer group and, 186–187
male
core identity and, 193–194
father and, 178
female child versus, 14–16
masculinization ritual and, 13–16
mortality of, 123–124
peer group and, 186–187
rebirth of, 58–59
value of, 123
Circumcision
attractiveness of, 70
lack of, 139
as substitute for castration, 69–70

Cognition, indigenes and, 40–47
Conception
concepts of, 56–57
multiple intercourse and, 150–151, 162
Copulation, oral, 90–96, 100–101, 109–110
Cousin, marriage and, 33, 140
Couvade, 123
Creation myth, 100–101, 115–131, 133–140, 142–147
Cult, male
Amazonian versus New Guinean society and, 165
latency and, 108
loyalty to, 30, 113
Cult hut, 28–30, 51
tenure in, 53
woman-proscribed, 31
Culture
goals of, 10
language and, 45
personality and, 9
primal ancestor and, 39–40
Cybele, awe of mother and, 131

Dama, 144
Daughter
marriage exchange of, 140
trading of, 149–150
Dead
collectivity of ancestor spirits and, 42
ghosts, 42
primal ancestors, culture and, 42
rebirth, 45
Death
ghosts and, 28–30, 39
heterosexual intercourse and premature male, 93
homicide, 146
Australian ban on, 26
pig indemnification and, 35
menstrual blood and, 78

nirvana principle and, 165
reincarnation and, 92
sorcery and, 41
suicide and, 121–122
symbolic, 148
view of, 42
Deerotization
  male child and, 15
  Western versus New Guinean society and, 188–199
Defeminization, 171, 188–199. See also Masculinization
Deity, 156
Dema
  intercourse and, 143
  Marind-anim and, 141
Dentate vagina. See Castration
Depression
  Bimin-Kuskusmin initiates and, 121–122
  emotional abuse and, 118
Dichotomy
  indigenes and, 42–47
  male-female, 84, 192–193
  reaction formation and, 122–123
Dispersion
  analogy and homology, 166–169
Divorce, 36
  absence of father and, 199

Earth, menstrual blood and, 134
Eating of semen, 120–121. See also Fellatio
Economy
  ceremonial pig killing and, 51
  hamlet and, 36, 38
Ego, 74–75
Emasculation, threat of, 15–16
En Am ritual, 127–131
Envy
  female procreation and, 14–16
  magic and, 35
  male, 49–50, 71–72, 179
  of mother, 128

penis, 14, 49–50
  Western versus New Guinean society and, 192–193
  of women, 94–95
Erewhon, fictional land of, 7–9
Eros, return to womb versus, 164–165
Eroticism
  fellatio and, 95–96
  infant, 176
  mother-child, 13–16, 102, 124–125
  Western versus New Guinea society and, 188–189
Europeans
  definition of, 1
Exogamy, 30–31
Extramarital sex, 103. See also Promiscuity

Family
  dynamic structure of, 185–186
  role of, 151–156
  structure of, 30, 32, 35, 62
  Western versus New Guinea society and, 198–199
Father
  Amazonian versus New Guinean society and, 162–163
  as "good" mother, 138
  harmful presence of, 124
  identification with, 185–186
  interaction with infant of, 176–177
  isolation of, 123
  male child and, 178
  paternalistic Europe and, 183
  rivalry and
    for mother, 181–182
    son and, 13–16
  weak, 74–75
Feces, ritual use of, 146–147
Fellatio, 90–96, 100–101
Female. See also Mother; Woman
  ancestor and, 142, 155–156

child and, 14–16, 31
dangers of, 31
envy of. See Envy
initiations, 143
libido and, 78
male versus, 46
puberty rite and, 77
ritual leaders and, 120
wish to be, 145
Female exudation, 51. See also Womb blood
Female identity, male child and core, 193–194
Female-male function
dichotomy and, 84
interdependence of, 128–129
reversal of, 135
Fertility
control of, 59
rite, 146–147
ritual control of, 192
Fetus
gender of, 122–123
origin of, 56–57
Fiji, 4, 167, 168
Flute. See Sacred flute
Food
economy and, 36, 38
feminine, 118, 121
masculine, 97, 139
taboo, 92, 96
Forest lodge ritual, 107–140
Bau A, 108
Maolima, 111–113

Gender
of fetus, 122–123
identity and
development of, 75–77, 177–199
dichotomy of, 122–123
family transactions and, 185–186
male envy and, 49–50
male insecurity and, 116

peers and, 186
Genitalia
infant interest in, 176
odor of
danger of woman's, 98, 128
vaginal, 66–68, 84
Western versus New Guinean society and, 197–199
subincision and, 69–70
Ghost
beliefs about, 39
fear of, 28–30
"Good" mother, 147
Government
influence of, 141
New Guinea and, 27–41
Greece, ancient, 94
homosexuality and bisexuality in, 155
initiation and, 112

Hair
cutting of, 119
ritual growing of, 63
top knot, 119
Headhunting, 148–149, 150
Heterosexuality
acceptance of, 115–116
difficulties with, 98–102
rejection of. See Homosexuality
weakening effect of, 82, 93, 109
Western versus new Guinean society and, 194–197
Highlands people, 24–26
Homicide, 146
Australian ban on, 26
pig indemnification and, 35
Homosexuality, 191, 194
Amazonian versus New Guinean society and, 161
enforcement of, 101
etiology of, 195–197
fellatio and, 90–96
forest lodge ritual and, 107–140

fostering of, 109
incest and, 102–103
Kimam-Papuans and, 141–156
lack of, 112–113, 129
　Bimin-Kuskusmin and, 115–131
latency period and, 14–15
Marind-anim and, 141–156
obligatory, 34
oedipal conflict and, 99–100
openness of, 142
ritual, 82
Sambia, 81–105
sociosyntonic, 195–196
warrior and, 15–16
Western versus New Guinean society and, 194–197
Hormone
　gender behavior and, 175
　oedipal period and, 182
Husband, loyalty of, 30

Illness
　avoidance of, 63
　beliefs about, 39
　male child and, 123–124
　menstrual blood and, 54
Image, body, 174
Impotence, 125
Incest
　brother-sister, 95
　forest lodge ritual and avoidance of, 107–140
　mother-son, 145
　prevention of, 100–101
　taboo, 74
Indigene, definition of, 1
Infant. See also Child
　baby purchase and, 130
　mortality rate and, 123
　sex identity and, 175–177
Initiation ritual, 2–11
　Bimin-Kuskusmin and, 115–131
　central aspect of, 5

cruelty in, 35
defeminization and, 49–64
female, 59
final Bimin-Kuskusmin, 127–131
Gahuka-Gama and, 59–64
Greek, 112
manhood and, 15–16
Sambia and, 81–106
Insanity
　Bimin-Kuskusmin and, 121–122
Insemination
　through abrasion, 109, 149
　anal, 109, 142–144
　feeding and, 94–95, 145, 146–150
　fellatio, 90–96
　multiple, 142
　　Amazonian versus New Guinean society and, 162
　oral, 109
　by patrikins, 151
Intercourse
　anal, 144
　avoidance of premarital, 107–140
　breast milk and taboo and, 56
　conception without, 136
　danger of, 54–55
　debilitating effects of, 5, 82, 93
　extramarital, 103
　oral, 90–96, 109
　serial
　　conception and, 149–151
　　prepubertal bride and, 149
　　semen-vaginal fluid mixture and, 145–146, 155
　vaginal, 143–145
　Western versus New Guinean society and, 197–199
Irian-Jaya, 19, 21, 23, 57, 94, 116
Isolation

forest lodge ritual and, 107–140
from women, 90–91, 148
Judaism, 156
Language
  aberrant, 134
  culture and, 45
  Papua New Guinea and, 1, 21
  sacred, 126–127
Latency period
  forest lodge ritual and, 107–140
  oedipal transition and, 14–15
  peer group and, 186–187
Law, Australian, 116
Libido
  development of, 174
  female, 78
  menstrual blood and, 66–68
  shift in cathexis of, 181
Life, male creation of, 148
Life span, 34
Little Hans, 177–178
Logic, 42–47

Magic
  causality and, 9
  envy and, 35
Maldevelopment of male child, 123–124
Male. *See also* Father
  aggrandizement of, 81–105
  Big Man and, 28, 30
  bonding and, 107–140
  creation of life and, 148
  cult of. *See* Male cult
  danger of marriage and, 130
  envy and, 49–50, 71–72, 179, 191–192
  equivalence between, 35
  existential flaw in, 164–165
  female versus, 14–16, 46
  insecurity and, 116
  life tasks of, 34, 167–168
  masculinity and. *See* Masculinity
  menstruation and, 49–79
  mortality of, 123–124
  original subjugation of, 158–161
  peer group and, 186–187
  phallic, 125
  rebirth of, 58–59, 81–105
  rivalry and, 81–82
  superiority of, 155
  transsexual, 74–75, 179
  Western society and, 186–187
Male cult. *See also* Initiation ritual
  Amazonian versus New Guinean society and, 165
  latency and, 108
  loyalty to, 30, 113
Male-female function
  dichotomy and, 31, 84
  interdependence and, 128–129
  reversal of, 135
Maolima, 111–113
Marind-anim, 141–156
  dema, 143
  family structure of, 151–152
  "good" and "excrement" mother, 145–147, 154
  homosexuality, 142
  location of, 141
  serial insemination, 142
Marriage
  age and, 34
  Amazonian versus New Guinean society and, 162
  arranged, 109–110
  choices and, 36
  cross-cousins and, 33, 140
  dangers for male of, 130
  failure of, 198–199
  menarche and, 36
Masculinization, 81–105. *See also* Initiation ritual; Insemination

Amazonian versus New Guinean society and, 171–172
Bimin-Kuskusmin and, 115–131
changed concepts of, 183
forest lodge and, 107–140
male child and, 15–16
passivity versus transition to, 164–165
psychoanalytic theory and, 173–199
rituals and, 13–16, 49–64
Western versus New Guinean society and, 188–199
Masturbation
proscription of, 125
ritual, 52
Maternal function, arrogation of, 128–129, 160
Matriarchy
Amazonian versus New Guinean society and, 169
myth of, 157–172
Maturation. See also Masculinization
ease of female sexual, 76–77
induction of, 59
lateness of, 53
male sexual, 81–105
Menarche
age at, 35
Amazonian society and, 170
child bride and, 98–99
marriage and, 36
ritual and, 59
Menstrual blood
castration complex and, 65–79
danger of, 54
death and, 78
decontamination of, 130
eating of, 125–127
fear of, 66–68
myth and, 66
womb blood versus, 126
Menstruation. See also Menarche

disruption of, 66–68
male, 49–64, 65–79
odor of, 67–68
Milk, breast
postpartum taboo and, 56
semen and, 91, 99, 136
Milk sap, semen and, 135
Misogyny, 14. See also Masculinization
Missionary
halting of orgies by, 147
highlands and, 24
influence of, 141
Mortality. See Death
Mother
adolescent unmarried, 199
Amazonian versus New Guinean society and, 163
betrayal of son and, 86
deerotized love for, 178–179
father as, 138
gradual detachment from, 183–184
incest and, 145
Kleinian theory and, 147
need to separate from, 164–165
oedipal rivalry for, 181–182
oral incorporation of, 152–153
patrilineage of, 151
primal, 142
primary identification with, 174–175
renunciation of, 137–138
reunification with, 74–75
ridding influence of, 49–64
separation from, 171, 188–199
sex as symbolic merging with, 76
symbiosis with, 173–174
symbolic breaking away from, 78
Murder. See Homicide
Myth
Amazonian versus New Guinean society and, 167, 171

Subject Index

indigenes and, 46–47
of matriarchy, 157–172
oedipal, 100–119, 141–142, 152
Narcissism
infant, 176–177
Native, definition of, 1
Necrophagia, 33. *See also* Cannibalism
Bimin-Kuskusmin and, 116
relative and, 26
Neolithic society, 17
New Guinea, 17–47
geography of, 18–23
Nibek monster, 61–62
Nirvana principle, 165
Nose-bleeding ritual, 87–89
fatherhood and, 99
wife's menstruation and, 98
Nuclear family. *See* Family
Numerical system, 40

Odor
attraction of mother's, 68–69
danger of menstrual, 68–69
danger of woman's, 98, 128
vaginal, 66–68, 84
Western versus New Guinean society and, 197–199
Oedipal transition, 2, 14
childhood and, 73
classic conflicts of, 181–199
Freud and, 99–100
hostility to father and, 178
and human condition, 197–198
latency period and, 14–15
menstrual blood and, 65–66
renunciation of mother and, 75–76
resolution of, 182
rivalry and, 72, 138
universal task of, 76–77
Western versus New Guinean society and, 197–199

Oedipus
fantasies and, 102
Sphinx and myth of, 153–154
Oral copulation, 90–96, 100–101.
See also Fellatio
Orgy, missionary halting of, 147

Pacification, Australia and, 16
Pain, initiates and, 35
Papua New Guinean society, 166–172
Papua New Guinea oedipal myths
Mae Enga, 152
Keraki, 102
Kiwai, 141–142
Sambia, 100–101
Papuan Gulf, 141–156
Parent, single, 199
Paternal figure, identification with, 74–75
Patriarchy, Freudian writings and, 131
Patrilineage, 151–152
Payback, definition of, 41
Penis
amputated, 144
cutting of, 62–63, 112
equivalence of breast to, 191
sacred flutes and, 89–90
strengthening of, 124–125
superiority and, 174–175
as symbol of nurture, 91
symbolic destruction of, 119
Penis envy
counterbalance to, 49–50
female child and, 14
Phallic worship, 144
Pig, 35
ancestors of, 119
economy and, 51
festival, 53
Population, 21, 79, 130
Post-menopausal woman, 125
ritual leader and, 129–130

safety of, 36
Postpartum sexual taboo, 56
Preoedipal period
  adult sex roles and, 72
  common influence on, 179–181
  distinction between oedipal period and, 182–183
  mother and, 147
Primal ancestor, 76, 115–131, 133–140, 145, 146
  female, 142, 155–156
  importance of, 39
Primal horde, 152
Primary identification with mother, 73–74
  need to overcome, 174–175
Primary inseminator, 94–95
Primary process thinking, 42
Projection, 184–185
Promiscuity
  Amazonian society and, 169–170
    New Guinean versus, 161–162
  anal intercourse and, 144
Protestantism, 156
Psychoanalytic concepts
  absence of oedipal period, 187–188
  of anal birth, 129
  attachment behavior, 174
  bisexuality and, 194
  of bleeding rituals, 70
  boys' pregnancy fantasies, 178
  boys' separation from females, 107–108
  castration anxiety, 68–70, 73, 165, 181
  collective unconscious, 166
  contrast with oedipal theory, 173–199
  converse of oedipal theory, 152
  ego identity, 198
  fear of menstrual blood, 67
  gender identity, 171, 175–182
  genital sexuality, 198
  homosexuality, 195
  latency, 108, 182, 186
  libido theory, 182
  male fears of vaginal engulfment, 195
  of male puberty rites, 68, 138–139
  narcissism, 176–177, 182
  need for father, 172
  oedipal period, 180–181
  oedipal transition, 75, 76, 180
    alternative concepts of, 183–186
  penis envy, 174
  preoedipal influences, 179, 182
  reaction formation, 192
  separation trauma, 163
  sexual anxiety, 171
  splitting of mother, 147
  superego formation, 182
  theories of individuation, 73–75, 173
  womb envy, 174
Psychoanalytic theory
  masculinization and, 173–199
  reexamination of, 13–16
Puberty rite, 68–73
  female, 77
  Reik and, 138–139
Purification, womb blood and, 58–59
Rage
  displacement of, 118
  emotional abuse and, 118
  intentional creation of, 137–138
Rape
  ritual, 146
  serpent and, 134
Rapprochement phase, 129
Rebirth
  Bimin-Kuskusmin and, 119
  gender identity and, 139

Subject Index

male sexual, 81–105
  child and, 58–59
  symbolic, 78, 148, 150
Reincarnation, 92
Religious center, 134–135
Ritual. *See also* Masculinization
  brutality of, 191
  dangers of, 52–53
  female leaders of, 120
  forest lodge, 107–140
  homosexuality and, 82
  initiation, 2–11
    Bimin-Kuskusmin and, 115–131
    central aspect of, 5
  male menstruation and, 49–64
  male-female reversal and, 135
  nose-bleeding, 87–89
    fatherhood and, 99
    wife's menstruation and, 98
  original power of women and, 130–131
  postmenopausal leader and, 129–130
  puberty, 68–73
    female, 77
    Reik and, 138–139
Rivalry
  father-son, 13–16
  male, 81–82
  oedipal, 138

Sacred flute
  ancestor spirits and, 53
  fellatio and, 90–96
  fertility and, 59
  male menstruation and, 51–53
  nama cult and, 51
  patrilineage and, 170–171
  true identity of, 89–90
Sadism, 125
Sambia
  initiation rituals, 81–105

first stage (Ais An), 85–96
  birth house, 91–92
  forest lodge, 92
  nose-bleeding, 87
  oral insemination, 90–96
  primary inseminator, 94
  secret of flutes, 89
  strengthening rituals, 86–105
second stage, 96
third stage
  becoming inseminators, 97
  puberty rites, 97
  terminal war raid, 97–98
fourth stage
  unconsummated marriages, 98
fifth stage
  cohabitation with wife, 98–102
  countering female contamination, 98
  problems with vaginal intercourse, 99–102
sixth stage
  countering mother-son incest, 100–105
  full manhood ritual, 99
  myth of Numboolyu and Chenchi, 100–101
  location of, 83
Secondary process thinking, 42
Secretion, vaginal. *See* Vaginal secretion
Semen
  agnates and, 109–110
  Amazonian versus New Guinean society and, 161
  anal "feeding" of, 149
  breast milk and, 99, 136
  composition of fetus and, 126
  fellatio and, 90–96

foods mixed with, 145–146, 150
growth induction and, 148
healing power of, 124, 148
importance of, 90, 148–151
indirect use of, 117
ingesting of, 93–96
loss of, 54–55
male maturation and, 81–105
milk sap and, 135
reproduction and, 40–41
skin abrasion and, 149
symbol of, 120–121
as symbol of breast milk, 91
Serial intercourse
  conception and, 149–151
  prepubertal bride and, 149
  semen-vaginal fluid mixture and, 145–146, 150–151, 155
Serpent, 134
Sex play, premarital, 111
Sexes, dichotomy of, 31–32
Sexual intercourse. *See* Intercourse
Sexual intimacy, 76
Sexual maturation, ease of, 76–77
Sister-brother relationship
  safety of, 33
  trust and, 95
Skin cuts, 119–121
  rubbing semen into, 149
Society
  complexity of, 10–11
  New guinea and, 27–41
  Western, 186–187
Sodomy, 142–143, 194
  preference for, 194
Son-father rivalry, 181–182
Son-mother incest, 145
Sorcery, 39
  death and, 41
  fear of, 28–30. *See also* Witchcraft
South America, matriarchy and, 157–161

Speech. *See* Language
Sphinx, 153–154
Spiny Ant Eater Rite, 119
Spirit, ancestor, 28–30. *See also* Witchcraft
  fertility and, 133
Structuralist theory, 42–47
Subincision, 69–72
Suicide, 121–122
Superego, 39. *See also* Primal ancestor
Symbiosis, mother-child, 73–74, 173–174

Taboo
  food, 92, 96
  incest, 74
  kinship, 90
  postpartum sexual, 56
Telefolip, Afek at, 133–140
Thinking, primary and secondary process, 42
Time perception, 40
Tongue, 62
Totem and Taboo, 142
Totemism, 170
Transition, oedipal. *See* Oedipal transition
Transsexual male
  envy of female and, 179
  weak father and, 74–75
Transvestite, 179
Tribal societies
  Awa, 58, 63
  BaMbreti (Africa), 166
  Baktaman, 27, 31
  Baruya, 28, 43
  Bedamin, 109
  Big Nambas (Vanuatu), 152
  Bimin-Kuskusmin, 31, 35, 45, 46, 50, 67, 104, 115–131, 163, 180, 192
  Chambri, 64
  Dobu, 46

Dogon (Africa), 159
Elema, 141
Etoro, 108, 109, 110
Fore, 33, 35, 64
Gahuka-Gama, 27, 34–60, 64, 79, 84, 88, 89, 90, 126
Gimi, 67
Gururumba, 39, 51, 54, 77, 79, 89
Huli, 144, 194
Iatmul, 58
Ilahita Arapesh, 65, 111–113
in Irian Jaya, 2
Kaluli, 108, 109, 110
Kapauku, 21, 44
Karavar, 39
Keraki, 66, 94, 98, 102, 141
Kimam-Papuans, 33, 63, 64, 78, 97, 119, 141–156, 160, 169, 191, 192
Kiwai, 141–142
Kowo (Africa), 166
Kuman, 31
Kutulu, 40
Kwavaru, 66
Kyaka, 194
Mae Enga, 25, 30, 33, 79, 152, 194
Marind-anim, 23, 33, 64, 78, 79, 97, 120, 141–156, 160, 169, 189, 191, 192
Mehinaku (South America), 158–172
Mundurucu Indians (South America), 158–172
Oksapmin, 31
Onabasulu, 109
Poro societies (Africa), 166
Sambia, 33, 50, 51, 55, 58, 81–104, 115, 157, 190, 194
Selk'man Indians (South America), 158
Seltamin, 27, 31
Siane, 78

Telefomin people, 133–140, 155, 192
on Trobriand Islands, 2, 27, 136
Wogeo, 52, 58, 60–63, 64, 69, 77, 79
Yomana Indians (South America), 158

Uncle, 140
insemination by, 149
mentoring of, 149
paternal function of, 33

Vagina
entrapment by, 144–156
fear of castrating, 160, 189
intercourse and, 143–145
sacred flutes and, 89–90
Western versus New Guinean society and, 197–199
Vaginal secretion
benefits of, 142–143
castration and, 142
serial coitus and, 155
Vegetal-animal boundary, 46
Vengeance, 35, 41
Vomiting, ritual, 49–54. *See also* Masculinization

Warfare
Australian ban on, 26
cannibalism and, 26, 133
Papua New Guinea and, 21–22
Warrior
homosexuality and, 15–16
initiation and, 85–96, 150
novice, 90–91
Weaning
age of, 124
pregnancy and, 163
Western society, male child and, 186–187
Wife, dangers of, 130
Witchcraft

beliefs about, 5, 39
cannibalism and, 26
child raising and, 125
illness and, 39
penis amputation and, 144–145
Woman. *See also* Female; Mother
Amazonian versus New Guinean society and, 161, 164
bewitched, 160
creation myth about, 100–101
danger of, 54–64
degradation of, 15, 31, 78–79, 81–105
desire to be, 104–105
equality of, 142–143
forest lodge ritual and avoidance of, 107–140
freedom from, 111–113, 117
importance of, 125–127
life tasks of, 36, 167–168
male envy of, 49–50
    child and, 179
myths of, 158–160

naturalness of, 104, 123
original dominance of, 116, 130–131, 136, 158–161
with penis, 129
positive attitude of, 55–56
post-menopausal, 125
    as ritual leader, 129–130
    safety of, 36
prepubertal bride and, 149
as primal mother, 142
protection of, 33
subservience of, 104–105
Womb
envy of, 192, 199
return to, 129, 164–165
symbol of, 88
Womb blood. *See also* Menstrual blood
menstrual blood versus, 126
purification from, 58–59
reproduction and, 40–41

Youth. *See* Adolescence